Alison Baines was born in C
Mount School, York, and New
and lives in London. She work
business, management and w
national newspapers, women's magazines and
programmes, and edits *Women in Management Review*.
She is actively involved in furthering equality between the
sexes in several areas, particularly through the Fawcett
Society.

ALISON BAINES

Success and Satisfaction

PALADIN
GRAFTON BOOKS
A Division of the Collins Publishing Group

LONDON GLASGOW
TORONTO SYDNEY AUCKLAND

Paladin
Grafton Books
A Division of the Collins Publishing Group
8 Grafton Street, London W1X 3LA

A Paladin Paperback Original 1988

ISBN 0-586-08756-7

Printed and bound in Great Britain by
Collins, Glasgow

Set in Sabon

Acknowledgements

I would particularly like to thank W. G. Baines for his loving concern, help and guidance; to express my gratitude to Dale Spender and Sarah Jane Checkland for reading drafts and commenting kindly and constructively; to thank Judith Kendra, who commissioned this book, for her sensitivity and patience and Gillian Beaumont for editing it most sympathetically and meticulously.

My thanks are also due to the many people who generously gave me their time, their thoughts and the fruits of their experience in interviews. They may not recognize themselves and their contribution in the text, but they pervade it and without their formative influence it could not have been written.

Contents

1

Starting Point

Ambition is a rude word: failure is taboo. Success fascinates and failure frightens us, a register of how closely identity is linked with achievement. But a third factor can complicate the picture: the desire for fulfilment. People who are torn between success and satisfaction live with dissonant public and private selves. Achievement seems to demand an unequivocal commitment they fear (or hope) they cannot give, and while it validates the public self, it might impoverish the private.

Ambivalence to achievement is rarely discussed except in children who underperform at school, but it is something which affects adults too. It is revealed not only directly in reluctance or refusal to achieve but indirectly in what amounts to self-sabotage, in ways which range from physical blocks like stress-related ill-health to a sense of invalidity, illegitimacy, artificiality or fraudulence in relation to success. The common denominator in such feelings is that there is a dissonance between the self and a formal public role, and it is in the discrepancy between public and private that ambivalence arises.

Of all categories of underachievers, women are the easiest to identify. Women's underperformance is often discussed in political and economic terms, focusing on legislative remedies and collective action. That, however, is not at issue here, partly because it is well and frequently covered ground but also because it distances the individual woman from the source of a dichotomy of which she may be more or less acutely aware, and because it puts the solution to these problems at an even greater distance.

Often the public and the private are distinguished one from the other in terms of the separation of work and the domestic sphere – which is not an adequate description of the diverse and personal private realm. But women's continuing association with the domestic realm makes the discrepancy between public and private selves sharper than it generally is for men and raises the issue of which is the true, the real, the natural self. So the contradictions between success and satisfaction (which is personal fulfilment but may register as failure on the scale of public achievement) are also more acute.

The impact of the private world on the public realm is often discussed only crudely, in sociological, political or economic generalities. It is quite true to say, for instance, that women are disadvantaged at work by sex stereotypes. But what does that generalization mean? How does it show up in real lives?

Most people do not see themselves as simply conforming to type: witness the number of women who acknowledge that women in general are discriminated against, but who feel they are not themselves victims of discrimination. This suggests that if, for instance, a woman feels she is being discriminated against, or if she feels somehow that she is not getting as much out of work as she wants to, she should do something about it herself. For a variety of reasons, this is not always possible: indeed, it is not usually possible. And one of those reasons is that in such circumstances women often feel personally at fault for not fitting in.

The fact that ambivalence towards public achievement is not part of the vocabulary of the public realm, with its stress on commitment, obscures that ambivalence and pushes it into the private realm where, unarticulated, it remains a potent source of inhibition. Women are particularly prey to it because it is reinforced by femininity, which asserts the connection between women and the domestic realm, but it is not exclusively a women's problem. Men, however, prefer to talk about this issue of ambivalence towards achievement in a dispassionate and objective way and to discuss it as a women's issue, perhaps because it is for them, too, a powerful conflict but one which they are even less accustomed than women to address.

The dichotomy of the public and personal realms is often also discussed in terms of masculine and feminine differences. But it is more useful to look at it in terms of the difference between public and private than between men and women. This is a distinction that embraces men's feelings too, and it is here, rather than between traditional male and female roles, that change is visibly taking place. And here, too, lies the opportunity for redressing the inequality which, by association with the domestic realm, women have suffered in comparison with men. It is perpetuated in the fact that ambition can be acknowledged less by women than by men: this secrecy reinforces women's ambivalence and sabotages their direct and unmediated pursuit of achievement.

Dale

Not all women are hampered by unarticulated anxieties over the possible price of commitment to their careers or to other areas of the public world. Can high achievers teach underachievers a lesson that is genuinely accessible to women whose material conditions seem far removed?

Dale Spender is an extraordinarily prolific writer, a leading figure in the women's movement, an academic, editor of an international journal, who lectures internationally and advises the boards of several different companies, in addition to commitments to campaigning and voluntary work.

'How is it,' Melissa Benn, who is a journalist, asked her

– on hearing that Dale had just completed another book in a month which had already seen the launch parties for two Spender *œuvres*, a lecture tour of America and a host of campaigning activities, in addition to her normal work-load – 'How is it that you can do so much?'

Dale, who had arrived at the dining club she had founded straight from the plane back from America, replied with her habitual air of innocence:

'Nobody ever told me I couldn't.'

There are three parts to the meaning of Dale Spender's apparently guileless response to Melissa Benn. Ostensibly she is saying, naïvely, that she did not realize there was any reason not to do what she has done or that there was any particular difficulty attached to joining the inter-national lecture circuit, founding a journal, raising thou-sands of pounds for charity, advising companies' boards and, particularly, writing prolifically.

But as a leading feminist thinker, writer and campaigner Dale Spender is also referring to the fact that many women are insidiously told that they 'can't'.

Encoded within her simple reply is a final meaning, in the context of her beliefs and writings, which challenges the cryptic prohibition against achievement. To people in receipt of the message that they 'can't', she suggests the response: 'Why not?'

What stops women?

What makes many women feel that they cannot work to the limit of their abilities? Superficially, it seems that women are given every opportunity and encouragement to achieve as much as they are capable of achieving. There is no explicit prohibition against this in the public sphere in a country in which both the head of state and the head of government are women; enabling legislation passed years ago lifted the legal barriers to women's entry to all sorts of walks of life; women might find themselves deterred from some occupations – like the schoolgirls who found opposition from careers teachers, careers officers and employers when they wanted to get into traditionally male jobs like banking and motor mechanics – but with determination they can overcome such obstacles.[1]

Yet women average only two-thirds of what men earn and work in fewer occupations and at lower status, though currently they are out of the workforce having children for, on average, less than four years of their working lives. Only six per cent of Members of Parliament are women and less than one in every five local councillors. An even lower proportion hold appointments on public bodies like committees of inquiry and government advisory committees.

If women are not told that they 'can't' do as well as men, then only lack of ability can account for their poor showing. Yet investigations into abilities show that they are evenly distributed between men and women. Therefore the prohibition is none the less real for being invisible.

What, then, is it? It is not composed of men conspiring to defeat women's ambitions for public achievement; it is not embodied in laws and regulations limiting women's access to the public realm; it is not simply the residue of post-war belief that a woman's place is in the home, nor the deterrence of the real and practical difficulties of women being the primary carers for others and running homes and organizing families, for it affects childless women and women without steady partners as well as mothers in settled relationships. It is a profound unease and ambivalence which is reinforced by the sense of being anomalous in the public realm.

Such a complex sense is itself part of the private realm, outside the concrete and simple conceptions of the public world. Hence the unarticulated sense of invalidity is perceived as an individual circumstance and peculiarity, rather than the common experience it really is. It is not understood to be a structural fault in a system which is not geared to accommodate women or the values of the personal realm.

Increasingly, men show a growing disaffiliation from the public realm: by wanting to play a larger role in their children's early lives, by wanting work which is more expressive of their individuality and forgoing the traditional rewards of gradual promotion and gently rising earnings, and by ameliorating the stereotypes of masculinity to which their fathers conformed. But if men are less aggressively ambitious, this does not mean they are obscurely torn over their working lives in the way women who want a career are.

For women in conventional women's jobs whose public lives are narrowly circumscribed, with little opportunity to expand their role or for significant promotion, such issues are similarly at a great distance. It is the women who are drawn to achievement but fear what it costs who are caught on the horns of an inexplicit dilemma.

Investigating and clarifying this dilemma means recognizing that it is a systemic problem, not an individual flaw. This means going beyond the particular to the general – yet not overlooking individual circumstances. For it is ultimately the voice of real, personal experience which speaks most clearly of the way ambivalence afflicts women's career development.

In order to counteract the insidious sense that they are, as individuals, unequal to the task of public achievement – success – women with careers have to be able to pinpoint and analyse the elements which undermine and sabotage their ability to work to capacity, which means being wholeheartedly engaged.

Direct prohibitions and contradictions, as well as being rare, are easy to define and discuss. How is the message

that individuals 'can't' constructed and delivered? Not
overtly.

The discrepancy between the apparent and the real in
what Dale Spender is saying illustrates how the inhibitions
which deter many people from resolutely pursuing
achievement operate, for it corresponds to the dualism of
the public and private realms in their lives.

The simple and the complex

The image of herself which Dale presents to the world is
that of a simple woman, surprised at the contradictions
she notes in the world about her. 'I find it curious'; 'I find
it interesting' and 'It seems to me remarkable' are characteristic prefaces in her conversation to pellucid observations on the idiocies of inequality.

Beneath the guise of naïve astonishment – and there for
all with discrimination enough to see – is a sophisticated,
highly informed logician's disposition. She does not dissi-
mulate. But Dale is an ironist, without cynicism but with
an enormous contempt for those without the wit to
perceive irony.

Qualities like irony are available to men and women
equally but are not exploited much in the public sphere in
which men excel, where literal interpretations are more
favoured. By comparison with the personal world, the
public realm is simple and direct. Its object is tangible
results, measured as output or achievement; these are
tangential to the private realm, which values feeling.
Whether or not irony is particularly a woman's prerogative, qualities which are most associated with the private
world are often described as feminine.

The growth of private values in the public realm

In recent years it has often been said in management
education circles that feminine qualities are increasingly
important at work. Certainly qualities from the more

complex private realm are increasingly seen to add value
to the activities of the public world. The swing to service
industries means that customer care is growing in importance, and major employer organizations like British Air-
ways invest time and money training their staff in the
basics of courtesy and concern for others. The growth of
entrepreneurialism and of intrapreneuring (mentioned in
chapter six) are other measures of the degree to which the
public realm is reshaping itself to incorporate values from
the private domain, such as autonomy. For a decade
employers have been encouraged to 'humanize' their
workplace, to increase employees' job satisfaction by
paying more attention to individual needs; more often on
economic than on ethical grounds.

At the forefront of this change in the public world –
from dismissing the private realm as unproductive to
trying to incorporate some of its aspects – is the stress on
qualities like creativity and wit. Recruitment advertising
uses 'creative' as a selling point for jobs in areas conventionally seen as the antithesis of creative, such as finance
and administration. Creativity has always been a strong
value-added factor in the commercial arts and related jobs
like advertising, marketing and public relations. And management academic and author Alistair Mant stresses that
wit is something the public world now needs. In discussing
the new generation of entrepreneurs and managers, whom
he describes as the 'mavericks' more interested in a career
in something smaller, more interesting, more unpredicta-
ble and difficult and more worthwhile than the big and
traditional corporations, he describes them as
'mischievous':

It has not escaped the attention of some of the big corporations
that the 'best' of the new people are virtually unemployable by
them. When T. J. Watson Snr wrote his famous letter to IBM
staff about the importance of 'wild ducks' in the corporation,
the company wags added 'provided they fly in formation'.[2]

This is an example of the way public entities like companies can believe that they accommodate and employ values from the private world, while in practice their behaviour is contradictory. It is not necessarily a conspiracy to lie on the part of the senior managers who articulate the corporate consciousness, but a measure of their tenuous grasp of reality. In just the same way many organizations believe that they employ women on the same basis as men, and knowledge of what constitutes equal treatment is often very vague.

Alistair Mant characterizes the young mavericks, the technocrats behind the Silicon Valleys and Apple computer corporations – which, he observes, they built up 'almost by accident, so absorbed were they by the technical challenges which faced them' – by their 'Monty Python' humour, and he is a great apologist for the value of paradox and wit.

Gaining face
So values from the private realm, sometimes described as feminine, are gradually appearing in the public domain, and one of the major differences between the two has been that while the public, masculine world tends to take things simply at face value, the private sphere more easily recognizes the difference between appearance and reality. It embraces paradoxes, contradictions, dilemmas and doubt, where the public world values action and decisions. The reward of the public world is success, which is achievement in the eyes of others, while the private realm offers satisfaction, which is a measure of achievement in personal terms.

'Man is least himself when he talks in his own person. Give him a mask and he will tell you the truth,' said Oscar Wilde.[3] In this apothegm the master of modern wit, although referring more to The Truth than to matters of fact, represents the need for providing the individual self with a vehicle, a protective outer skin, or a persona for public appearances. He was referring in particular to Man as Artist, but in the course of the twentieth century the aesthete's sensibility has spread from Bohemia out into the world at large, and the conditions first felt by artists of all sorts now inform the attitudes and expectations of people whose work is not creative in the strict sense.

The stress on individuality in contemporary society means that the individual must not clothe herself in an obviously artificial persona because the private values of integrity, authenticity and sincerity validate her in the public world – in society, at work, in the public eye. If people do not seem natural, they do not seem trustworthy. On the other hand, to seem natural is not necessarily the same thing as being so. Therefore complex forms of self-presentation are required of anyone who goes out into the public world; these are crucial to the creation and maintenance of self-confidence, which is similarly crucial to success.

On the question of the correspondence between confidence, honesty and persona, Erving Goffman, a social scientist who analysed in detail the way people construct and interpret behaviour in everyday situations, discusses 'face', applying the oriental concept to Western behaviour:

A person may be said to *have*, or *be in*, or *maintain* face when the line he effectively takes presents an image of him that is internally consistent . . .[4]

When a person senses that he is in face, he typically responds with feelings of confidence and assurance. Firm in the line he is taking, he feels he can hold his head up and openly present himself to others.[5]

[But:] Should he feel he is in the wrong face or out of face, he is likely to feel ashamed and inferior . . . Felt lack of judgmental support from the encounter may take him aback, confuse him, and momentarily incapacitate him as an interactant. His manner and bearing may falter, collapse and crumble. He may become embarrassed and chagrined: he may become shamefaced. The feeling, whether warranted or not, that he is perceived in a flustered state by others, and that he is presenting no usable line, may add further injuries to his feelings . . . [6]

This description bears close relation to many descriptions of lack of confidence among women, and to the sense of fraudulence that women managers describe.

Face is an important concept for women; this is evidenced literally through their use of cosmetics and metaphorically in the sense of invalidity expressed by women who are anomalies in an organization or structure in which their 'face does not fit'. In such circumstances women must use an appropriate persona but must also cope with the sense that this is a false position, since it is not their natural, real face.

Appearances and realities
The simplicity with which Dale Spender appeared to answer Melissa Benn's question illustrates these paradoxes of appearance and reality; in her ironic subtext, Dale was suggesting that most women are in effect told that they 'can't' do what she does.

In a culture which overtly encourages women to enter traditionally male spheres, which has abandoned marriage bars and permits equal access to education, it is difficult to locate the sources of the message that prevents women engaging themselves at full stretch in the public world.

The fact that it is not explicit makes it harder again to argue with simple-mindedness in the public world which can deal only with material evidence, recognized as 'objective' fact. Ostensibly, the enactment of equality legislation in the mid-1970s means that it is no longer lawful for women to be refused opportunities on the grounds of their sex alone.

Neither is it lawful to exceed a speed of seventy miles per hour on motorways; nor to trade in general goods on Sundays; nor indeed to defraud, rob or assault another person.

Legislative change does not immediately lead to a change in habits; it only makes something an offence. In the case of equality of opportunity for women (as distinct from other 'minority' groups), the offence is very widespread and the remedy very limited. Research by the Equal Opportunities Commission, which is responsible for monitoring and advising on equal pay and sex discrimination, shows that few cases are taken by comparison with the amount of discrimination that exists and that one of the main reasons is employees' fear of recrimination from employers. Not only is it difficult to bring an equal pay or sex discrimination claim; it is difficult to meet the requirements to make a claim, difficult to present a case, unlikely that it will get anywhere without legal representation and, even if the claimant wins, not worth it. At 1986 figures, most people who won cases where they had been refused a job because of their sex were awarded £100 for injury to their feelings. The laws stand on the statute books, but in practice they are not of much use to working women.

So changing the law has not changed behaviour, yet behaviour changes constantly with economic, technological and demographic development. The balance between the sexes is shifting so that there are significantly more men than women in the younger age groups and these, in turn, are changing in relative size, with the number of teenagers now falling rapidly, so that the mid-1990s will have a third fewer young people than the mid-1980s. The impact of AIDS on the population has also changed behaviour from the libertarian and sexist attitudes prevailing into the late 1970s. There is a direct correspondence between women's position in relation to sex with men in the mid-1960s and mid-1980s; in the one, saying 'No' was the popular advice on the first line of contraceptive defence; in the other, it is a defence against disease. Women in the 1980s have more choice of sexual partners and more power to refuse them. However, that is not necessarily replicated in an increase in political or economic power.

A teacher in a South London comprehensive school reports that the student body there is one-third girls to two-thirds boys.[7] The result is not, however, that girls have gained power or visibility in relation to boys but that they have become a muted group in the classroom – no improvement on the position Dale Spender reported in the 1970s when she found that teachers in mixed schools gave a disproportionate amount of attention to boys and largely ignored girls, without being at all aware of this.[8]

Success and satisfaction
The contrast between success and satisfaction and between the public realm and the private is also the difference between order and randomness, between intention and accident and between control and chaos. One illustration of this is the connection between success and power. For instance, one method recruitment organizations use for assessing achievement is the number of people under job candidates' direct or indirect control, for the ideology of success speaks of absolute control.

In its way the ideology of privacy also seeks absolute control, this time through personal freedom which denies the power of others, suggesting either a world so small that the individual is much bigger than events in it, or a way for the individual to distance herself and make uncontrolled external events unreal by elevating subjectivity over all sense of what exists outside the self.

Both the pursuit of public acclaim and the retreat into a private world are in this sense similar responses to the same doubts and are attempts to give shape and meaning to life. Whether either is a good strategy is open to debate, but if the proving ground is the question of what meaning can be ascribed to a person's life then it is perhaps a safer bet to choose, if a choice has to be made, the strategy most likely to seem meaningful to the self rather than to others.

On this analogy, the pursuit of success is like trying to turn life into art, to shape life as a message to others, while the quest for fulfilment is an attempt to come to terms with nature rather than to control it, with the object of understanding how personal experience fits into a wider context.

Women in the public world

Women's interest in careers – and so implicitly in success – is demonstrably strong; this is shown in the rising number taking business and professional training as a foundation for management careers and similarly in those gaining manual skills in traditionally male areas like the construction industry.[9] Networks for women in manual and non-manual occupations have sprung up to cater for the demand for contacts, training and support and women's magazines have greatly increased the number of pages devoted to work-related subjects.

The position of women at work has changed since the middle of the century in terms of numbers holding paid jobs and, immediately after the equal opportunities legislation of the 1970s, in pay as a proportion of men's average earnings. But the belief that women are going out into paid employment in large numbers for the first time is mistaken. The growth in women's employment since the Second World War ought to be seen in the context of a dramatic fall compared with a hundred years earlier, as the idea that it was unseemly for a woman to go out to work took hold.

Women are not currently gaining ground by being appointed to better jobs. The proportion of women in

senior administrative and professional positions has stayed
constant over the century; the proportion in clerical and
retail jobs has risen sharply, and the proportion in skilled
manual work has plummeted.[10]

Despite the popular idea that the career woman is a
contemporary phenomenon, the proportion of women in
the population who dedicate themselves to their jobs has
fallen with the rising number of women having children.
Because there are now more men than women under fifty
in the population, women have a wider choice of partners
than in earlier generations when they outnumbered men,
and this is related to the fact that nine out of ten women
have children now compared to seven in the 1930s. In a
number of areas women from the last generations, where
there was structural spinsterhood, who are now retiring
from their careers are leaving a gap in senior positions.

Although women are not participating equally in the
public world, government statistics, historically insensitive
to their participation in the labour force, show that their
experience of public life is changing.[11] There has been no
real proportional increase in the number of women now
in paid work compared with a hundred years ago,[12] but
the jobs women do have shifted from being largely connected with a domestic support role – as servants, for
instance – to cover a slightly broader spectrum of occupations.[13] And although feminization had devalued occupations like clerical work, women have been enfranchised
and thereby released from the political category to which
lunatics, felons and minors are consigned.

The impact of this on the values and expectations of the
public world can be seen in, for instance, men's attitudes
to work and family life. There is evidence that they want
more involvement in family life.[14] There have, too, been
other developments marking the need to accommodate
women – for example, the introduction of maternity leave

and the massive increase in part-time work during the 1970s.[15]

But the greatest effect has been on women's own lives. The differences between male and female interpretations of how to act and how to be in the public world have been increasingly closely defined in the rising volume of literature investigating how women compare with men.

Egalitarians and feminists

Although the male-surrogate style is not now the only legitimate one for working women, the degree to which it still exerts a strong influence shows how uncertain women are in it and how unaccommodating it remains. Male surrogacy has been adopted because masculine styles are more strongly associated with success than feminine manners and also because of the danger of discrimination, which means that many women have been at pains to minimize or deny the differences between them and men. There remain, even now, many women who have penetrated previously male bastions and the upper echelons of power and responsibility (or feel they have) who deny significant differences between the sexes and insist upon personhood before womanhood.

Frances, a senior BBC producer in her twenties, commented:

There is nothing that debars a woman from being as effective a manager as a man. When it comes down to it, what in fact distinguishes between people is personality, not sex differences, and I think it's dangerous to make women a special case. Women are just as able as men.

Her view is representative of many similarly successful professional women in all walks of life; it is often articulated, for instance, by both men and women in public service, where there can be a strong sense of equality of opportunity which is not underpinned by an awareness of the working conditions of most women in Britain. It shows the difference between believing in equality and supporting feminist values.

This sort of view is understandable enough. While the public world – the realm of political activity, visible achievements and civic responsibilities – was associated with and defined by men, a woman's position within it was anomalous. If women conformed to feminine norms they risked exclusion from their particular fields of endeavour for inappropriate behaviour. Therefore they had to minimize sex differences.

Separating success from masculinity

The means of making achievement available to women have been debated for a long time. Sarajane Harris-Richard, a senior civil servant whose job takes her outside the cloisters of Whitehall into collaboration and negotiation with industrialists, financiers and foreign governments, articulates the employers' argument against facilitating women's entry to the public realm through greater participation in more senior jobs. She questions

the extent to which it is actually right for organizations to make the sorts of concessions entailed in positive action for women at the cost of their own efficiency and effectiveness. I work in an internationally competitive environment; we're up against the Japanese, the Germans, the Koreans, whoever. And most of these societies offer a great deal less equality to women than we do. And when it comes to doing business in the world, they're extremely effective and one of the reasons is that people in these countries put in levels of commitment which are probably greater than anything you get in the UK and certainly greater than anything you could possibly get in a situation where you are saying: 'Well, people have to have lots of time off for maternity leave and part-time working and flexible hours and all that sort of thing.' That's all very good and dandy and nice in human terms, but may be at the price of our continuing decline as a nation.

The can-we-afford-to-be-nice argument is predicated on an idea of the economic and social order which developed under nineteenth-century industrial capitalism; in a post-industrial society, things are different. The argument against positive action also sees women as a special-interest group or as a secondary labour force with marginal rights and limited responsibilities, to be called upon to meet sudden surges in demand and then dispensed with.

The growth in part-time working by women encourages that view and is reinforced by the background to British management, historically untrained, gerontocratic and ill-prepared to meet swift and radical technological change. However, under the new technological industrial regime part-time working, job-sharing, home-working, consultancy and self-employment are becoming very much more widespread.[16]

So there are changes in working patterns which could help to promote women in the workforce by legitimizing the flexibility they need for a successful integration of family responsibilities and working life. However, it is understandable that many managerial women, who attained their position under more or less adverse conditions, are reluctant to argue a special case for themselves and for other women.

Women as managers

But not all women managers think this way. In particular, women who are actively engaged in helping others into better jobs tend to see women as a special case, not as a minority but as a particularly disadvantaged sector of the workforce, with special qualities to offer.

Ruth Poppleton trains women for and in management:

I think that as a woman manager I've developed a particular style which is quite different from most male managers, and it's quite difficult to achieve because our models tend to be either of male managers or of aggressive women managers, which is very unfortunate. But there aren't many good models of women managers about. That's possibly why some women do fall into the stereotype of being seen as aggressive, because, possibly, that's the only model they've got other than as an ineffectual manager.

Some of the qualities that women can bring to management are very undervalued: like good personal relationships; like promoting co-operation; like encouraging good teamwork and within that, encouraging people within their group to achieve their full potential in the job, which I think is very often not done because of managers fearing competition from their staff. Whereas I think that certainly I, and perhaps quite a lot of women, are not very frightened of that because we're not very status-conscious and we're more interested in working as a group: achieving in that kind of way rather than personal achievement.

Jane Conniff, who also runs courses for women at every level from manual workers to senior management, agrees:

I think a lot of women have natural management qualities. They're nurtured into looking after people, and management is about looking after people. It's seeing that they do their job, but it's actually people. One has to be fairly patient as a manager sometimes. And I think women learn to praise, too, and I think that's something you need to do as a manager – something that men find difficult. And men can often shout at work; I know a lot of people think that losing your temper is actually an effective way of managing.

But Judi Marshall, author of a study of women managers' identity problems, comments that the danger of claiming special talents for women as managers is that these talents can be construed as invalid management techniques, and therefore used to debar women from management positions.[17]

The idea that women do have a different style, not

only in management but at work and in the public world generally – in politics, for example, it can be used to suggest that if more women were returned to Westminster, a different ethos would prevail in Parliament – is rooted in the association between women and the private world.

The implication of assuming a more co-operative, less competitive style at work among women is that women operate on the values of the *Gemeinschaft* (the realm of the private community of family and intimates) even within the *Gesellschaft* (the social and economic realm). It assumes that women instinctively aim for communal achievement rather than an individuated success. Another interpretation – also suggested by the detailed account Ruth Poppleton and others give later of women's lack of confidence in their jobs – is that women are intimidated from pursuing the goals of individual success, entailing the risks of personal failure, and prefer instead the relative security of co-operative enterprises. Like Dale Spender, they believe women get the message that they cannot engage fully and actively in the public realm.

What drives people onwards and upwards?

Motivation theory, an area within social and personality psychology, suggests that people's behaviour is determined by the degree to which they desire success and fear failure. For each individual, the balance of the two forces is different. Those who desire success more than they fear failure will take more risks and strike out on their own, backing their own judgement: they are the entrepreneurs and the mavericks; those who fear failure more than they desire success will hedge their bets and play much safer. Whether it is possible to claim that women on the whole fall into one category rather than the other is a contentious area, but the idea that women prefer working with a group and under a co-operative rather than an authoritarian regime conforms more to the notion of fear of failure than desire for success.

As Judi Marshall points out, such distinctions amount to saying that women are not managers, since managers are people who tell others what to do, take decisions and lead a team. She gives similarly short shrift to the argument that women have only to be patient and the day will dawn when their special qualities will be recognized and rewarded; this is based on reference to the fact that the proportion of women undergraduates in business studies is growing; however, the number of women in management does not reflect the increase in management-educated women. Women qualified, and even experienced, in management are often shunted into specializations away from the mainstream of line management and industrial relations experience which would be appropriate for a career path leading to a board appointment, or a role in the upper echelons. Instead, they are still clustered on the bottom rungs of the management ladder, or pushed off it into consultancy work and self-employment.

The distinction between personal and political

Another way in which women are perceived as having different interests from men and being more personal, particular and private in their orientation is the assumption that they are less politically than socially motivated, although the distinction between the two is never very clear. British political parties have traditionally resisted selecting women as candidates out of a sense that women are anomalous in this particular public arena and would not be taken seriously, although evidence from the electorate contradicts this.[18] It is claimed, for instance, that women are less interested in or able to cope with the backstabbing and machinations of political life – although in other contexts women are stereotypically portrayed as the manipulative sex.

But many women corroborate this, describing themselves as interested in social but not political issues: a Europe-wide survey showed that when women and men were asked whether they were interested in politics the men declared themselves to be more so than the women, but when they were asked whether they were interested in important social issues, women came out of the survey just as intelligently concerned as men.[19] This is in line with the way women's concerns are popularly characterized as more immediate, practical and personal, men's as more abstract, theoretical and broader-ranging.

The same distinction was noticed by Rayna Reiter, an anthropologist who studied the distinction of male and female lives into public and private spheres in a small French village, and whose book on the subject has become a contemporary classic in the literature. She found that the women's lives were structured round kinship, in terms of both their family and their ancestors, with the central relationship being with their mothers, while men's relationships made everyone, including kin, into colleagues. The women spent their time in their own homes or in the village shops, while the men went out: to work, to the café and to nearby towns. Reiter noted that in a peasant community, while men have access to their own homes, women do not, except under well-defined terms, have access to the public realm:

Women's reaction to such domain-ance is to invert it. They perceive the public areas as the sites of great play-acting . . . [They consider the public world, outside their private territory, silly.] . . . The arenas and roles forbidden them are discounted as unimportant. They do not see the public sphere as more powerful or imposing than the private one.[20]

On this analysis women lack interest in politics because it is perceived as a masculine domain.

One of the changes in the balance between the public

and private realms in contemporary life is the number of women entering the public sphere. If this gives rise to certain difficulties for women it affects men too, principally perhaps in having to adjust to women working more than before.[21] Men seem to perceive women as equal citizens to a greater extent than previously, to adapt to different domestic and private demands and to some extent to redefine their roles.[22]

Yet for men the issue remains largely one of being reactive, whereas for women the opportunity to enter the public realm means taking the initiative, which for many women entails a more radical transformation than men undergo.

Going public

How do women indicate the contradictions implicit in entering the public world? One line of inquiry has been through what is popularly known as fear of success, which has used motivation theory to interpret imagery of the consequences of success as showing that women are afraid of achievement because of the conflicting requirements of the social construct of femininity and that of being successful. It has also been linked with psychoanalytic views of women as less self-reliant and independent, with the implication that until they make up, by an effort of will, for these deficiencies they will not deserve the rewards of public achievement.[23]

The problem with this thinking is that it again suggests a male-surrogate style for women and is based on the notion that, in wishing to enter a public domain largely occupied by men, women must accept the terms on which men operate in that domain rather than looking for ways of negotiating a workable and satisfactory agreement between the opportunities and requirements of both ways of being – female and public.

Being ladylike

What is femininity if it stands in such opposition to public achievement? In terms of sex stereotyping, which is an index of the social construction of femininity, women are seen as more sensitive, supportive and intimate than men.[24] As consumers women are more disposed towards romance, fashion and fantasy than men are supposed to be (although increasingly there are categories of men who employ the semantics of fashion and image, particularly in the rock and media worlds; if they are called effeminate it is a misnomer, since they are not divesting themselves of masculine styles and privileges but acquiring and exploring a new vocabulary which has been traditionally available only to women).

The idea of the opposition of masculine and feminine is based on the assumption that there are fixed or learned character attributes which are meted out, some to women and others to men, with little overlap between the two. But it is misleading to view masculinity and femininity as poles of a single spectrum. Psychological research into sex roles and attitudes in the 1970s indicated that masculinity and femininity are not so much poles as different axes of personality measurement; so people can be both very masculine and very feminine; or very feminine but not very masculine; or neither particularly feminine nor masculine.[25]

Femininity is also associated with feeling and subjectivity as masculinity is with action and objectivity; in the same way, the public and private realms are characterized as masculine and feminine respectively, even though everyone participates in both. The private world is that of the self; the public, that of others.

The world of the self precedes the world of others as the globally subjective sense antedates an objective view of the world. Child psychology generally holds that the child copes with the shock of learning that there are boundaries to the self – and therefore boundaries over what the individual can control – according to her relationship with her mother. Feminist psychotherapists in particular suggest that because the relationship between mothers and daughters is different from that between mothers and sons (and this is in the broader context of the different social attitudes towards girls and boys, men and women) the sense of me and not-me, inner and outer, and hence of public and private is not the same for girls and women as for boys and men.[26]

The difference, at its simplest, is that girls are guided towards a nurturant, supportive, sensitive role in which they react to the initiatives and needs of others before expressing their own and that the earliest relationship in which girls are encouraged to take their first altruistic, self-denying steps is in their relationships with their mothers who, because they give so much support to the men in their ambits, are themselves in desperate need of support; their only source of supply is commonly their daughters.

Boys, on the other hand, are guided towards exploration, which entails self-discovery. Thus a little boy has more opportunity to learn his own strengths and weaknesses, while a little girl learns how to supply other people's needs. Roughly speaking, this process produces men who are not highly sensitized to others' needs of them and women who have an uncertain sense of who they are and rely on others to define them by demanding responses.

The constraint of feminine self-awareness
Thus women are afflicted by certain fundamental forms of self-consciousness to which men are immune and often oblivious. Women look to others for reassurance and need support while men, constantly supported both by individual women and by a whole social order, feel unconstrained by such needs.

This can explain why women seem to form more intimate relationships more often than men; why women seek reassurance in ways that seem unnecessary to men, who often construe this as vanity or affectation; and why also women are more occupied with issues of image and appearance, not only in consuming fashion and beauty products but, for instance, as great consumers of soap opera and romantic fiction. Both these categories of fantasy offer a specific form of reassurance or validation by presenting detailed information on how lives are lived.

Women, as consumers of romantic fiction, can constantly check that 'this is me', 'this is not-me'. By contrast, the heroes of fiction for men are much more action-orientated. This, with the narrative element generally, preponderates over psychological or emotional development. In line with the general notion of what is masculine and what is feminine, fiction for men is about what happens; fiction for women is about how it feels.

Women's relatively less certain sense of self leads to another constituent part of femininity: the importance of image (fashion, make-up and style) and attractiveness. This is often interpreted as vanity, but for an individual with an unreliable sense of self, adopting and discarding different images is an obvious choice. It is seeking identity through the complicated route of manipulating the way others see you, pursuing it via self-presentation rather than unselfconsciousness, which is less and less available in contemporary society with its stress on individualism and consumerism.

The availability of material from which to construct images – through the mass marketing of clothes and make-up and more generally through the growth of consumer choice to be exercised in finely discriminating between different brands of the same product – reinforces this, as does the latitude society now allows for adopting different images. There is, for instance, a return to less gender-specific forms of clothing, with men being put into skirts by Jean-Paul Gaultier and women commonly wearing jeans. Since the 1960s, cosmetics and fashion magazines for men have been continually launched; although they have not yet taken a mass-market-sized sector, the expectation that men and women will grow more alike in these areas remains strong.[27]

The development of style magazines in the 1980s is one indication of the ways in which, among younger men, conventional masculinized behaviours are modified. They developed from rock magazines to embrace questions of visual style and behaviour in ways which were traditionally the province of women's magazines, with fashion spreads, merchandise information and softer features angled around personal interests rather than the factual data supplied in men's hobby publications. Their readership is more evenly split between the sexes than that of publications aimed at women or at men only.

Within a society which has become much more self-conscious than its antecedents, where there is a new importance and a new potential for personal fulfilment, women are less certain of their individual identities than men yet seem to have more options for exploring self-fulfilment. This is not only a question of visual style: men, for instance, cannot bear children, which has been considered one of the centrally fulfilling experiences of women's lives; although men can raise them, they exercise that option in far smaller numbers than women exploring what are traditionally male roles.

The sources of prohibition

The ways in which women are inhibited from taking up the opportunities before them are diverse and subtle, and hence either obscure or entirely invisible. For instance, women managers are reported as being more aware of – and to a lesser extent more prepared to articulate – the degree to which, by comparison with male managers, they organize their time less efficiently and have more trouble in identifying priorities and enforcing decisions.

Women often feel unconfident, but (probably wisely) do not necessarily indicate this. The result is that they do not get the supportive feedback from the public world which they need to perform to capacity. This again is an area that has been identified in management training, but there remains a shortfall in the degree to which men managers are able and willing to respond to women's needs, not least because these demands run counter to the traditional ethos (competitive and aggressive, independent-minded and dominating) of management in particular, business in general and capitalism broadly.

Much of the debate on the ethos of the public and private worlds has been inspired by Marxist sociologists' interest in the impact of economic structures on both the masses and the individual. Historically there has been an association between feminism and socialism, where the community of interests is evident and the conflict of interests palpable: both feminism and socialism are commitments to advancing the needs of an underprivileged mass; but where feminism has often loyally served the needs of socialism, socialism has felt less wedded to feminism's best interests.[28]

Masking the private

Women often seem partially to resolve the conflicts of being raised feminine and entering the public world – most often paid employment – by masking their uncertainties. The masks are various and entail the danger of reinforcing stereotypes (if these are their models) and restricting individual expression. For instance, women in supervisory, managerial, professional or executive roles are often perceived as highly organized, thorough, efficient and hard-working (but not as gifted, creative or original) by men and other women alike. Women at work are prone to being characterized as competent and reliable rather than gifted (and giftedness is associated with independence of thought and risk-taking). Therefore women are applauded as excellent lieutenants, but rarely promoted to captain.

Another aspect of this reputation women have acquired for thoroughness and hard work is a range of activities which actually get in the way of achievement; women sort and order things, list and plan – but do not execute. Victoria Wood, the playwright and performer who discusses in chapter six how she procrastinated over work, found herself sorting nails into boxes and cleaning out the telephone mouthpiece with cotton buds. In her more detached moments, she questioned the value of such activities for a woman with a television series to write.

Women dissipate their energies in other ways, and one of their chief obstacles to achievement is the claims of the personal, private world, particularly those of family and children. With the lack of childcare and social services in Britain, women with family responsibilities, as parents or as carers (for elderly or infirm relatives, for instance) have to negotiate compromises such as working part-time or working from home, or even giving up work altogether. One of the major criteria for achievement in the public world is commitment, construed by companies as loyalty, consistency (track record) and status (pay, responsibility, power). Part-time work, low pay and discontinuous work histories all debar women from meeting these requirements.

It is a problem for women to be anomalies in a male world, and constructing a mask or persona is an incomplete solution; those who adopt this strategy feel fraudulent, insecure and highly fragmented although they may not in reality have much choice about presenting themselves in a particular, artificial way when that is acceptable to their colleagues and is a condition of entry to the public world.[29]

For women, then, entry to the public world is relatively more complicated and problematic than it is for men. Women feel less certain, more in need of support, validation or authorization, less confident and less wholeheartedly engaged in their roles. The alternative is to retreat from the challenge of the public world, back into traditional roles which are very widely perceived as unsatisfactory.[30] This, however, is not the answer; we must synthesize a new solution.

Yet because the issues involved are so diverse and so radical, that synthesis is not merely a matter of adjusting domestic relationships and expectations (any more than feminism is centrally concerned with who does the housework). It is not to be found in merely proselytizing or informing men and women of their new opportunities to reorganize their working and family lives. It means reconstructing femininity – a radical change for all the individual women actively trying to find a place in the new territories of the public world opening up to them for the first time.

Already the problem is generating its own solutions. There are collective remedies (assertiveness training, support groups and networks) and there are individual remedies (therapy). There is also the effect of economic, industrial and technological change to be taken into account: while it cauterizes the flow of job opportunities, particularly for women, it also catalyses social – and particularly occupational – change. The effect may be to validate some of the strategies women have employed, such as freelancing, home-working and consultancy, part-time jobs and job-sharing. The redefinition of work and leisure also entails the redistribution of labour in the family and offers the opportunity to remake roles at home. Changes in the private world entail corresponding alterations in the public; advances in equality in one area lead to more equality in the other, just as inequalities in the private world mirror inequalities in the public realm. The woman overburdened with domestic chores cannot achieve so much at work: the woman denied success at work may look for satisfaction at home.

Bending gender rules

The first version of the solution to be tried out was in the 1960s and 1970s, when 'unisex' was a high-street fashion and androgyny its theoretical companion-piece. It was not an effective solution to the conflicts of the different satisfactions of the public and private spheres, partly because of prevailing economic conditions and social attitudes but also partly, perhaps, because it essentially asked of women that they look and behave like boys, which meant abandoning much of what is valuable about womanhood. It also offered men very little in the way of a new deal. But it was part of a process which laid the foundations for the current social, economic and techno-logical conditions which can foster a new definition of public and private, individual and society, male and female.

The problem for women who feel invalid in the public realm is that this is often not only an uncomfortably sensitive issue but one which is particularly hard to articulate. Because of this, and because feeling invalid contradicts so much of what the public realm accepts and supports – and particularly the ideology of success – it is difficult to negotiate a satisfying career.

The issue is made more complex because there is no final authority to appeal to. The world of work, and the larger public world of which it is a part, are, in a capitalist society, not centrally and hierarchically organized. So there is no collective bargaining on behalf of all women, only discrete negotiations in different workplaces and, at most, in different industries and unions. Beyond that there is no one to talk to and individual women must negotiate their own solution to the difficulties of participating in public life.

The question remains unanswered: What is the nature of the prohibition against women being successful and prolific? The exterior obstacles are not sufficient to deter women from fulfilling their potential. The interior obstacles, the inhibition against direct self-expression, are much harder to discern.

British women are reluctant to express personal demands directly. They are in general more comfortable working collectively and altruistically: ambition is not a feminine quality, nor is competitiveness. But achievement does not necessarily depend on rigid, limited and cold qualities like these. Fulfilment, on the other hand, is an acceptable goal for women, though they are often unable to pursue it outside the personal realm.

For the exceptions like Dale Spender there is no problem with inhibitions, only with prohibitions. But Dale is not British. The interior barriers are a problem for diffident and confused women like Geraldine, Rebecca, Louise and Jillie (whose experiences are recounted below), who appear efficient, successful and confident but feel frightened, resourceless and blocked. The price of success is stress, and for some it can prove too high.

All these women are educated, middle-class Anglo-Saxons. Not all are British, but in Britain this obscure, difficult and dangerous question of acknowledging women's ambivalence and sense of invalidity in the public realm is more immediately apprehensible than in the bluffer, more robustly egalitarian new English-speaking democracies. The English tradition of self-deprecation is a useful vantage point from which to survey the many avenues through which women apparently damage their own best interests.

The solution to the problem of why women do not do better lies in integrating the private (feminine) and public (masculine) experiences of the world, for it is the split between the two which breeds the idea that they are inherently opposed and that achievement in one can be gained only at the expense of the other. This categorical attitude also suggests that a choice must be made, for it rejects paradox, ambivalence and complexity; hence it suggests that some people are suited to the public realm and deserve success, while others can find fulfilment only in the private realm. How has this attitude developed, and how has it affected women over the centuries?

2
History

Then and now

Sometime around 350 B.C., eleven Teutonic warriors were
buried with their shields, swords and spears at what is
now Tecklenburg in Westphalia. Three also had bows
with them, and these were all women. At other sites, too,
in East and West Germany and in Czechoslovakia, the
bodies of women warriors from some two thousand years
ago have been found, dressed in trousers, bearing arms
and killed by sword strokes.[1]

There are European traditions of women warriors and
warrior queens: some where the written record seems to
be borne out in the archaeological record, like Cartiman-
dua or Boadicea, others, like the Amazons, with no
corroboration for their mythic existence.[2] The occupation
of soldier or adventurer has attracted women down the
ages: Eleanor of Aquitaine went on a crusade, accompanied by her ladies dressed as Amazons; the painter
Artemisia Gentileschi fought at the siege of Bologna, and
The Maid of Zaragoza fought famously in the Peninsular
Wars. In the eighteenth century a number of women
became folk heroines by disguising themselves as men and
joining the army or navy – usually, they said, to follow
their husbands or sweethearts. The most famous was
Christian Davies, an Irishwoman who spent more than a
decade as a man in the British Army until she was
wounded at Ramillies. Women were recommended for
decoration for their military service as late as the nine-

teenth century; however, their status was never as assured as that of male professional soldiers and sailors. Often their decorations got no further than recommendations; many, including Christian Davies, had difficulty in claiming the war pensions to which they were entitled.[3]

But the fact that some women could escape into men's roles, that roles were not so sharply defined according to gender and that there was no absolutely enforced connection between women and the private sphere, does not mean that in the past women generally had much to do with the public realm. Evidence for the private realm is, however, slender.

'The position of women seems to have been high,' remarks Nora Chadwick about the Celts,[4] but she says little more to support this, for the evidence is slender: classical historians vary in their reliability and wrote generally not from first-hand but reported experiences.

The writers of annals and historians leave some clues about the position of women outside the empires of their days, commenting now and again that they were venerated and consulted in the decision-making process. The evidence for women's role in religion and magic is perhaps stronger: there are more accounts of priestesses than women warriors. Burials reveal women laid to rest with splendid grave goods about them, but do not give the precise occupation of the woman thus inhumed: ruler, priest or wife. The myths which survive these eras of the European past show women in all these roles, and more. Women, witches and goddesses tutor and protect, aid, abet and oppose heroes throughout the world.

But just as the Celts are obscured from us by only limited participation in the public events of the civilized world, so were women. The process of recording events, the growth of historical records, has focused on public life. And just as women are largly absent from the historical record, so there is no clear account of how the public

and private realms were distinguished until relatively
recent times.

The classical conception of public

The private realm was defined as the absence of public life
for much of recorded history. Aristotle, in his *Politics*,
considered the matter of the distinction of the public from
the private in terms of the difference between the part and
the whole, and his view was that the individual, the private
part [*idios*], belonged wholly to the state: 'We must not
regard a citizen as belonging just to himself: we must
rather regard every citizen as belonging to the state.'[5]

Because he saw that people preferred to live in communities and that the good of the community was also the
good of the individual, Aristotle described man as a
political animal. But the optimum size for the political
community, the *polis*, was 'the greatest surveyable number
required for achieving self-sufficiency'. This meant that the
polis had to be of a size which allowed its political leaders
to know every citizen personally.[6] In terms of mass society
– which Aristotle specifically denied the description *polis* –
this translates into describing man as a social animal.

In this public world the anonymity of the individual in
a mass society was absent, for it was a community in
which decisions were based on personal knowledge. It also
denied the opposition between the individual and the state
which now shapes the distinction between the public and
the private realm. The *autarkeia*, self-sufficiency, which
Aristotle considered proper to the *polis* is a quality very
similar to the independence fostered by American rugged
individualism, which belongs to the private realm. In
comparison with the ideal citizenry of classical Athens,
contemporary Western society produces people who aim
to be islands, entire unto themselves.

The personal realm is associated with the natural realm
and the public domain with the artificial. Women and

children have been conceived in many cultures as being more 'natural' than men, in the sense of being governed by nature and less self-controlled.[7] Even in a society such as Victorian England which on the contrary elevated middle-class women to a more cultured status than men, the opposition of women and the artificial public realm was maintained by associating women with the family and domestic sphere.

This is all part of the contemporary idea of the private, personal realm as the realm of freedom, unconstrained by the social controls required by the public world. It reverses the classical conception of the difference between public and private, to which women were wholly confined.

Greece and Rome

In classical Greece women were excluded from public and political life. The exceptions to the rule were the *heteira*, the courtesans, at whose salons, it seems, reputations were made and lost and policy formed and discussed, as later in neoclassical France. But the *heteira*, if capable of influence, were still only informally associated with the political domain. Their chief area was recreational and leisure activities, which in contemporary terms were categorized as play [*paidia*] and recreation [*anapausis*], which was refreshment after work, and leisure pursuits [*schole*] – intellectual recreation: an occupation in its own right, but one undertaken for its own sake and not from any sort of necessity. *Schole* was a valuable activity, *paidia* and *anapausis* mere amusements.

In Roman society women were similarly debarred from taking a full and active role in public life, though there was scope to be a power behind the throne. Roman society also apparently allowed women greater occupational freedom than did the Greek city-states by and large, though these varied in the latitude they allowed: for instance, Athenian orators were contemptuous of the freedom with which Spartan women conducted their lives. Roman epitaphs commemorate women secretaries, clerks, stenographers, teachers and doctors, though women were expressly forbidden to be bankers or to work in precious metals.

The Romans also looked askance at the licence with which Etruscan women behaved. Contemporary Greek and Roman writers commented on practices like husbands and wives dining publicly together and Etruscan relics depict men and women in couples in life and in death. Respectable Etruscan women seem to have been free to go out alone in public, while their Roman and Attic contemporaries kept strictly to their quarters. They also had their own personal names, and inscriptions record both patronymic and matronymic. Nevertheless, in Etruria too the connection between women and domestic life was strong. Women's tombs were distinguished from men's architecturally by placing their funeral couches within house-shaped chests.[8]

So the connection between women, the domestic and the private world was firmly and early established. As classical influences merged with the North European heritage to form the kingdoms of Dark Age and medieval Europe the association between women and home continued, reinforced at different periods by Pauline Christianity.

Developing conventions of femininity

There continued to be examples of women resisting or remaking convention and entering the public realm or creating spheres of influence which were not commensurate with the personal and familial. In 1308 women were recorded as eligible for election as Deputies to the assembly of the estates at Tours. Joan, the Fair Maid of Kent who married the Black Prince, romantically affected the dress of the *bonnes amies* of the brigands of Languedoc and with her ladies-in-waiting attended tournaments dressed in male attire of particoloured hose, tunic and short cape and sporting a dagger. In seventeenth-century England the pamphlets 'Hic Mulier' and 'Haec Vir' prescribed the duties of women and men respectively, the former being a polemic against the freedoms available to women which the author saw as unnatural (its subtitle was: 'Being A Medicine to cure the Coltish Staggers in the Masculine Feminines of Our Time'; here the idea of gender ordained by nature appears, if metaphorically, along with the idea, to which we shall return, that going against nature in this sense should be treated as an illness). The courts of love, in earlier times, were established and run by women.

There is evidence also for women working as academics, in the professions and as artists, in roles outside privileged court circles. In 1322 Jacoba Felicie was prosecuted in Paris for lecturing without a licence, while at the university in Bologna Novella d'Andrea lectured in medicine from behind a screen in order, it was said, that her students should not be distracted by her fabulous beauty. Meanwhile Christine de Pisan was earning her living as a writer, the first women credited with doing so.[9]

But such women were the exception to a rule of subordination to and dependency upon men, and one of the pillars that supported that order was the vast proportion of most women's lives devoted to child-bearing. This is why the introduction of reliable contraceptive devices for women has made such a radical change in their lives. There are other elements in this critical change: the reduction in infant mortality; the shift from labour to capital; the increasing wealth of the industrialized nations. But these factors only lifted the pressure on women to be continually pregnant in order to ensure the survival of enough children to provide the labour necessary for society and for a secure old age for the parents.

The growing sense of a split
The modern sense of a distinction between public and private has grown up with industrialization. As the romantic

sensibility developed in response to the influences of rationalism and the Industrial Revolution, so did a sense of a natural order from which people were being removed by the rise of the cities, the growth of communications – including, for the first time, mass media – and the alienation engendered by mass-production processes. The slum conditions in which many of the labouring classes lived seemed, to the Victorian social reformers and those they influenced, unnatural. These and other conditions entailed by an industrial society, such as living at a remove from the countryside, were seen as a corrupting influence, not only oppressing (not to say curtailing) the lives of those most immediately affected – the labouring classes – but insidiously pervading society and destroying its moral fabric.

Intrinsic to this process was the corruption of commerce, and specifically the idea of money as the root of all evil. This lived alongside the work ethic which seemed to imply that the fruits of labour were wealth and that poverty was the result of lack of moral fibre. This idea was moderated by the association of money with vulgarity. Genteel manners varied in importance in direct proportion with the growth of the bourgeoisie and later of today's mass lower middle class.

One of the foundation stones of genteel life was women's dependence on men. In particular it was not ladylike for women to go out to work, although the 1851 Census shows that a quarter of women did so, while the earliest census information on married women in paid employment showed that in 1911 one in ten had paid jobs.

Technology and the home
In London in 1850, one in every five households included servants. Where the wealthier classes had long had servants to sustain their complex households and their many possessions, the poorer classes in the industrialized countries now also had more complex domestic arrangements.

Housework made an appearance as a major factor in women's lives as a result of moralizing social reform and aspiration which insisted that you did not have to be rich to be clean. The poorer classes, who were then in the majority, were required to demonstrate their commitment to these middle-class values and the deserving poor, as distinct from the indolent, wicked or hopeless, were characterized by their godly cleanliness.[10] The greater part of domestic work had previously involved looking after household animals, growing, preparing and cooking food, scouring and storing a few cooking utensils, making and maintaining clothes and looking after people, including preparing and applying everyday folk remedies.

From the mid-nineteenth century onwards the domestic order was transformed by technology with the installation of city-wide piped water, followed over the next hundred years by the introduction of other power utilities, gradually enabling this new class of housewife to avail herself of labour-saving devices such as the vacuum cleaner, the sewing machine, the washing machine and the cooker. However, the existing burden of housework was not fully offset by these innovations, while it was massively increased by the rise in standards of cleanliness and order.

This burden has continued over the period during which women have also taken on new responsibilities in the labour force and in the public world generally so that now a woman in full-time paid work, averaging thirty-five hours a week, spends a further twenty-eight hours a week on housework.[11] Since the 1950s it has been recognized that women bear the burden of a dual role when they participate in the labour market because entering the sphere generally designated for men – the public world of work, politics and civic affairs – does not correspondingly reduce their responsibilities for the private realm. These responsibilities are not officially recognized because they are considered private.

The divorce of work from home

The separation of home and work has for most people been a relatively recent and slow process. The majority of men worked at or near their homes in the long eras preceding the Industrial Revolution, when agriculture was the economic base and manufacturing largely took place in cottages rather than mills or factories. In the Lancashire cotton industry, when spinners first left their cottages to work in factories they were allowed to hire their own assistants and thus imported their families into the mills, continuing the old arrangement of work in a new location.

The greatest volume of women were employed in domestic service, an occupation which shrank only after the First World War. Families found it acceptable to send daughters out to work when the work was similar to what they did in their own homes, and they were joining another household. Going into domestic service was not going 'out to work' as we now conceive it, involving going into the public realm. In the nineteenth century factories also adopted the household model for girls working away from home, offering dormitory accommodation so that they lived and worked in the same location. Nineteenth-century sweatshops, which began the tradition of piecework and outwork for women which continues in the garment industry to this day, allowed local girls and women to take work into their own homes, while country girls lived with the owner of the sweatshop, as family servants.[12]

In Victorian middle-class family ideology women were supposed to be dependent creatures; this was exhibited by their economic dependency. Unmarried women were the responsibility of their nearest male relative. In practice, of course, not all men could provide for all their female dependants. There was therefore a grouping of middle-class women particularly shamed by having no one to care for them: governesses, companions and others in a variety of occupations who left home to remove the disgrace of their employment from the family – some going so far as to emigrate. The problem was exacerbated by the greater number of women in the population as a whole, which has been reversed only in generations born since the 1950s.

Aristocratic or upper-class women still retained their lines of communication with the public realm through their influence on politics; the women of the labouring classes were largely excluded from public life – until the rise of the labour movement led to working women taking political action by going on strike – but had access to social life. They could go alone among strangers in the street and in the factory or workplace. The vast increase in illegitimate births in the new industrial cities was an indication of the fact that young women were living among strangers and outside the communities which had organized family life and regulated behaviour in previous generations. There was a great rise in prostitution, which absorbed many girls and women, sometimes as a temporary shift or second job. But for respectable women the public world was at one remove, and they became associated almost exclusively with the domestic sphere.

Heart and home

Women now are still responsible for feelings, for care and concern, for sensitive responses in the private realm, for the emotional health care which is beyond the scope of the public realm but on which it depends. The interaction of the public and the private world in the critical but elusive terms of women's relationship with love, romance, emotions and sentiment are discussed by the American scholar Jessie Bernard in a book she wrote in the 1970s on women's roles. She says:

The importance of this supportive, expressive function, or 'heart', was highlighted as the brutality of the new economic system – the *Gesellschaft* [business world] – began to make itself increasingly felt. The home came to be seen as a protection against the harshness of the outside world . . .

One of the major functions of women's sphere, therefore; was to . . . [supply] the balm needed to heal the wounds inflicted by the outside world. It made life in the male world tolerable.[13]

Therefore the problems women face in entering the public realm are not only practical matters of conflicting roles and demands on time. The most intransigent question is how the values of the private world are cultivated if the traditional division of public from private along male/ female lines is dispensed with.

If the source of love and the remedy to the depredations of the public world is women, who is to provide these things for women who go out into the public world as much as men do? If women generate the private world by keeping separate from the *Gesellschaft*, what happens to the private realm if they leave it? On the other hand, if women are orientated exclusively towards the values of the private world, how can they make any impact on the public world and how can the public world, with its particular object of success, satisfy these needs?

Attitudes to the past

We venerate Renaissance men and women, whose breadth of scholarship and ability impress us, because we no longer have access to their diversity of talents and pursuits. The spread of leisure to the labouring classes, with the reduction of the working week and increase in annual holidays, has not replicated the cultivated pursuits of the leisured classes of earlier epochs: leisure time is used more for entertainment [*paidia* and *anapausis*] than for improvement [*schole*], since under present conditions of work people need to be relieved of a consciousness, which they find more or less oppressive, of the public world. The retreat into the private realm is often a retreat into the safe vacuity of entertainment – the average man in the UK watches nearly twenty-four hours' television each week, and the average woman even more.[14]

Nevertheless we are fascinated and awestruck by the productivity of great minds, even though generally we make no attempt to replicate their efforts or outputs. We feel perhaps irrevocably dissociated from conditions which could produce minds capable of such universality by the growth, since the Renaissance, of information produced by the proliferation of specialisms and different areas of expertise. This growth in information is not the same thing as an increase in knowledge, but the effect of specialization is to make it difficult to distinguish the accumulation of data from contributions to the body of knowledge.

Art and illusion

At Nostell Priory near Wakefield hangs an allegorical painting by an artist successful in the eighteenth century though less well known today, Angelica Kauffmann, which shows her trying to decide between painting and music, lured by the muses of each. It seems vain by today's standards, for an admission of such vocational uncertainty, particularly in the arts, is often interpreted as a confession of rank amateurism. To the mind steeped in the values of professionalism the dilemma portrayed by Kauffmann suggests a lower ceiling of aspiration and excellence than that available to the artist undivided over her vocation; we do not really allow equivocation in matters of work, especially of the higher callings. Practising art in all its forms is considered a privilege, particularly because it is seen as an activity of inspiration and talent more than skill and practice. We reserve a special category of work for artists, who have to renounce the ambivalence permitted in other jobs because art, despite its commodity value, is revered as something of a mystery in a technological world. It is a private area, because it is not contaminated by the prevailing conditions of the *Gesellschaft* and because it is taken to signify a giftedness which has access to a higher intentionality.

Although genuine artists of all sorts, including entertainers, are suspended from the normal imperatives of work – in that their output can be irregular, their temperaments erratic and they are permitted to be unreliable, while employees are not – the simplistic expectations of the world of work – supreme intentionality and control – are nevertheless read into art in the naïve viewer's expectations.

Rather in the way that it is difficult for us to believe that strangers or people in the public world can be uncertain, prone to make mistakes or to act in the same imperfectly shaped flow of events that we perceive in our private experience, so people looking naïvely at works of art interpret them as somehow minutely planned and skilfully executed. This reveals the degree to which we still measure their success (perfection) by the standards of professionalism: we exaggerate the skill the artist has in shadowing forth things unseen. We think: 'How did she know to place that there and not somewhere else?' Editing out the degrees of spontaneity and accident, we see a piece of work executed to the standards of precision engineering. We read these values even into what is conceived as the artist's special relationship with the unconscious, and as a mass public we take art and culture terribly seriously and tend to disapprove of jokes and humour, if indeed we perceive them at all in our preference for interpreting cultural works literally and searching for a particular meaning in them.

This is how people interpret works of art when they are distant from them: they are not participating in or reliving a work but are perceiving or viewing it as separate from them, over a distance.

For example, the modern (conventional) theatre, with a proscenium arch framing the action for an audience sitting in darkness watching a stage illuminated like a dream, was developed in the last century. The growing self-consciousness triggered by the rise of industrialism and mass society led to a sense of the artifice of theatricality and the importance of creating and maintaining an illusion in order for the audience, the perceiver, to be at one with the art presented.

The suspension of disbelief brought about by theatre, performance or exhibitions is not created immediately by the conditions in which they are presented, for whenever there is an audience it makes its collective presence felt. In addition, therefore, to harmonizing with the work or works of art presented on public display, the individual must also accommodate the collective response. But the public, mass response is likely to be less sophisticated, more simple and more literal than individual responses.

Private consumption of art is more direct and immediate; reading, watching videos and television or looking at paintings you own, drawings or artefacts allows a direct response unmediated by other people's presence and opinions. But as an unshared experience it lacks the validation of others' opinions, is not enhanced and refined by being discussed with others and is likely to be unexpressed.

Fragmentation and expertise

We generally disparage occupational diversity: dilettantism has negative, not positive leisure connotations, even as social forecasts increasingly outline the value of exchanging one unitary career − a single occupation in a single industry − for a multivariate career embracing periods of study and updating, periods of community work and paid employment and self-employment: a self-determining working life. But not to focus exclusively on one activity is still perceived as decadent rather than

enriching; as evidence of lack of seriousness and responsibility – a correlative, perhaps, of its risk of financial
insecurity, for employers reward a clear and steady track
record. Because of the conflicting demands of family and
work as well as different socialization, women follow a
unitary career less often than men.[15]

With the rise in the numbers of women who have
children, fewer women can pursue a completely uninter-
rupted career. In mid-Victorian England, a third of all
women remained unmarried for life; by 1961, eight in ten
women in the twenty to forty age group were married;
today the proportion stands at nine in ten.[16] And while in
the 1920s sixteen per cent of married women were childless after ten years of marriage, by the 1950s the proportion had dropped to ten per cent and ten years later to
eight per cent. Hence the number of women who can offer
work their undivided attention has fallen during this
century and by comparison with earlier centuries. The
idea that contemporary feminism has created a greater
number of career women is a modern myth.

At the same time, the way public values are infecting
the private sphere can be seen in the single-minded passion
with which some hobbyists fill their leisure time. They
transfer, and even exaggerate, the values of work to
unproductive activities and products – sailing, DIY, building models, sports – validating them by making them seem
necessary, but at the same time making them rather joyless
to the beholder. They lose the quality of play by being
shaped after the fashion of work.

The necessity – drawn from the constrained conditions
of the labouring and middle classes who lacked the wealth
that was largely the means of self-determination – which
validates these activities is precisely the one which characterized the private domain to the classical mind. The
public world was available only to those who could choose
freely what activities to engage in and how to dispose of

their time. The classical conception, then, was that the public realm was free; the private, restricted. The modern conception reverses that.

One of the grossest restrictions of the public domain is the culture of professionalism: this is a correlative of the increase in specializations and the growth of expertise, in which occupations and jobs are broken down into their constituent parts and organized into smaller ambits.

This proliferation of areas of expertise necessitates, in turn, the development of bridging skills in interdisciplinary subjects. There is, for instance, much cross-breeding in the academic world, with hybrid specializations straddling different fields of knowledge.

Part of the fragmentation of experience is brought on by increasing complexity. The more we know, the less it can be grasped by individuals: hence our admiration of the Renaissance minds which could embrace science and technology and the arts, which seems to us a colossal stride. One of the axes along which attitudes and experiences are polarized, particularly in terms of occupation, is in the gulf between the arts and sciences.

The complexity of the world, which we deal with by progressively breaking it down into workable units, also increases the sense of operating in a large and confusing environment, largely beyond the grasp of individual comprehension and control.[17]

Hence the public world is seen as overwhelming in some respects, while the private is by contrast comprehensible. The private domain is proportionate to personal existence, whereas the public realm is on a scale which dwarfs individuals. The difference is bigger even than that symbolized by public buildings compared to private homes.

The hugeness of public life combines with the apparent inability of ordinary people to bring it under control, into order. It is a vast and chaotic element from which issues a stream of events. The impact of this disparity between private and public proportions on personal life inclines the individual to feel increasingly helpless about the public world. If it is too complex to grasp in its entirety, it is correspondingly too complicated to act upon effectively. Its complexity, its proliferation of specializations and technologies obscure to the layman, is one reason why field independence (see chapter three) is a measure of how well people cope with the public world. By comparison the private sphere is compensatingly manageable, and this effect is strongest for those who feel least at ease and potent in the public realm.

The professional mystique

The world of work is governed by the culture of professionalism. Although not all jobs are professional, many are being professionalized – labour market research shows that people with craft skills, for instance, increasingly need new technology or cross-trade skills. Jobs are dignified with obscure, technical-sounding titles which create a mystique about the content of the work – rat catcher becomes rodent operative. But manual labour, even if it has a separate and more personal culture, is influenced by the culture of professionalism through the people who supervise and manage.

There is an implied agreement between employees and the organization they work for, which is more salient in managerial and professional jobs than in skilled and unskilled manual work but which permeates all levels of an organization: that employees will maintain consistent standards of performance and behaviour. At lower levels, they are judged on timekeeping and absenteeism; in jobs where more autonomy and a less concrete product are at issue, people are measured by their attitudes and track record, which means their history of successes, an increasingly nebulous concept which management writers recognize as more and more dependent on style and image than on demonstrable achievement.

The entry criteria for executive, managerial and professional careers are less uncertain than the standards on which promotions depend. Employers look for relevant experience and, at point-of-entry jobs, qualifications.

In support of this, in parallel to the fragmentation of the public world which has produced a proliferation of specialisms and areas of expertise, the new professions of trainer and consultant have arisen. These straddle the realms of education and work and are an example of the operation of the fragmented, specialized public realm on the individual. Just as parents are rendered inexpert in matters of childcare by comparison with paediatricians, child therapists, health visitors and the other professionals who can intervene, so jobs are increasingly tricked out as sophisticated, complex and expert by consultants and trainers who, to improve efficiency, reorganize or describe functions in a workplace, analyse work and classify it according to (sometimes quite tiny) categories of activity.[18] The net effect is to mystify job components and to make work less accessible to the inexpert, particularly the untrained. Training can involve the denial of common sense, partly on these grounds and partly – particularly where health and safety are involved – because it must never leave the obvious unstated, as trainers must take into account the lowest common denominators in workforce skills and abilities.

Another example of professionalization and specialization encroaching on jobs is the degree to which they move away from ordinary language into jargon, using either technical terms or, if those are not available, phraseology which identifies job-holders as group or team members, rather as in-jokes underline shared experiences. Professional language in particular, and public language in general, depends on passive constructions and impersonal voices ('It is to be applauded . . .').[19]

Metaphors from sports, military activities, and increasingly from computing are an illustration of professional speech: to interface; to push buttons on; to debug; state of the art . . . all these are used principally to confirm the speaker's membership of the set of 'professionals' and secondly to create a sense of active engagement and centrality for disciplines and activities which cannot be understood by ordinary people.

The investment in expertise, emphasizing the degree to which individual jobs are different from each other and mutually incomprehensible, is strongly supported by two major contemporary issues: economic insecurity, which places a heavy premium on having and holding a job; and the satisfaction of feeling that there is something special about your job, that it could not be done by just anyone, that it needs someone with special abilities.

The professional culture is by definition impersonal: it is driven and guided by necessity rather than freedom and the abilities it demands are in clear contradistinction to the personal realm: discipline rather than spontaneity; seriousness rather than humour. It is obscure and intimidating rather than open and welcoming to inexpert outsiders; it requires intentionality and instrumentality rather than accident, intuition and expressiveness. It insists that people must conform to norms rather than define themselves idiosyncratically in dress, in behaviour and in speech. It cannot interpret metaphor, sophistication and multiplicity but demands literalness and simplicity. Hence it is, in this extreme and traditional form, at an increasing distance from personal life.

People show that distance in many different ways. They adopt personae at work which fit with the roles they are required to fill more than the personalities they cover. Consequently there can be a considerable difference in the way people behave and feel at work and in their private lives. So long as work and private life are separately maintained there is no dissonance, but it can be difficult if they overlap. Why do women seem to find the dichotomy more painful than men?

3

An Unstable State?

As we have seen, the dynamics of the contradiction between women and the public world were set in motion in the nineteenth century when the division of the public from the private sphere became more concrete than before, the association between women and families and the private sphere was established, and the idea of feminine women as frail and fragile grew up as a prime reason for women's confinement to private and domestic roles. It was said that education would damage a woman's fertility; it was thought that women were naturally unmoved by sex, and a host of other myths were propagated about their innate difference from men. Women were considered both to lack physical stamina and to be psychologically less stable, and hence to need protection from exposure to the world outside their own private realm.

The two major lines of inquiry into the distinctions between the public and the private in modern times have been the political and social, and the psychological. While Marx and Engels fathered the first, Freud stimulated the second.

Freud started by investigating hypnosis as a cure for the hysterical illnesses from which so many of his women patients suffered, thus making women a central subject for psychoanalysis. In his earlier days Freud did not challenge the prevailing ideology which conceived of women as frail creatures, and his account of the feminine psyche as debilitated by comparison with the male and his corresponding idea that maturity in women was acceptance of their unenviable condition dominated psychology and psychiatry for the greater part of this century.[1] Because so many women were drawn to these professions, and because so many were treated by them, they became an early target for feminist critiques.

Feminism took issue with the idea that women needed to be treated to fit into society, rather than that society should be changed to fit women's needs. By the 1960s psychiatric remedies were being used to pacify increasingly large numbers of women. In the 1970s, feminists began to question the mass application of Valium to sedate a generation troubled by the growing contradictions between the opportunities nominally available to them in a consumer, libertarian society and the social and personal restrictions placed on them in practice.

One reason why feminism was influenced by Marxism and politically allied with the left was that Engels's studies of family life and writings on the role of women were among the first to view women as something other than separate, idealized and marginalized creatures. Another was that this strand of socialist thought, allied with the political programme developed by the left, put together descriptions of women and family life which were recognizable to women with a compelling programme for action.

Nevertheless, feminism and the left are not the same thing, and not all feminists are socialists. One difference is that while socialism is a political movement, feminism pays more attention to the personal. Hence, while public and private in political terms refer to ownership, by the state or by individuals, in personal experience the difference between the public and the private is the difference between self and others. Where from a political standpoint the family and social relations are part of the private realm, in personal life they are halfway towards the public, the realm of strangers.

Psychology is all about the personal, since it takes the self as its subject. It explains how people work in much closer focus than political analyses. Where political thought, and most sociology, look at the effect of economic, political and social structures, psychology looks at the influences of people upon people – at the way fathers and mothers affect their children, rather than the way the family is subordinated to the state. These two traditions are not completely distinct: for instance the Chicago school of sociology took up a method of studying people that was closer to psychology in that it investigated people close up and in depth, interviewing them and reporting what they had to say, while for its part psychology has tried to turn itself into a science and to produce 'hard' data by doing surveys and relying on statistics, getting away from the 'soft' data of individual cases.

Both sorts of data have their uses, because, although case studies have the advantage of presenting everyday life and offering something with which the reader can identify, they have the disadvantage of being particular, while hard data pull back from the immediate and particular case to look more generally and to get an overview. The problem is that these kind of data are seen as representing the truth because it seems more objective and therefore more scientific. Yet statistics are no more true than personal experience, are open to interpretation and can easily be misleading, since they are mystifying to many people. Hard data does not always show how it was collected, analysed and interpreted, and although it depends on subjective factors it seems more reliable – because it is methodical and thorough within its limits – to a culture that trusts the mysteries of science and technology rather than the instincts of art.

Fact and fiction are only two ways of looking at the

same thing, but the public world relies on facts and does not easily admit fiction, which is for the private realm and hence associated with leisure and entertainment, not work. Personal experience and case histories are closer to the style of fiction than of fact because, although factually accurate, they are more openly subjective. The public world is inclined to view this as inadmissible evidence.

The weaker sex?

Social statistics have seemed to support the idea – derived from the ideology of the Victorian family – that women are less stable and more frail than men. An analysis of all first admissions to mental hospitals in 1975[2] showed that twelve per cent of women but only eight per cent of men were likely to be admitted to a mental hospital during their lifetimes.

This, however, disguises the fact that men are more often cared for in the home, but adult women who cannot look after themselves are hospitalized. More men than women under the age of eighteen are admitted, which perhaps reflects the greater number of younger women cared for in the home, while other data show that women stay in hospital longer than men, again perhaps an indication of the fact that, while women care for discharged men, fewer care facilities are available to women at home.[3] Men may also be more reticent about emotional problems, while doctors may be more disposed to diagnose mental ill-health in women than in men if they think women are more prone to it.

This belief in women's emotional frailty found perhaps its fullest expression in the Victorian convention of the male breadwinner supporting a genteel, economically inactive wife. The idea that this was the norm in families has persisted even into the 1980s, when this model applies to less than five per cent of the UK population.[4]

There were always exceptions to these rules: unmarried women who had to support themselves in service, by going out to work in factories or sweatshops, or by taking in work. The surplus of women in Britain was also consciously exported – between 1862 and 1914 emigration societies helped 20,000 women to emigrate,[5] the ladies to marry colonial administrators, the women to find mates among the other ranks. Those women who began seriously to seek an education of the same calibre as their brothers were warned that developing their intellects would correspondingly reduce their fertility. It was thought that the expressive qualities central to femininity – warmth, sympathy and nurturance – were cancelled out by instrumental masculine qualities like analytic thought and debate.[6]

The view of women as subnormal according to male standards persisted across much of this century. For instance, psychological research into motivation published as late as the 1960s[7] dismissed women in a single footnote, which commented that the theory when applied to women produced nonsensical results: this was not taken to show any flaw in the theory. Only gradually, under pressure from within – because so many women had become psychologists, psychoanalysts and psychotherapists – did researchers begin to investigate why women appeared so often as statistical anomalies and to adjust theoretical constructs to take account of these findings. At first there was a tendency to build a parallel account for women, but gradually, as investigations failed to show conclusive evidence of measurable differences in ability between the sexes,[8] theories were adapted to describe both.

Men and women are now seen as much more alike than they were thought to be a century, or even a generation, ago. But differences remain. Some can be accounted for by discrepant experiences in daily life: for instance, women still have the greater part of household and family responsibility but the lesser part of rewarding paid work; others can be explained by the different ways girls and boys are brought up and educated and the resulting disparity in what is seen as appropriate to each.

One survey of how well people feel discovered that two-thirds of men reported that their health was good compared with only half of women questioned at the same time;[9] one in seven women, but fewer than one in ten men, thought their health was not good. Similarly, slightly more women report chronic ill-health.[10]

These differences reflect women's different physiology and the fact that pregnancy increases their contact with the medical profession. They also indicate that women have different attitudes to their bodies, their health and themselves generally.

Pain without a cause

In some senses our bodies are our selves. The two are generally coterminous: our bodies are the principal medium through which we experience the world and the main means by which we express ourselves.

Following in the footsteps of Freud, investigators have looked at the way our corporeal selves reveal our inner selves, at how gesture bespeaks unconscious meanings and motivations; while students of body language try to decode the meaning of posture, glance and voice.

Psychoanalysts have also been interested from the first in psychosomatic disease, seeing in it the physical correlative of psychological conflict. The remedy for the illness, in this reasoning, lies not in treating the symptoms but in uncovering the cause.

Many illnesses are now thought to have a psychosomatic component: a memorandum from 500 doctors in the UK to the Secretary of State for Social Services suggested that eighty per cent of illnesses were psychosomatic in origin,[11] while surveys of general hospitals' patients in the US suggest that up to a quarter of patients and ten per cent of people claiming disability benefits in 1970[12] were suffering with psychosomatic symptoms.

Yet there is some resistance to recognizing psychosomatic origins in illness. Some members of the medical profession have a practical and material bias and are uncomfortable with ideas of counselling, so they look for and treat organic disorder only. Some sufferers think that psychosomatic illnesses are not 'real' and therefore resist that description; or they need to feel that their illness is an exterior factor and cannot accept the personal responsibility entailed in recognizing its psychological origins. There are also class differences in attitudes towards the sources of disease. A study of cancer patients found that while those from the middle classes favour more psychological accounts of the disease's onset, think that psychological treatments can work, and believe they personally can have some effect upon or control over their cancer, working-class sufferers see it as a physical illness only.[13]

Stress is considered to be the chief cause of psychosomatic ill-health and is implicated in a very wide range of illnesses including cancer and heart disease, but this has been treated as a masculine domain since it has been associated with job stress and particularly with managerial roles. One area under scrutiny for psychosomatic rather than organic origins in women is a gynaecological disorder called 'chronic pelvic pain'.

The precise number of women suffering from chronic pelvic pain is difficult to estimate, since the condition is differently described by different doctors. A review by a psychologist and an obstetrician[14] cites studies variously showing that seventy-five per cent of women at a gynaecology outpatients clinic had pelvic pain with no physical abnormality to account for it; sixty-three per cent of those given a laparoscopy had nothing visibly wrong with them; in only a third of cases, in one study of women diagnosed as suffering from pelvic inflammatory disease, were the diagnoses borne out by laparoscopy, while another study showed that nearly half (forty-seven per cent) of women so diagnosed were found to have nothing visibly wrong when laparoscoped.[15]

The fact that many women suffer chronic pelvic pain without anything obviously wrong with them suggests that there is no single, undiscovered cause. There is probably a variety of different causes. One is that it is a symptom of undetected disease. Another is that physiological changes which do not indicate disease, such as vascular congestion, are interpreted by the sufferer as pain. Psychological studies of self-attention (or self-awareness) have proposed two different kinds, the public and the private (see chapter four); people who score high in private self-attention are psychologically and physically more attentive to themselves. This might explain why some women notice inner changes of which others are unaware, and why they might interpret these sensations as deviations from a norm and therefore experience them as painful.[16]

A third explanation is that some pelvic pain has psychological origins, and this is the traditional psychoanalytic account. Some psychoanalytic writers have seen psychosomatic pelvic pain as a conflict about femininity. The old Freudian view was that such symptoms showed that the sufferer had not come to mature terms with her feminine condition but was rebelling against it and envious of men. The contemporary psychoanalytic view is that femininity is at odds with society and engenders conflicts in strongly sex-stereotyped women who identify too closely with it.

Conflict about femininity

In this context, psychosomatic symptoms are just one example of the ways in which women express the psychological dilemma of sustaining themselves in both private and public realms. Calling this a 'conflict about femininity' suggests, rather dismissively, that such women have not resolved problems which are part of a normal process of development, for it echoes early psychoanalytic ideas about women's innate psychological differences and suggests a norm of adjustment in which women can find fulfilment under existing conditions. But more recent psychoanalytic and psychological work takes a different view, starting by seeing women as constrained by anachronistic sex stereotypes and social roles.

The 'conflicts of femininity', then, are not to be resolved by women coming to terms with their sexual functions – that is, gracefully acquiescing to the demands made on them by men, children and society at large. These conflicts are indeed the conflicts of society at large; but women have the opportunity, and problem, of facing them first. They are problems centring not just on sex but on the frontier between public and private.

Phobias

Phobias are another indicator of the clash between public and private. They are not exclusively women's problems, but women are more commonly incapacitated by them. A national survey of agoraphobia[17] found that one per cent of the population suffered from it to a degree that caused them a significant problem, and most agoraphobics are housewives. There is some indication that the circumstances which may predispose men to be alcoholic or sociopathic make women vulnerable to phobias.

The panic attacks which characterize phobias have their origins in anxiety states. No one escapes from anxiety and stress completely, but phobic responses are extreme reactions. Agoraphobia, for instance, can effectively prevent some people from participating in the public world at all. They cannot go out to work; they cannot go out shopping; they cannot go out to parties.

In other cases phobias do not prevent the sufferer from

doing any of these things, but they make it uncomfortable.[18] If the phobia represents contradictory motives in the phobic, it shows a heightened awareness in those who experience it as a discomfort; while it acts as a solution, if an imperfect one, for those whom it prevents from doing things they want to do or feel they should do.

The psychopathology of everyday life

Phobias, severe or mild, probably affect only a few hundred thousand people in Britain, but they fall into a continuum of anxiety- and stress-related symptoms which affect many more people. For instance, compared with the few people whose fear of spiders is a disability, many will readily admit that they dislike spiders. Some of the conflicts between the public and the private sides of life are described as 'normal', either because they do not prevent people living their lives or because they are considered so widespread as to be a condition of everyday existence.

Relatively few women are so ambivalent about the public world that they cannot go out at all; but many are conscious of it as a hostile and possibly intimidating environment. This shows, for instance, in their shyness about public speaking or their nervousness walking home alone at night. Home Office statistics show that women are twice as afraid as men of being attacked by a stranger, although men are five times as likely as women to be seriously wounded by an attacker.[19]

In *The Psychopathology of Everyday Life* Freud looked at the ordinary ways in which ordinary people cope with ordinary conflicts – the tricks our minds often play on us. He enumerates, for instance, mistakes in speech, in reading, writing and memory – the things we call 'Freudian slips' – which are similar to the tendency to use the wrong name or word which precedes the onset of agoraphobia:[20]

Two women stopped in front of a drug store, and one said to her companion, 'If you will wait a few *moments* I'll soon be

back,' but she said *movements* instead. She was on her way to
buy some [castor oil] for her child . . .

. . . A lady once expressed herself in society – the very words
show that they were uttered with fervour and under the pressure
of a great many secret emotions: 'Yes, a woman must be pretty
if she is to please the men. A man is much better off. As long as
he has *five* straight limbs, he needs no more.'[21]

It might seem that the more exaggerated psychosomatic
diseases which produce disabling pain, symptoms or phobias are more serious than the everyday psychopathol-
ogies. Precisely because these are not so pronounced and
can be described as 'normal', they can be invisible. Yet
they indicate an ambivalence which might not be clear
either to the ambivalent individual or to those around her,
but which will shape her actions. And because they are
'normal' and widespread they are intrinsically worth investigating, since they appear in the everyday lives of millions
of people who do not suffer from phobias or psychosomatic diseases.

Inner obstacles to achievement

For many women the inner obstacles to achievement are
not apparent. It is easier to identify the external barriers.
But a sense that you are doing something wrong, that you
therefore somehow do not deserve or are unable to achieve
what you would like to do, is quite widespread – even
among women who have apparently achieved a great
deal[22] – and reveals a sense of invalidity and illegitimacy
in the public world which inhibits action.

   That sense of invalidity is also perhaps represented to a
degree in women's self-reported lower general health, the
greater numbers of chronically unwell women and wom-
en's higher rates of absenteeism (though there are other
factors involved in this, such as the strain of a dual role in
the family and at work and the fact that comparisons of

working men and women must take account of the great differences in occupation, status, age distribution and remuneration). It is certainly present in the lack of confidence – discussed widely in women's groups and networks – women reveal to trainers trying to encourage them to apply for promotions more often.

A diffuse lack of certainty, lack of confidence, sense of fraudulence, doubt or ambivalence are serious obstacles to women engaging fully and effectively in the public world, but they are hard for the individual to define and counter. Because these experiences are diffuse and personal, not amenable to translation into hard data and therefore not likely to be recognized in the public realm, women are confused by them and see them as a personal, not a public problem. It makes them feel stupid to feel held back but not to understand why.

Geraldine

For more than two years Geraldine had a job with a prestigious managerial title in a respected voluntary organization. But gradually things began to go wrong. She found her work getting so far out of control, for reasons she could not understand, that she believed she had suffered a stroke. She was increasingly seen as incompetent by the people she worked for, who eventually began to take steps to fire her. Finally she resigned, partly to forestall further damaging action.

The circumstances surrounding this unhappy episode were that she had a heavy workload and little support either from below or above. She had to contend with very poor office facilities and with reporting to several different bosses, all of whom had different ideas about what she should be doing. In this situation, her strengths as an employee worked to her disadvantage: she was meticulous and persistent, when she needed to be able to organize her work according to priorities. She also wanted autonomy, but because – given the number of people she reported to – she had administrative difficulties she would have bene-fited from guidance and a manager who was prepared to take personal responsibility for her.

Geraldine came to London from South Africa in the 1960s, had a baby and in the seventies settled into a permanent relationship with Kevin and a series of low-paid but highly committed jobs in voluntary organizations.

These jobs were a good compromise for her. As well as the prevailing ideology in her youth, which militated against taking work too seriously and disapproved of the pursuit of wealth, she had imbibed the ideology of her childhood: that men showed how they valued women by protecting and providing for them; hence women who provided for themselves had been unable to attract a man. Voluntary work was a respectable occupation for a lady, since it suggested she was working out of commitment, not for money.

Unfortunately, salary scales in the voluntary sector were calibrated on precisely that assumption, and as times got harder through her thirties she began to feel the financial strain. She and Kevin bought a nearly derelict home in a smart area which they had to renovate by their own efforts. Her home life was not comfortable, even if the address sounded good.

In her late thirties she set about trying to consolidate and organize her experience. She broached the idea of marriage with Kevin, who turned it down, but she got round the problem by always referring to him as her husband. She tried to expand her job into areas which would be more prestigious and might provide a basis for promotion, but had too much routine administrative work to accomplish this.

She began to struggle away from femininity, which had not brought the promised results, towards feminism. But the attempt to turn herself into a self-determining woman was complicated by the fact that it was a move forced upon her by disappointing circumstances rather than something she had discovered with delight for herself.

She worked very long hours in an attempt to move the mountain of work growing on her desk, and also because her home was so comfortless. But however long and hard she laboured, the pile never diminished and she was beset both by constant and conflicting demands and by increasing complaints about her tardiness or inefficiency.

She therefore doubled her efforts. Always conscientious, she now attended to every minute detail of her job and also began monitoring her activities, keeping records of every letter and phone call and an account of every hour of the day. This was partly so that she had a rebuttal ready for those who complained of her standards of work.

Her job involved taking minutes and giving verbal reports at meetings, and as the stress grew her ability to speak fluently decreased. She spoke increasingly slowly and deliberately, with many pauses; but more and more often she had to apologize for losing her thread. She was unable to field questions or to recall information she was asked to give. She arrived with larger and larger piles of paper, representing longer and longer periods of preparation, which repercussed on the amount of her normal work she got through. Her work rate slowed further as she got more anxious to do the job properly, to be able to prove she could do the job properly when challenged, and to be seen to do the job properly.

The result was that her incompetence became more apparent.

At the same time, she grew increasingly fatigued. She began to take days off, hoping that she could recover enough energy to make some impact on the monstrous amount of work accruing. Finding that rest was not helping her to cope and that her speech problems were not improving, she went to the doctor, who thought she might have suffered a minor stroke, unusual as this would have been for a woman in her thirties. She was sent for a brain scan and advised to rest and, on her return to work, not to overdo things.

As her speech problems grew, her social skills declined. In proportion to her increasing need for allies in the organization, she became less able to win friends and influence people. She found she lost her thread, blanked out or could not find a word even in ordinary conversations; she also had trouble following what people were saying. As a result she seemed awkward and disjointed.

The situation was now beyond recovery. After a few weeks off work she returned, but was still unable to perform effectively. After some weeks, her part-time assistant was sacked after Geraldine had suggested that she was the reason for the problems in her office. It became increasingly apparent that Geraldine herself would be next, and she started thinking of looking for another job. However, she did not resign – probably partly because she was so demoralized that she was uncertain that she would be able to find another job, but also because she was reluctant to feel driven out and needed to recover her position.

She stayed for a further six months before resigning on the grounds that her workload did not permit her the time she needed to find another job – just in time to pre-empt her dismissal for incompetence.

The personal is political
Geraldine had good reason to identify with the sense of women's oppression which characterizes some feminist writing, but it would have been a giant conceptual leap for her to see lobbying for legislative change as relevant to her situation. Her problems did not present themselves as political, and it was therefore hard to see political remedies for them. They felt, and were, personal.

Yet the connection between the personal and the political is consistently stressed, not only by feminist writers (it was Robin Morgan who coined the slogan: The Personal Is Political) but by social critics like Christopher Lasch and Richard Sennett, who argue that what seem to be the conditions governing private experience are in fact general social conditions and therefore should be seen as political, not private.

Idiosyncratic as the particular details of Geraldine's case seem, they illustrate influences on women's working and public lives. The remedy lay only in her own hands, but the sources of her difficulty were not all of her own making. They were in the ideologies which had shaped her expectations, and chief among these was femininity.

Her problems with language exemplify the 'blocking and fogging' characteristic of the hysterical personality under stress[23] and she was also prone to slips similar to those Freud described. She preferred a dramatic organic reason to a psychological one, insisting on having had a stroke, because the physical explanation was an exterior circumstance for which she could not be blamed, while the psychological alternative entailed accepting personal responsibility for the mess her work became. But accepting personal responsibility was not an option for her because she did not understand by what mechanism she had created the mess. Had she believed she was responsible for it without understanding why, she would also have had no means of knowing whether or not she would do the same thing again in a new job. Therefore she had to see herself as the victim of bad luck.

Refusing to recognize a psychosomatic cause for their symptoms is also a characteristic of hysterics (which is one reason why it is difficult to estimate how many illnesses have psychological rather than organic causes).

Field dependence

The connection between being unable to choose the right word and to organize work may also relate to 'field dependence', a psychological trait which has been associated with feminine-typed personalities.

Field dependence means the ability to abstract specific information from its background. Studies of field dependence have generally used visual-spatial tests (for instance asking people to pick out a shape from background detail) in which men have been found to perform better, though there is evidence that where the test is verbal rather than spatial the difference between men's and women's performance disappears.[24] There is also evidence that androgynous women (described below) are as field-independent as men. Cultural differences in field dependence show that it is related to social structure, increasing with the degree of authoritarianism and conformity;[25, 26] it is therefore linked with sex stereotyping.

Field dependence had also been related to personality type and it has been claimed that field-dependent people have low resistance to social pressure, are more suggestible and more conformist. It has also been argued that they are more dependent than average on others and prefer working with people to working autonomously.[27]

Simple minds

Field independence is also associated with cognitive complexity, the ability to tolerate anomaly and ambiguity. Its opposite, cognitive simplicity, requires conformity.

Simple personalities are categorical, reason in black and white and find it difficult to accept ambiguity or to think in terms of alternatives. Such people conform more easily to a sex stereotype precisely because this is a simple view. Low abstract reasoning ability and high field dependence would be congruent with this personality type, while complex personalities are organized around more diverse thought processes, with greater ability to discriminate between stimuli and to synthesize and integrate disparate items of information into a complex whole. Complex personalities are more able to tolerate ambiguities and discrepancies because they do not derive the rules by which they operate from their environment as much as simple personalities do, so they show up as being less field-dependent.[28]

Self and non-self segregation

Another framework for field dependence is self and non-self segregation, a measure of how far people distinguish between 'me' and 'not-me'. People high in non-self segregation rely on internal cues, while those low in it depend on an external frame of reference. They are more sociable and more inclined to identify themselves with other people or groups. They are more prone to define themselves by reference to categories; to say: 'I am the sort of person who . . .'. High non-self segregation is associated with stereotypical masculinity, independence, assertiveness and an analytical approach, while low non-self segregation is linked with stereotypical femininity, sensitivity to the needs of others and the desire for social approval.[29]

This is similar to the distinction between public and private self-attention (discussed in chapter four): private self-attention leads people to define themselves in terms of their inner condition rather than their environment. They are less suggestible, acting on what they feel rather than on what they feel is expected of them.[30] The two sorts of self-attention, public and private, are not exclusive; a person can be high in private self-attention in one context and high in public self-attention in another.

Men and women who are strongly sex stereotyped tend to be intolerant of ambiguity and cognitively simple, while those who are androgynous or cross-sex-typed (women with masculine character traits and feminine men) are cognitively complex and much more able to tolerate ambiguity, conflict, ambivalence and contradiction.[31]

Sex-role stereotyping is an attempt to reduce anomalies by applying rigorously black and white rules to experience. It elevates rules over experience in an attempt to make sense out of what otherwise seems an overwhelmingly complex mass of information.

But the experience many women have had of leaving the home to go out to work within a society which has generally supported the idea that women's true place is in the home and with the family has engendered a conscious-ness of confusion, ambivalence and conflict, which has had its effect on the degree to which they remain sex-typed. There is an association between feminism and androgyny – women with feminist views are generally more androgynous than those with traditional views, who are more feminine-typed.

Androgyny

The concept of androgyny was much in vogue in the 1970s. It derives from measurements of how far people conform to the stereotype of masculinity or femininity, which showed that everyone has both masculine and feminine traits. Masculine-typed men have few feminine traits, and feminine-typed women have few masculine traits. Androgynous people have a good balance of both.

Further investigation indicated that androgyny is asso-ciated with benefits in many areas of life, including mental and physical health and achievement. But the definition of traits has changed in the ten years over which investigation into sex roles has been carried out. One recent study suggests that while feminine traits in men and women are not related to their mental health, masculine traits are associated with good mental health in both sexes.[32] In women they are associated with high self-esteem.

It has also been suggested that field dependence is related to spatial and analytical abilities, which have been investigated in the course of trying to define sex differences. Women have been seen as more verbal while men seem to be more numerical and spatial. Field independence is related to the ability to sort information; therefore to analytic skills. Although verbal skills go with analytic thought in the left hemisphere of the brain, an area in which girls achieve dominance earlier than boys, so do numerical and spatial skills, which are associated with abstract thought.

If this account is applied to Geraldine's case it suggests that her problems could be traced to femininity, which encourages women to be field-dependent and hence more easily confused by large amounts of information. The degree to which she was feminine in orientation also made Geraldine more inclined to do things by the rules – she was meticulous rather than able to put aside what she could not do, and kept scrupulous records which absorbed even more of her scarce time.

It accounts too for her failure to adapt to meet circumstances as they changed. Instead of modifying her style of working as it became apparent that it was not appropriate, and finally, instead of leaving when it became clear that the situation could not be saved, she went on beating her head against a brick wall. She continued, in other words, to play by the rules even when the circumstances contradicted them, because she could not be flexible and discard the rules she had learned. She was, however, trying to change by taking an interest in feminism.

Self-attention
Another possible factor in Geraldine's problems with language is self-attention. She had every reason to feel unconfident since she was unsupported, asked to achieve too much, and too conscientious to throw out some work

in order to get through the rest. Her isolation also meant that she was left to question her own abilities more than she might have had she been well supported and directed.

Psychological theories of self-attention and the way it regulates behaviour use models from work on artificial intelligence to suggest that people have standards against which they monitor their behaviour, in line with the feedback they get, to reduce the discrepancy between what they do and what they think they should be doing.[33] But when the feedback is inconsistent with the standards to which they aspire they can enter a 'negative feedback loop', in which their attempts to bring their behaviour into line with what they expect has instead exactly the opposite effect, consistently exacerbating the degree to which they fall short. In other words, the harder they try, the more they fail.

In Geraldine's case, being unable to speak fluently, both losing words and losing the thread of what she was saying, was triggered by the discrepancy between what she expected to result from her behaviour (her hard work and attention to detail) and what actually happened (she was accused of incompetence and threatened with dismissal). This led her to distrust her senses and scrutinize her actions from an external standpoint. Therefore she was not able to speak, or to behave, unselfconsciously, fluently or directly. Just as she monitored her behaviour by keeping meticulous records of how she spent her working time, so she policed her speech which, just like a computer memory being overloaded, both slowed her down and increased the number of malfunctions. The effort to produce the right phrases, on top of the effort to maintain her confidence in the ability to do the work, was too much for her to sustain.

She was aware of a discrepancy between the way she perceived herself and the way the people for whom she worked saw her, and this made her feel invalid. It was this that she translated literally in suggesting that she was suffering from the after-effects of a stroke, a problem of the brain rather than the mind. Conventionally psychologists would label this sort of reaction 'hysterical'.

Hysteria

The 'blocking and fogging' of thought and speech illustrated in Geraldine's difficulties, in some cases in the onset of phobias and in everyday Freudian slips, could be described in terms of public and private self-attention. It is also a characteristic attributed to hysterics.

The classical and medieval idea of hysteria was that it was a symptom of a womb detached from its proper position in the body, and out of this concept Freud's association of conversion symptoms and feminine sexuality developed. The ancient remedy for the wandering womb was to fumigate the vagina with pleasant fragrances while applying noxious odours to the nose. In the last century thousand of women who were thought to deviate from the norm of femininity had to undergo surgical removal of their ovaries or clitorises.

'In the light of the statistics on gynaecological surgery among hysterical women, one wonders if modern practices are qualitatively different,' comment two writers[34] on the discovery that one characteristic of hysterics was their high rate of gynaecological surgery. This is interesting in the light of research on the number of women who have normal appendixes removed because they are suffering from pelvic pain. While it is not surprising that doctors and surgeons disposed to deal with the soma and not the psyche resort to surgery for patients whose pain has no clear organic cause, it is alarming to find a relationship between surgery and hysterical personalities which have been described as 'super-feminine' by a psychologist who, though thinking mainly of eating disorders like bulimia

and anorexia, rightly warns that femininity can damage
the health.[35]

Femininity

The association between hysteria and femininity is ancient
and close, and it is this which accounts for women's
supposed frailty and instability. Hysterics are said to be
field-dependent, to have poor recent memory, vigilance
and attention[36] and to be more suggestible, all of which is
linked with high public but low private self-attention.[37]

Like the hysterical personality, field dependence as a
personality trait looks as if it might be a result of sex
stereotyping. Both feminine women and hysterics are more
likely to identify with other people or groups and to be
more conscious of the way they present themselves and
less aware of their own inner development.

Women are not necessarily born, but are certainly made,
different from men in these respects. Femininity is profoundly concerned with self-presentation and belonging to
a group and it predisposes women to define themselves
generically, as being this or that sort of person, which
underpins their interest in standards by which they can
measure themselves.

One of the major preoccupations of femininity is a
concern with image, which can most easily be identified
through fashion, style and appearance but which more
profoundly relates to the attention women give to projecting their persona and to their self-presentation in the
public world, in the social realm just as much as in the
realm of strangers.

4

Acting the Part

Usually when people feel they are acting a part they are uncomfortable. Although in complex and diverse urban societies it is only by playing the appropriate roles that people can cope with the opportunities they are offered, they still feel it is dishonest and inauthentic. More profoundly disturbing than the half-acknowledged guilt at deceiving others is an uneasy sense that playing social roles corrodes the self, for permeating Anglo-Saxon societies is an idea that personal identity should be absolutely consistent. Femininity, as an acquired behaviour, undermines the possibility of presenting a monolithically integrated self to the world.

But consciously and skilfully projecting a persona, as well as being potentially a great asset in professional and social circumstances, can reinforce the private self.

Kathryn Pogson found that applying her professional training to her personal life provided the solution to the problem of starting a career in the highly competitive acting profession. She had been unemployed for a long time but the turning point came on a day when she felt so hopeless that she found herself not even trying to convince a director of her ability at an audition for a good part:

As I came out I thought: Kathryn, you just shouldn't have bothered going up for that job, because there was no way you were going to get it. I sat there just giving out: 'Well, I've been out of work for so long and I don't get jobs . . .' And I thought:

they don't like you as it stands now, you're not getting the work. There's something that's not working, so do something about it. So I went off to Lucie Clayton and did a modelling course, but I thought: okay, doing this course I have to be up at nine o'clock every day, I have to be the other side of town and I have to look great. Every day I have to do a full make-up, I have to be co-ordinated in my dress, I have constantly to be aware of how I'm looking and the whole bit. And although I'm very much against that packaging type of deal, I was doing it to say: I'm not getting in where I'm at, therefore I'm not going to go home and whinge about how stupid they are; I'm going to go back in and look different, and say: 'You didn't like that – okay, how about this?' Until I get my foot in the door, until I can afford to go into interviews dressing as I want to dress, until I could say: 'Yes, you've seen my work, this is how I am.' But at that time I couldn't afford to do that, because it wasn't working.

Then I started modelling for a few months, earned some money, bought some clothes. And the first interview I went for, I had six-inch stiletto heels on, I had a tailored suit, I had a hat, gloves, the whole works. The Works. And I kept thinking: let him do all the work, Kath . . . don't do anything, just sit here and look fantastic. 'Cause I looked fantastic, 'cause I'd been taught the make-up . . . and I got the job. And that got me working again and I never went back to modelling. I kept doing that [presenting a glamorous image] for a while because being out of work for such a long time, I couldn't afford to come home and be miserable about it. It was just a question of saying: okay, then, change it, derail yourself . . .

She used showbiz tricks to give a performance of Kathryn Pogson, Actor, that got her work as an actor. She was at once both Pygmalion and Galatea, both Svengali and Trilby. And this act of creation, which entails a self-observing consciousness, is something common among women when they present themselves to the world.

Self-presentation has been a central issue for women since long before it appeared as a career factor. Women have consciously constructed and managed their image to the outside world as a way of coping with the conflicting demands of the public and private realms – they have, for instance, worn cosmetics in different societies from very early times, and one function this serves is to mask the individual with a protective colouring. The geisha's face-paint eradicates from the features not only imperfections but idiosyncrasy and personality, presenting not an individuated identity but an image determined by its social context.

Everyday Western make-up is applied to accentuate the facial features, which are one of the principal means by which we are identified (especially by strangers, since people who know each other well recognize each other by movement and outline when they are too far away to see distinguishing details like faces or familiar clothing). But the selection process for which features to choose and how to accentuate them depends on convention. Make-up is contradictory in many senses: if it is used to make a person more attractive it must fit the persona and look natural, according to conventional conceptions of the natural. But even if it is unapparent to the eye of the beholder, the person wearing it knows of the artifice it constitutes. And whether or not it is noticeable to the beholder, make-up betrays a vulnerability in the wearer. It speaks either of an unease at going among strangers great enough to demand some disguise, or it suggests a dissatisfaction with the natural self, which we conceive of as the true self.

The uses of beautification

Make-up seems to have served as protection from the most ancient times. It seems that kohl rimmed the eyes against brilliant sunlight in ancient Egypt, as it still does in Asia. It was also associated then with death, as cosmetics were used in mummification.[1]

As well as standing as a sort of guild emblem, the cosmetics used by the *heteira* of the Greek city-states may have served a protective function in resolving the contradiction of being public women in a society in which women were unpainted, unenfranchised and associated with the domestic realm, which was then explicitly separate from the public realm; later, women in salon society, which functioned around the courtesan and her circle, used elaborate make-up. During the centuries in European history when country and court were largely demarcated by naturalness in opposition to artifice and sophistication, both men and women at court used paint and powder, patches and masks to enhance or disguise themselves. In the seventeenth century, women in polite society completely masked their faces to protect their complexions when they went outside. Cosmetics permeated the ordinary lives of respectable women in the nineteenth century, when powder and rouge were discreetly employed. The beauty industry was just beginning to grow, and moneyed women could have early plastic surgery – for instance, the removal of the lowest rib so that they could wear more tightly laced corsets. By the 1930s facelifts were available to those who could afford them.

At the same time, special surgery for women developed to cosmeticize their temperaments. Thousands of ovariectomies were performed on American women between 1860 and 1890 to correct a variety of conditions ranging from 'eating like a ploughman' to 'erotic tendencies' and 'simple cussedness'.[2] This extreme of cosmetic improvement, where it was not punitive but carried out with the patient's consent or, like cosmetic surgery today, actively sought, illustrates the degree to which the protective function of cosmetics is a double-edged weapon. Just as the lead content of pre-modern cosmetics endangered health; just as now private plastic surgeons may also perform female circumcision (using the justification that daughters whose mothers insist on it might as well benefit from the reduced risks of infection in hygienic conditions and the available anaesthetic of Western clinics rather than being subject to traditional methods); so the cosmetic mask preserving privacy can undermine the sense of self thus protected, by constant comparison with public ideals of the beautiful, natural and acceptable which do not match private realities. The insidious habit of conforming to those ideals, against which feminists in the 1970s deployed plainness, naturalness and honesty, can constrain and deform.

Another element in the cosmetic surgery used to improve women's appearance and tame their temperaments is the masochism which, in the early days of Freudian psychology, was axiomatically part of femininity.

Sexuality, pleasure and pain

The association between women's sexuality and masochism goes back a long way, and the absolute point of differentiation between pleasure and pain in sex has never been clarified. This is partly because the nature of pain is itself unclear, with apparently wide differences in individual tolerances as well as differences between ascriptions of sensation; some people interpret as pain feelings which to other people are simply feelings (a point which was implicitly touched on in the discussion of pelvic and psychosomatic pain and the connection with self-monitoring).

The association between pain and femininity is still profound. Particularly when viewed from an objective standpoint rather than subjectively felt, identifying marks of femaleness such as menstruation and childbirth involve pain, and the idea of penetration is also suggestive of violence. Femininity connotes acceptance, patience, endurance and passivity as the obverse of sexual allure; it suggests that women operate under some instinct for pain. Because of this, women themselves are sometimes unable to distinguish for certain between the conflicting influences at work upon them, and many victims of violence suffer a sense of guilt and suspect themselves of having been implicated somehow in the crime committed against them.

Some women are condemned for their style and the cosmetics they use to attract others by cognitively simple people who want single, direct relations between cause and effect and hence ascribe simple motives to behaviour. A particular target for this sort of criticism is women who do not conform to conventional feminine dress: it comes from both men and women, though usually from older women to whom public recognition of female sexuality is disturbing.

For instance, in a broadcast discussion of violence against women at work a traditional-minded, conventionally feminine-style older woman contended that in going out to work and leaving the home women had invited violence, because this constituted a challenge to men which negated their chivalrous instincts. She argued that if women returned to a solely domestic life, men could resume their 'natural' chivalrous behaviour and violence against women would disappear.

Make-up, with its obvious intention of increasing attractiveness, has also been a target for moralists, to whom the inference of women's active sexuality was unwelcome. Make-up has been seen as subversive – the more usual adjective is 'immoral' – not only because it contravenes the feminine injunction to be natural but because it suggests, at the very least, receptivity to sexual encounters. Further inquiry into the strong feelings elicited by certain uses of clothes and cosmetics from some traditional-minded or conventional people leads towards a sense in which clothes and cosmetics used with some – even if discreet – sexual intention are threatening. They turn the tables on the feminine prescriptions of passivity and receptivity. Just as the degrees by which pleasure shades into pain in sexual activity are imprecise, so the distinctions in sexual availability between suggestion and statement are uncertain and depend very much on the beholder; but overt or aggressive sexuality, perhaps particularly in women, is a potent defence in the world of strangers.

Decorative men

Providing a means for women to be in public distinct from their natural, unpainted state in private is not the only function of cosmetics, nor is it one which only women may use. Cosmetics are used elaborately by men in different societies – for instance in contemporary African tribal societies and in prehistoric and early Near Eastern communities, judging from the grave goods men were buried with. Men use face- and body-paint and masks in tribal cultures to disguise themselves from supernatural enemies and evil spirits; warriors paint for war parties; shamans paint, decorate and dress themselves to encounter spirits. Just as household portals and village or compound walls are guarded with painted or applied spells and charms – in written characters, in sacred clothes or garlands – so tribal men are disguised with paint and costume when they leave the security of the community and go out into the wide world.[3]

Cosmetics can be used to mask out individuality or to emphasize aspects of the persona in the features of men just as well as women outside tribal cultures. Some of the protective functions which cosmetics serve for women also work for men; not only face-paint but face-masks too. For instance, Tuareg men cover their faces with a mask where the women do not, and this affords them a privacy within the family which anthropologists have likened to the way other men hide behind the morning paper.[4] Cosmetics protect the private person by replacing personal identity with a stylized image, as stage make-up illustrates, with its emphasis on some features so that they can be seen at a distance and under strong light, but are masked at close quarters.

Actors and entertainers do professionally what to some extent everyone does naturally in presenting an image of themselves in public, and in learning their craft actors become conscious of how they achieve their effects. But for both trained, professional performers and for ordinary social actors, it is important to turn in a credible performance. Where it is incoherent, uncertain or ambivalent, it is ultimately unbelievable. And credibility is fundamental to reputation and to achievement.

Shyness

One of the difficulties people often experience in the transition from private to public is shyness or embarrassment. It is a very common problem: one study in America found that nearly half the population felt shy.[5] Shyness, embarrassment and self-consciousness also indicate lack of confidence and are related to women's difficulties in entering the public world, most obviously in areas like public speaking. The key to public performance and social control is self-awareness (or self-attention).

Two forms of self-awareness have been identified. Public self-awareness is a sense of how you seem, while private self-awareness is a sense of how you are. Public self-awareness is concerned with your image; private self-awareness with your motives and meanings. These are not opposite ends of the same spectrum but independent dimensions of personality, so that people can be high in both public and private self-awareness, or low in one and high in the other, or low in both. Neither public nor private self-awareness is related to intelligence, ambitiousness, anxiousness, activity levels or impulsiveness, nor is one sort more socially desirable than the other. Both are inversely related to self-esteem – the higher you are in either private or public self-awareness, the lower your self-confidence – and positively related to emotionality. Experiments to depress or elate people showed that those with more private self-awareness were more deeply depressed, but not more elated, than people with more public self-awareness.

As well as being disposed to deeper depression, people high in private self-awareness are more reflective and more likely to use imagery in both personal and impersonal problems, while people high in public self-awareness are more sociable. People can be both thoughtful and sociable, though not at the same time.

People who are high in private self-attention are less suggestible than those who are not and are more able to come to an independent conclusion about what they feel.[6] Experiments show that placebos are not as effective on people high in private self-attention; their analysis of their feelings is more reliable than that of people lower in this quality. They are more able to define their feelings and less likely to be confused by or unaware of them. For instance, people with low private self-attention were experimentally induced to think that when they felt angry or afraid they were experiencing the side effects of a drug they had been given, whereas people with high private self-attention were not fooled.

Investigations into private and public self-awareness do not report distinguishing between men and women. But relating these ideas to other ways of construing psychological sex differences suggests that they might be in line with the general idea that women are interested in motives and the inner, personal realm; men generally are not. The correspondence between the traits that relate to field dependence and femininity, like suggestibility and depression, suggests that there is some overlap between what has been called characteristically feminine and different sorts of self-awareness. In being more aware of self-presentation women show high public self-awareness, while their interest in human psychology suggests high private self-awareness.

The British psychologist Ray Crozier suggests that the difference between shyness and embarrassment is that shyness is a result of feeling that you fall permanently short, while embarrassment is the consequence of particular occasions on which you fall short. He points out that for society as a whole shyness is a means of control, since individuals have to monitor themselves if they are not to contravene complex social rules, and that it increases the more society emphasizes individualism – in other words, the more people are made conscious of themselves as separate and different from other people.

Taking part in society has not always involved such complex and detailed surveying of the self. Richard Sennett suggests that until the eighteenth century, people felt and behaved in ways which are no longer available to us.[7] The distinction between a valid, real, private self and an artificial public persona did not exist until industrial capitalism ravaged the social order. Until then people had not elevated one sphere of life over the other; both had been sources of satisfaction.

In public they were guided by codes of civility which meant, for example, that perfect strangers could talk to each other without the least embarrassment within the conventions, strict by our standards, of dress and behaviour.

Contemporary emphasis on individualism and difference, however, has broken down the conventions governing public behaviour and appearance, just as it has introduced a greater variety of dress and manners, with the result that people are more self-conscious in public than their ancestors were because they are being evaluated more on personal than on social criteria. They also have more decisions to make about how to present themselves, how to project a persona, than when public life was much more governed by convention.

In the past in private – which meant in the home –

people were informal, not aiming at public standards of behaviour. This is also the realm called 'off-stage' by Erving Goffman, who proposed that contemporary social actors present themselves in everyday life in occupational roles in a way analogous to the way professional actors play dramatic parts.[8] In the home they are in a natural state; in public they are in society. The effect of industrialization was to elaborate this distinction between the natural and the civilized into a split between the real and the ideal, with the home as the tranquil centre of the *Gemeinschaft* in opposition to the *Gesellschaft*. But in its earlier form the sense of self by reference to which we operate in modern society was not present in either the natural, private sphere or in the civilized public sphere; nor did people look for intimacy in the public realm, in which they saw themselves as actors with defined roles but without the sort of self-consciousness that afflicts us when we now see ourselves as actors.

Our forefathers did not expect to be as realistic in their public roles as we demand. Crises of confidence were not in evidence in earlier periods because confidence – personal, economic or political – was not the crucial factor it has become as individuality has dragged self-presentation to the fore. Just as dress was not personalized but tended generally to indicate a role or rank, so people were not subject to the close scrutiny common now. In contemporary society credibility has perhaps replaced reputation, not only denoting achievement, which is still a measure of worth, but also connoting sober moral values. Credibility, which functions on confidence, is important both in the commercial sense and also in terms of the impressions individuals create. The need for credibility means that as social actors we must turn in coherent performances, performances in which there is no dissonance or anomaly. This means concealing the complex, inconsistent private self, yet displaying openness and sincerity. The obviously impersonal person is not seen as trustworthy in a society which stresses the value of intimacy and individualism, although the disengaged, independent individual, whose behaviour might not be so different, is respected.

Masks and personae

Seeing ourselves as actors makes us feel uneasy because it seems a false position. Contrasted with personal goals of intimacy, naturalness, self-disclosure and transparency, the grander gestures of the public arena – politics, public speaking, even presentations to colleagues at work – seem unnatural, artificial, overblown and invalid. What unnerves us is the discrepancy between the persona we have to adopt to appear in public – the image we present, however much we claim to be unaffected, natural and unconscious of our effect – and the person it masks, which we feel is the real, the true self. This is one of the signs of the 'imposter phenomenon', in which people feel they will be caught out at work and revealed as inadequate. They do not account for the success they enjoy as something earned but as the result of good fortune.

   Not everyone who has constructed a public persona feels an imposter. Peter Marsh is chairman of a major advertising agency, a successful self-made man whose first career was as an actor. His involvement with advertising means that presentation, image and persona are the content as well as the means of his work, and he discussed this with Professor Anthony Clare in the radio series *In The Psychiatrist's Chair*. Here he described the minute detail in which he orders his life, including planning social occasions precisely. He accounted for his rejection of spontaneity by reference to theatrical performances thus: 'You can only be spontaneous when you've got the framework . . . it gives you the opportunity to be able to deal with the unexpected and turn it to great advantage, so people are not discomfited.'[9] Peter Marsh's rigorous organization of his life is inspired by his ambition. 'You become totally intolerant of anything except achievement,' he told Anthony Clare.

The pursuit of public acclaim was also the inspiration behind the career of a man who became an MP and held office in a Labour government, until he faked his own death to escape into reclusive private life. John Stonehouse claimed that this was because he had undergone a transforming revelation about the fakery of his public persona compared with the sincerity of private life, but he was jailed for the financial misdemeanours which accompanied this revelation. Anthony Clare says of him:

He was always being something other than he was and, in a paradoxical way, his insistence that he had two personalities was again being something other than he was. He didn't have two personalities. That was him. He was still the same John Stonehouse: voluble, manipulative, verbal, intelligent, and not really facing up to himself.

The discrepancy between people on the outside and people on the inside: what I was saying to Stonehouse was: that is a truism. You are describing all of us.

With the rising importance of authenticity and credibility the public world increasingly values sincerity, but it is hard to sustain there except through complex procedures of presenting a sincere persona, which is nevertheless not the same thing as being sincere. Like acting, political performances take place on a scale which is larger than life, because they are designed for an audience. Hence there is an inherent contradiction in trying to act sincere, as politicians must, which for some people in the public world is too great to sustain. The persona develops as a protective mechanism for private people going into the public world, but it can become a carapace for the self which fits so badly that it has to be discarded.

Although it might seem that acting would exaggerate the elements that disturb us in presenting ourselves in the public realm, professional actors are a curious exception to the general rule. Superficially they seem to work in conditions likely to undermine confidence and create a great discrepancy between the personal and the public self. Their world, with its star system and strict hierarchies of power and authority, emphasizes the individual, but deprives him or her of the sense of mastery which is an important element in self-esteem by making jobs very scarce (only a quarter of all Equity members are in work at any given time) and often dependent upon selection at an audition or on the basis of a reputation created as much by public or fickle critical opinion as by recognition within the profession; by incorporating periods of unemployment, sometimes long and sometimes frequent, between periods of intensive work; and by requiring actors to tamper with their personalities and to practise the art of self-consciousness to a degree that would seem, at first sight, excruciating.

Of course there are signs of strain – just as in playing a public or social role – related to shyness and lack of confidence. Actors suffer from stage fright; they dry; and they face identity crises and alienation, as the British actor Simon Callow illustrates when he talks about how, as a young actor at the Drama Centre, he found his acting restricted by his persona:

This stranger called Simon Callow was getting daily more remote from what was going on inside. He had a career of his own. 'Blah blah blah,' he'd go, and people would laugh or agree or hate (quite a lot of that); but no one would ever have believed that behind all that was a cowering, desperate, sobbing creature, beating with tiny fists on the door of life and feeling doomed to perpetual exclusion from the human race.[10]

Later, in a student play he co-authored and co-directed, he found himself with no time to think about his own performance:

Suddenly, for the first time, I was acting. Not performing, or posturing, or puppeteering. I was *being in another way.*

At a stroke the mask I had screwed on to my face fell away. I was free, easy, effortless. For the first time since I'd arrived at the Drama Centre I understood what playing a character was. I was giving in to another way of thinking. Giving in was the essential experience ... 'Leave yourself alone,' they'd been saying to us since the day we arrived. Now suddenly I was.[11]

So he discovered an authentic, valid self through performing and going through the looking glass of self-consciousness. It seems paradoxical, but Simon Callow is a professional, as distinct from a social, actor.

He mentions that acting is different from performing, which is what the social actor does. But as his experience shows, the integrity uniting his inner and outer self and giving the private person access to the public world is an elusive discovery: one which ultimately can only be learned, not taught. And curiously, just as the experience of the professional actor is opposed to that of the social actor, so the woman actor also seems to reverse the position of most women in society.

Juliet Stevenson is a leading actor with the Royal Shakespeare Company. She explains how the experience Simon Callow described – of being trapped in his own image of himself – affects women actors:

What he's talking about is something that happens all the time. Probably in any organization, but certainly in our business, people walk around and very quickly stick labels on each other. 'I am the small funny man', 'I am the political activist in this company', 'I am the camp reincarnation of Noël Coward.' It's a way of protecting yourself, a way of making your mark and coping in a large company and large organization.

But a lot of women I know do tend to resist it rather than collude with it, because it's not in their interest. We are, as actors, absolutely at the mercy of the imaginations of our employers, and it's not in any actress's interest to allow herself to be identified with a mould or labelled because it will restrict her work . . . And it's already very restricted.

The theatre is the metaphor Erving Goffman uses to investigate how people present themselves in ordinary life, giving performances 'on-stage', in work 'roles' and going 'off-stage' into the private world where there is no audience, and for centuries it has been a favourite metaphor that 'all the world's a stage'. It exaggerates features of public and social life and presents them objectively, at a remove where they can be considered.

For women actors, in some respects, the contradictions of femininity are also larger than life. But at the same time, this seems to help some to resolve them. Juliet Stevenson puts the restrictions of stereotyped images of women in the context of the theatre, identifying problems for the woman actress who conforms to an image that conflicts with her private self:

There was an actress recently who I'm fairly sure was given a large part because she's extremely attractive, and she had a great deal of difficulty with it. The director didn't help her; her fellow-actors didn't help her either, she came in for a lot of stick. So a year later she was asked to leave. Or her contract was not renewed, which is the same thing. This sort of thing is very, very personally destructive.

Jane Lapotaire's success in *Piaf* was instrumental in her achieving fame, although she already had strong professional experience and the good opinion of her colleagues. She offers an example of the way success can prove an antidote to the disadvantage under which women work:

Piaf was written by Pam Gems and directed by a man, Howard Davis. What was interesting was that Piaf was the main protagonist. The men in the cast suffered a role reversal . . . They were very expressive about the difficulty of being in a play where a woman was the leading character. I had to work extra hard off-stage to keep the company together. I don't mean that there was any aggression or antipathy, but ironically the problem was spearheaded by one's social existence as an actress. In Stratford, it's normally left to the leading man to say: 'Hey, everybody, come and have dinner tonight.' And I suddenly realized I was in the position of making the suggestions about where the company should go to entertain itself . . . I made an extra effort to involve the men because as subsidiary characters they were suffering what women normally suffer . . . and they were far more vocal about it than we would be because we have a history of accepting the minor parts.

In Shakespeare, for every eight men's parts, there is one woman's part. Even *Antony and Cleopatra*, it's Antony's play, and Lady Macbeth is a very small part . . . Women do not have the experience of being the motor for the play, i.e. when the play starts, the woman is responsible for the rhythm, the pace of it, the energy of it. We don't have that experience. The boys do. They play their Hamlets. They play their Lears, their Othellos. Even Rosalind, who is perhaps the biggest female role in Shakespeare, is not on all the time.

As Jane Lapotaire shows, theatre mirrors life and even exaggerates in its representation of women. But acting out that mirror-image seems to contradict rather than reinforce the narrowness and difficulty women have with public roles compared with men. It is as if, by directly and consciously addressing the way they create their image, women actors gain a clearer view of the difference between their pretend, public selves and their real, private self.

Women actors are not immune, though, from all the confusions besetting women in society. Even actresses with a battery of professional techniques for making distinctions between what is real and what is illusion, what is self and what is stereotype, can easily – maybe dangerously – be confused, and playing other women can add to that. Juliet Stevenson says:

It's impossible to separate off Juliet Stevenson and her roles because . . . it's like twiddling knobs. If you imagine yourself as a radio set: there may be some parts which demand parts of your personality which may not be much in evidence, but which exist. Like the whore in you, or the peasant in you, or the barrister in you. A part may require you to really tune that up in yourself, and really turn down other parts.

I really do notice that I behave slightly differently if I'm working on one sort of part rather than another, because you're readjusting areas of your personality. You don't switch on and switch off. No, it's a question of realigning yourself – or your centre. It's never possible to cut yourself off completely.

So even for a professional actor, the distinction between public and private self is not clear-cut and easy to maintain. For a social actor, without the battery of technique and the clear context of a script, a stage, a play, acting under the injunction to be an authentic, a sincere individual, it is even harder.

How acting helps

Juliet Stevenson sheds some light on the professional techniques that clarify for women actors the difference between illusion and reality, public and private selves, authentic self and persona. She sees the chance to explore different potentials in her own personality through practising her profession as a positive personal benefit, not an erosion of self: 'It's terribly illuminating, I think it's one of the things I love most, because you discover your own possibilities.' She also distinguishes between her own personality and the way she draws a role from an aspect of it, and her persona as an RSC player. This she sees as:

Very dangerous. Because although one is resistant to the idea of having a professional identity, you do slip into it and to a certain extent you need it to protect yourself. But of course the danger is that hand in hand with that will go dishonesty. You have to be very careful about watching the way you use that persona.

But what of men who use make-up and masks to construct their stage characters? What impact does this have on their sense of themselves?

For Robbie Barnett this distinction between the professional persona and personal identity is an even more complicated and important issue. His performances are partway between the protective artifice of theatre acting and the complex authenticity of social performances. Although he has taken straight acting roles in theatre and cinema, his training, most of his working life and his intense interest are devoted to mime and clowning. Here the distinction between personality and part are blurred:

In variety, you lay technique on the table ... for instance, clowns are stylized, not realistic in an acting sense. So the audience can take or leave it. There's a great exposure for the variety performer.

Clowning is very depressing and frustrating. For instance, early on, I used to do eight hours' clowning in supermarkets. My character was based on the charm of being slightly insulting and intimate and would get an intimate response, with women telling me they wanted to take me home to bed: it was a slightly naughty intimacy. The freedom was available only because I had the licence the traditional make-up gives.

Afterwards, I'd get changed and leave and see the same women and say hello, expecting in a way that they'd carry on, perhaps they'd take me home ... And they didn't even recognize me. When they realized who I was, they were embarrassed. I felt depressed – rejected. It was only certain parts of my personality they'd accepted.

Or perhaps it was only certain parts of him that existed in a coherent form in public performance. For the variety performer, clown or comedian, whose act is his persona, whose persona is a specific and real dimension of his personality, the dilemma is that he makes sense on-stage but not off it: he risks feeling vibrant, big and real in the limelight; hollow, dissociated, unfulfilled out of it.

For the variety performer who works from her or his

own personality, the boundaries between the public and private selves are encroached upon more than for the classical actor. 'Everything has to be terribly close to what you are – anything that's inauthentic shows up immediately. It's a terrible magnifying glass,' says Robbie Barnett.

Using images and making a performance out of being in public is something that is strongly identified with the modern artefact of youth culture. Camp has overflowed from its theatrical confines – particularly via the mass audiences for rock and pop – into street life and is another illustration of the parallels between professional and social acting and of the complex distinctions between individual, private self and public presentation of an individualistic persona.

Robbie Barnett points out the paradoxical difference between being natural and seeming so. He is conscious of having to maintain a distance to achieve an effect. He comments too on the fact that what looks natural changes over time, which is also a point made by Richard Sennett, who traces the shifting balance of public and private through changes in the relationship between street and theatre since the eighteenth century, comparing the way in which people present themselves in public. In contemporary society, too, changing fashion also means that what looks natural at one point looks artificial later. Style changes.

Contrasting the conventions of performing in the popular performance arts with acting in the classical tradition, Robbie Barnett thinks that 'You flatter the audience's intelligence more by playing a style than by playing naturalism, though actors get a much greater high out of sustaining naturalism.' He gave as an example a time when he was working in continental shows. He had two roles: as a clown and as a magician. After his performance as the magician, an Italian clown took him aside and said: 'Don't ever do that again. That's acting; don't try to persuade the audience you are a magician. To act is to insult their intelligence.' Robbie's job was to be a clown pretending to be a magician.

He explains more about the contradictions of giving a performance which is a projection of his own personality and not a role or character created by an absent author: 'You are playing big because you're playing to 3,000 people, some of whom are over 500 feet away. And you have to play yourself because any moment of fabrication shows.' He amplifies this by contradicting the popular myth that clowns' faces are their trademarks and are patented on eggshells:

But among real clowns, there is no question of anyone taking someone else's make-up because everyone's face is different and make-up only accentuates your features. It's like stealing a gag: you can't steal a gag; you have to do it differently because it only works one way for one person.

The idea of originality, so closely linked to the notion of individualism, does not apply in popular art; but authentic rather than novel presentation is important. Miming and silly accents are false notions of clowning:

So is the funny voice: the effective clown – it is his own voice when upset. When I first started, the other clowns used to take me out of the ring and say: 'Why don't you use your own voice?' I was making my voice cockney out of embarrassment. Finding your own voice is the crucial criterion of authenticity.

In acting as in life, for Robbie Barnett's comment here is something that other people talk about later in this book in relation to pursuing their careers.

As Robbie Barnett's view of how popular artists work shows, when the distinctions between performance and personality are reduced the relationship between performer and audience is closer, the performer's respect for the audience is greater, and his defences in distinguishing between life and art, or rest and work, are sometimes dangerously reduced. Performing in variety comes much closer to performing in everyday life, which is perhaps one reason for the familiarity of comic and variety performances – aloofness would not work; the collusion, the knowing exchange between performer and audience, must take place – and is certainly why such performances are regarded as entertainment rather than Art. The idea that any ordinary, unpractised person could do it is clearly fallacious; there is nevertheless the feeling that everyone, in some sense, does it.

The private person in the spotlight

Victoria Wood sees herself firmly in the variety tradition and is conscious of the craft involved in her work, both in writing and in performance:

I work hard on being good. I take a lot of trouble when I'm writing. And as to anyone who thinks there's no particular skill to entertaining – a good entertainer needs technique, timing, breath control, good skills, good material, energy, and wanting to entertain as opposed to wanting to be acclaimed: a warm personality with aspects of both sexes in it, like Tony Hancock or Max Miller.

Because she is both writer and performer, she has two perspectives on the question of creativity. Unlike an actress, she is not an interpreter of someone else's work; nor, as a performer, does she play a comic character:

All I'm ever trying to do is to be like myself; more like myself than I am really . . . But that's a great satisfaction for me, to go on as myself.

It comes naturally from me, it's not a devised effect. I always write my own material, I always write what I want to say at the time I want to say it. I behave in the way that I feel it's natural to behave, given limitations of a stage performance, with all the technical things that implies. So if I changed – and we all do change – the stage persona would change, because it's always in tandem. I know that a lot of performers do fix on a false image of themselves, which I'm really not trying to do . . .

I'm not too struck about being recognized in the street because I'm not naturally extrovert off-stage. All my extrovert side is on-stage. I cope with it fairly well because I have to cope with it. At first I used to pretend it wasn't happening and be very shy. If people said: 'I know you', I just used to back away . . . but now I try to say: (heartily) 'Yes, you do know me, yes, I'm Victoria Wood, thank you very much' and pass on. It's just a way of dealing with it. That's the most false part of all that I do, pretending to be jolly with people I don't know at all. People come and poke you in the street and you have to try and be nice about it when you're trying to buy a paper or pay for some petrol . . . I get a lot of – just people looking: they think, 'Who . . . ? Oh, I know that person.' They don't know who you are; they just think they've seen you somewhere. It's not so bad if people come up and know you. But if they come up and say: 'Where do I know you from?' I don't know where you know me from. It's all right; I'm just glad I'm not Sting, or someone like that, because I think their life would be absolute misery.

She also shows that performing professionally can integrate public experiences with private identity when social acting would divide the public from the private:

I've always been terribly self-conscious and I've always thought people were looking at me, even before I was on the television. So now I've sort of got an excuse to think they're looking at me, I'm much less self-conscious. And because I'm always dressed how I want to be dressed, and not like one of those people who's terribly glamorous one minute and then not the next, so whenever they go out they think: 'Well, I'll have to be glamorous now because that's my bit on the television.' I don't have that pressure.

She confirms that her public persona does not disintegrate but in fact strengthens her private identity:

The performing side has a good effect on the rest of my life. Because if I can go on-stage to a thousand people and keep them happy for two hours, then it's a bit pathetic if I can't tell the coalman to bring me an extra bag when I can see he's forgotten one. I've got a terrible timidity about dealing with people, but I think: 'Well, this is stupid, dear. If you can go out and play comedy, which is the hardest job in the world, then you can complain if somebody cracks your cooker or something.'

But the positive effect of the performer's persona on her personality is earned at a cost that social actors do not have to pay. In addition to the higher premium paid in the effort that goes into creating and sustaining the performance, there are also higher costs for failure. Comparing her style as an entertainer with acting or comics who assume characters, she says:

I would say the rewards are greater, but the penalties are greater, because if the idea is to go out as yourself, or to make people think that's you, then when it doesn't go well, for whatever reason, it's you people don't like. You can't say it was the director, or the play, or the woman behind me dropped a plate of cutlery. All you can say is: they didn't like me, which is a very hard thing to come to terms with.

But then the rewards are, if you go out and it goes well, you can say then: well, they like me . . . 'She's nice.' And that's why you're doing it anyway, because you want people to like you.

In stand-up comedy, you're very vulnerable. That's why there are so many suicides and drunks and things, because it's hard. It's a really hard job to do.

The projection of the private self into the public world can be difficult, not only for the professionals but also for those who must do it socially. And the opportunity to get away without giving a good performance is shrinking as it becomes a crucial factor in more and more jobs. Women are often more deeply unconfident than men, but are perhaps better able to project the simulacrum of confidence. Yet that is not the same thing as being genuinely confident in your abilities.

People presenting a social or professional persona are less accomplished than performers at managing these different selves, and may not see themselves as a whole but feel instead a split in their experience between the public and the private world. Women's nurturant, affective function in the private world is at a greater remove from their efficient public selves, since masculine attributes are not inherently contradicted by the public realm. Women, then, are more disposed to feel that their public selves are a show and a sham, insincere, false and constraining and they may put them aside when they exit from the public stage, just as they kick off their office shoes and change their clothes.

People who feel that they assume a public self for the occasion may also feel insecure with it, for while it permits them to enter the public world wearing the appropriate mask, it does not allow them to participate fully and authentically. They are not bringing their whole self to bear but mediating the exchange between self and the world through a practice which lets bits of the self through, exaggerating some characteristics and obscuring others: exactly as cosmetics do.

The purposes of disguise are not only defensive. Projecting a persona, or wearing make-up, also puts people at a distance from the public world they enter. People who are not what they seem are also in a position to manipulate those who see only their appearance, not their reality. Women have conventionally been derogated as manipulative, and manipulating people is one of the few resources open to those to whom no sanction or force is available.

5

The Mirror Crack'd

The conflict between public and private for women constantly comes back to a question of femininity, which is more or less identifiable with private virtues and is therefore contradicted by public values. So what is femininity if it causes so many women so many problems?

Under surveillance – and self-scrutiny
A woman must constantly watch herself. She is almost continually accompanied by her own image of herself. Whilst she is walking across her room or weeping at her father's death, she can scarcely avoid envisaging herself walking or weeping. From earliest childhood she has been taught and persuaded to survey herself continually ... Her own sense of being in herself is supplanted by a sense of being appreciated as herself by another ... One might simplify this by saying: *men act* and *women appear*. Men look at women. Women watch themselves being looked at.[1]

It might seem presumptuous for John Berger to speak thus on women's behalf and to characterize their lives as walking across a room or weeping over a man; but the serious omission from his account is that it fails to state clearly that what lies behind this preoccupation with self-presentation is not mere vanity but the consciousness, unavoidable in many public circumstances, that women are very often the object of men's gaze, as another writer admits:

That erotic scopophilia, love of looking, which characterizes the human male serves as an anticipatory response to sexual possibilities. Whether he is sitting in a café, waiting for a train, walking through a shop, looking at a painting, or watching a movie, the male uses his eyes for visual consummations which are clearly sexual even if they do not lead to orgasm. Compared to men, women are less often stimulated by sensations of sight or hearing; they tend to rely more on direct physical contact.[2]

Men are naïve viewers of women. They do not, on these accounts, conceive of themselves as performing the act of watching in the self-conscious way John Berger ascribes to women, though they are made uncomfortably self-aware if a woman breaks the collusion by indicating that she is aware of being observed and challenging this.

Men and sensitivity

One of women's principal dissatisfactions with men is what they feel to be their insensitivity,[3] which is often described as an inability or unwillingness to communicate with others, leading to impoverished intimacy. In response to such charges levelled against them in the 1970s, and using the means developed by women such as consciousness-raising groups, some men challenged this stereotype and conscientiously developed more expressive behaviour.

To many women such responses seem naïve, for learned feminine behaviour accustoms women to a complex life in which they are able both to respond to personal and intimate exchanges and be aware of the way others perceive them. Men, with instrumental rather than expressive socially constructed roles, often cope but slowly with this new dimension.

A consequence of the public self-awareness entailed by femininity is that women, accustomed to seeing themselves through others' eyes, may more easily develop the facility for seeing things from other points of view. However, the dark side of this ability is that it erodes women's subjectivity, disposing them to be more suggestible and to see all things from all perspectives, taking a stand on none. This is a disadvantage in active engagement in the public world, since action derives from a standpoint.

But this feminine ability to identify with other people and to see other points of view has positive values, one of which is that it makes people more interesting. The exterior evidence of hard data lies in the proportionately large number of women drawn to working with people and in occupations involving assessing other people, their motives and their meanings: most UK marriage guidance counsellors, for instance, are women.[4] Analyses of the greater amounts of self-disclosure in conversations between women also support this, and show that they also talk about friends and family more than men do.[5]

A further complication of the position in which femininity places women, and one which again disposes them to more personal and interpersonal sophistication, is the association in the West between women and naturalness. Anthropologists have investigated this train of thought and have argued that because women menstruate, bear babies and lactate, they are conceived of as closer to nature (that is, closer to the animal kingdom).[6] Against this is the influence of Mariolatry and the cult of virginity and purity, combined with the association between women and cultivated artistic and literary pursuits, which represents women as ethereal and spiritual, free of the bestiality of sexuality to which men are subject. Both these opposing ways of conceptualizing women imply a lack of artifice or artificiality which is at odds with the self-consciousness created by femininity.

Thus femininity creates a strong sense of self through others' eyes (public self-awareness), a strong empathic sense and an injunction to be natural, free from artificiality and unselfconscious. (One quotidian example of these contradictions is the way make-up is often used to achieve a natural effect – a contradiction in terms.)

The result of all the 'erotic scopophilia', and the permanent self-consciousness it engenders, is women's keen concern with self-presentation. This is apparent in their behaviour, dress, make-up and image (the style or fashion different women adopt) to the detriment, as John Berger says, of unselfconsciousness and, ultimately, of acting confidently. It is catered for in goods marketed for women, from romantic fiction to fashion spreads in magazines, from advertisements idealizing images of women and family life to soap opera.

Romance

Just as it has different forms, so romance has different functions for women, from escapism to realism. While the American soap opera focuses on appearance, with images of unattainable splendour in glamorous domestic sets and clothing, the British soap opera concentrates on everyday behaviour, holding up sanitized but ordinary lives for inspection. However, although the trade in soap operas from America to Britain is – with the exception of sagas like *Upstairs, Downstairs* – largely one-way, there is also a very considerable export market for the British brand: *Coronation Street* can be seen right round the world. So the different types of soap opera do not only reflect local cultural differences but also show that there are different sorts of romance to meet different needs.

Nor are there national differences in romantic fiction in print according to Jacqui Bianchi, editorial consultant for Mills and Boon, leading publishers of romantic fiction. Stories from British authors are translated and sold worldwide without any further modification. Even for the American market, only the spelling and unfamiliar words are changed. Mills and Boon spread across all age and socioeconomic groups, so romantic fiction is shared by abroad cross-section of the female population.

Most authors of romances are women: there are only two men among Mills and Boon's 168 authors, and Jacqui Bianchi notes their difference in visual fantasizing:

Males find it very difficult to write from a woman's point of view without being patronizing, or at any rate without giving away some clue as to a certain degree of detachment, and detachment is the one thing you can't have when writing such a book. Favourite example: quite often in romantic fiction there is the scene where the heroine is standing in front of a mirror inspecting herself for flaws. It's one of the traditional ingredients. A female writer will use it as a description of the finer shades of the heroine's hair colour, her hairstyle, her nail varnish, whether or not her clothes are suitable for the projected occasion. Now, almost invariably with males, the girl's in her bedroom. You get a glowing description of her figure, which invariably describes her behind. Women aren't interested in other women's behinds as a general rule, though men are; and also, if you are looking at yourself in a mirror, even if you are inclined to look at your own bum, you do not necessarily find it easy to do so. Even if books come in under the name of Lucinda Thistlethwaite, instantly we know that it's a man.

Why do love stories work for women? The essential collusion between author and reader rests on 'a form rather than a formula. It is boy meets girl, boy loses girl, boy gets girl. The reader is invited to identify with her, and her perceptions for the space of the story become the reader's own.' Another important element is the explanation of motivations in the story; in real life this is an injunction on people to confess their private lives, especially in relationships and about sexual matters.[7]

The function of fiction
Conventional romantic fiction acts as an antidote to women's sense of their own predatoriness, which supports

the injunction on them to be natural, naïve, instinctual
and unselfconscious. Jacqui Bianchi comments:

It's sex without responsibility. There is also a social backlash
effect – the last real high point of romance in the movies, not
just in books, was during the 1930s and '40s when not only
were men 'on the absent' and therefore more desired, but women
had to take responsibility for their own lives and their own
decisions to a greater degree . . . I think there are still traces in
the more absolute behaviour of some heroes of the idea:
'Wouldn't it be nice to stop making decisions; wouldn't it be
nice to be looked after' . . . Where I part company from the
propagandists is that in accepting what is quite openly a limited
point of view for the duration of the story, our readers are quite
well aware of what they are doing. They are choosing to
surrender that much responsibility, that much detachment, when
they begin reading the book. We have discovered that, except in
extreme circumstances like the miners' strike, which hit the
pockets of some of our most devoted customers, in general the
more depressing the economic scene, the higher the sales of
romance novels rise. There is an inverse variation between the
gloom of the general outlook and the sales of our books.

Valerie Hey, a feminist who has written in support of
romantic fiction, considers that it offers a solution, even if
only in fantasy, to the contradictions of femininity. For
instance, it permits sexuality when femininity does not:
'At least within the pages of Mills and Boon, *Jackie*, *19*,
etc., are permissions to exist, to feel, to *have* pleasure (that
most illicit of emotions, as far as women are concerned).'[8]
She points out that since young working-class women do
not have an income which permits them independence,
marriage is an economic as well as a social necessity and
is seen, still, as 'destiny'. But it is an unexciting destiny.
Romance is a way of applying elements of real-life relationships but editing out the oppressions by stopping at
the moment when sexual uncertainty is over and nothing
will happen except that the couple will live happily ever
after:

Inside the genre of romantic fiction, the female domain of emotionality/nurturance is central. The site of female powerlessness is transformed into female powerfulness where women are seen to be in full control; ... this crucial site of female subordination is validated, valorized and glamorized ...

... the ideologies of romance reflect rather than create the contradictions that women experience. Is it not understandable that women, for whom monogamous romantic love is the only socially sanctioned adventure in life (apart from motherhood), should find so absorbing and necessary a literature ... that is committed to invoking the pleasures of the magical unknown and revoking the realities of the not so magical known?[9]

So romantic fiction is for its readers a parallel world in which private values are explicitly supported, rather than being subordinated to the necessities of the public world. It also reaffirms the importance of destiny. It solves the prohibition imposed by femininity on sexuality, for instance, by showing the hand of fate at work; lovers in romantic fiction are predestined, a truth manifested to its protagonists in the way their judgement is overridden by instinct and even their actions cannot outwit their designated ends. Women are gripped by instinct, in the face of which their intellects are unavailing. It is the triumph of nature over culture.

The difference between romantic fiction and adventure fiction mirrors the distinctions between stereotypical femininity and masculinity: popular fiction for men functions through instrumentality; the action's the thing. Romantic fiction for women is an adventure in feeling: what happens is only the vehicle to carry the protagonists, and with them the reader, into different emotional states.

Val Hey is also interested in gender disaffiliation: the way young women look for an identity outside the social construction of femininity, for instance in the way androgyny is manifested in the streets rather than in personality theory, through (for example) the development from 1970s unisex styles into phenomena like cross-dressing.

Gender identities

Studies tend to show that sex differences really begin to emerge only in adolescence, and crystallize in adulthood. It is during their teens that girls learn to be feminine. Adolescent girls modify their vocational expectations and their school interests, losing ground in mathematics, science and technology subjects in which, until then, they often outperform boys. Their behaviour in some respects exaggerates the feminine traits they will show later.

Val Hey sees gender identity being created through affiliation to a group, entailing experiences of which some are separate and some are the same for girls and boys. What the feminist social critic Angela McRobbie calls 'bedroom culture' for girls is one example of an experience divorced from boys' gang and street culture, private and antithetical to male public life, on which Val Hey comments:

Girls [in their bedrooms] were into looking at romantic literature, pin-ups, experimenting with make-up, discussing boys, in their separate space – they weren't really out on the street, and if they were, they weren't really there on the same terms as men: the whole idea of the street being taboo for women – witness the concept of the streetwalker, the idea that the streets are not safe, which is true – act as a whole set of controls operating to keep girls in their bedrooms out of the way. I don't think they have the same rights to occupy territory, public territory anyway. I've also written about pubs because I was quite interested in pub cultures and what happens to women who enter those spaces . . . the way encounters are sexualized.

She points out that sociological studies of subcultures tend to exclude girls and women and argues for a wider investigation of youth and subcultures:

What happens to the vast majority who don't actually join, in any definite sense, these subcultures? Where are they? The literature can't assume that they represent a mediocre, incorporated, silent type. It has to look at what they do and, rather than focusing on style, on display, on outfits, on gear, on what they look like, these stylistic guerrillas, look at what they do and where they do it – look at the chip shop, at babysitting – and thus incorporate an understanding of courtship rituals, dating, and the importance of romance for men. These concepts of chivalry, being the protector: I know they're double-edged, and they're often rationales to keep women down, but they have some emotional meaning for men, which doesn't operate at the level of the rational.

It's a very potent myth that men protect women, and they've got very contradictory and esoteric ways of showing that protection. The tendency is just to view men as total oppressors, but if that's the case, you can't account for feminism, you can't account for any resistance. It just makes women out to be total victims and I'm very against that line; it's just too bloody politically pessimistic, and it doesn't match with reality as I live it and see other women living it.

So sex stereotyping is not just for women. Men are also constrained by both their own ideas and women's about masculinity, just as they, in their ways, are moved by romance and fantasy.

Femininity is not a problem for women only. Feminine cultures exclude men: sometimes because they exist only in their absence, sometimes because they are created as havens in a patriarchal world, but often because men are unfamiliar with feminine traits except to the limited extent permitted by their experience of expressive, intimate relationships in couples. Families often assign men stereotyped roles. Men become suspicious of what is feminine in their personalities, fearing to unlock a Pandora's box.

The association of feminine traits with the private realm, with the greater sophistication, complexity and diversity demanded by intimacy, means these are correspondingly anomalous in the instrumental, practical public domain, which demands simplified personal relationships – roles rather than personalities. Men, with their greater investment in the public realm, are inhibited from opening up to the complexity of the private sphere, partly simply because they are often exposed to it for less of the time and hence are less accomplished in handling it, but also because they fear, not unreasonably, that venturing into this new terrain might make them see the world in new ways which would sunder them permanently from the simple, direct, action-orientated perspectives of the masculine world. They suspect, in other words, that developing feminine traits in the public world would be disadvantageous; so they confine their feminine characteristics of intimacy, subtlety and emotionality to their personal lives, just as women who work in the male public realm keep their private and their public selves apart.

Do men feel like women feel?

Language research into whether women are more verbal, more articulate, less logical and less able than men to justify their standpoints by reference to reason and facts has found that this is not true. Women are more fluent than men, less likely to interrupt themselves with 'ums' and 'ahs', and men are just as involved in the emotional aspects of what they talk about. But women and men tend to give a different priority to their emotional responses: where, for instance, women presented with a picture of a baby seal and a club would be likely to say first: 'That's terrible. I hate that picture', men would say: 'I don't think you should do that', and then say: 'That's terrible.'[10] Although men are sometimes accused of being dissociated from emotionality, some complain of being excluded by women arrogating the prerogatives of sentiment and sensibility. However, the fact remains that these do not occupy the same place in men's minds as in women's.

The way we look

The issue of style and fashion remains central to the question of gender identity. In an era of mass-produced fashion, the values of style are to do with creating visual identification from the available materials. Val Hey comments:

Feminists adopted uniforms like dungarees, so-called casual and comfortable styles – because it's hard to handle the contradictions of the power of appearance and sexuality – so you move out into a neutral uniform in a way. But I think there's now a move back to look at the pleasures of dress. The left's discourse on fashion contains two basic strands: one, that fashion is indulgent, hedonistic, anti-progressive, and upholds capitalist values. It implies: what we want is a rational sort of dress. Opposed to that is interest in the pleasures of the irrational.

Clothes and cosmetics as indicators of identity have grown in importance with the cult of individualism. Style is a signature of identity and creates an image from existing elements, employing wit, reference and even metaphor (for instance in clothes which consciously evoke those of an earlier era or clothes with a political message, like Katharine Hamnett's ecological T-shirts).

The way we present ourselves to others is based on the way we perceive them. The image of persona people project is calculated on how they imagine it will be interpreted, and so is the way the image or persona is subsequently managed.

Popular wisdom claims that women are better judges of character than men, just as it believes that women are more intuitive. This can be explained by the fact that women are more observant of others, which also accounts for their greater self-awareness and, consequently, greater skill in self-presentation.

An image or persona is constructed through the detail in which it is presented. Like cosmetics, clothes are sets of information used to create and manage a persona, as are behaviour, tone of voice, gesture, vocabulary, eye contact, stance, posture and position.

Investigations into interpersonal perception have found that people judge others more on the expressions on their faces than on what they say. It has been suggested that not only are attitudes towards other people communicated non-verbally, but there is a taboo on expressing them explicitly.[11] The fact that people believe not what others say of themselves but the way they seem to be and the way they look supports the importance of image or persona in the public world.

Since faces are important in creating an impression, make-up is a powerful means of creating responses in strangers. Stereotypes are attached to some features (for instance, one study found that women with bowed lips were seen as demanding and promiscuous)[12]. But it is expression above all which determines how people respond to each other. Women are better at interpreting emotion in photographed faces and use more facial expressions when asked to imagine themselves undergoing different emotional experiences.[13] As well as providing evidence for the claim that they develop observation and self-presentation more than men, this shows that women are more accomplished social actors.

Style

Style is an indicator of the importance of individualism and the stress on self-presentation as the outward manifestation of a unique inner constellation of traits and talents. The antithesis of stylish are mass-marketed designs, not for the cheap and raffish connotation they originally implied when only the poor wore clothes that were not tailored exactly to the individual, but because, unmodified, they represent a failure of the individual to identify her- or himself other than negatively, by general reference to being 'this type of person' rather than in detail. Modified, even off-the-peg chain-store clothing can be stylish.

The primary signal of conformist dressing is that the wearer's personality is not immediately in evidence and therefore falls under suspicion of not being clearly differentiated. Carefully tailored clothing may be distinguished from similar mass-produced designs too subtly for an uneducated eye, while mass-produced clothing can serve only utilitarian purposes. It is useful for covering nakedness and for moderating the extremes of temperature but it offers no further values, such as originality or discreetness. Just as a growing number of people value food for its aesthetic appeal rather than its mere necessity, so more and more people select clothing on less utilitarian criteria.

The stylish and the playful

Style has a great deal to do with consciousness. If you know what you are doing, your image operates as stylish even if it cannot be deciphered in detail. Style also has to do with confidence. Without confidence, clothing seems not to fit the personality but merely to be put on, and people who wear styles which do not fit their self-presentation draw attention principally to the discrepancy between what patently they wish to seem and what they really are. A bad fit is always unsatisfactory, both materially and metaphorically.

On the other hand, clothing which proclaims itself as costume or mask, stating that it hides or disguises the self – such as flamboyant cross-dressing or exaggerated fashion – can serve exactly the purpose the wearer intends, giving her or him the confidence which makes the style look authentic to the beholder. Originality is also closely identified with stylishness, most obviously when it is highly unconventional; but it does not have to be achieved ostentatiously.

Moira Goodall, a dress designer who talks later about the way she has integrated her private and public selves, creates suits for both men and women with a sober exterior but with unexpectedly brilliant linings, or set off with tiny details of stitching such as a zigzag of thread to match the cloth across the top of a pocket or on a cuff. Understatement has always been stylish.

Style in fashion and clothing is one of the ways social actors create the personae in which they appear in public, and people for whom the gap between the public and the personal is wide enough for them to be conscious of it need a persona to bridge it. The persona is the simplified self – reduced from the inconsistencies, contradictions and complexities of the private self – which is presented to the social and public worlds.

Wit
Wit is an important element of style, in the sense of understanding and using contradictions and anomalies like puns and paradoxes. Anomaly often figures prominently in contemporary unconventional style by interposing items from a different frame of reference: Ray-Ban sunglasses used with flounces of luxury fabrics like lace and satin, or the safety-pin body-decoration of the punk era. The shock of matter out of place is a useful device in contemporary styles, which go to further and more complex extremes than mere contrast. Contrasting colours work to enhance each other, but contemporary style tends to abandon homogeneity and uniformity in favour of challenge and contradiction: the problem of interpreting an image as coherent – and hence as internally consistent even if not on the surface – is thrown back to the beholder rather than solved by the wearer. The beholder must decode the image, which is presented like a puzzle which those in the know can understand while outsiders remain baffled or shocked. This operates most obviously in

subculture dressing. Although the concrete instance of this challenge may paradoxically be a uniform in subcultures, where identifying marks of group membership is an important function of clothing, it is fundamentally an emblem of the importance of individuality in a mass society.

There is often, too, a theatrical element in dressing which links these exterior ways of creating an image to the self-presentation in behaviour, for instance in contemporary street fashions. This idea of unfixed images, put on by the individual as circumstances dictate, is also embedded in the notion of transient fashions and short-life clothes. Here the element of play is to the fore and contrasts with the serious and utilitarian intentions of conventional dress.

Style has grown to encompass areas of life which in earlier eras were ruled entirely by convention. Clothing, for instance, is moving away from formality. The bowler hat has disappeared from City streets and more people are wearing leisure (private) clothes for work. So the values of novelty and individuality are manifested in everyday life.

Convention

There is plenty of evidence to show that convention occupied a proportionately greater place in determining behaviour in earlier generations than it does now. History also suggests that in the past people were taken much more at face value, as mentioned above. Convention was a protective device for the personal realm. In writing about women soldiers, a woman historian suggests that formerly it was enough simply for a woman to adopt male costume and styles of behaviour for her to pass as a boy,[14] though in the last century such passing off was a more radical challenge to convention than it is now, when women and men can share styles – witness the hobble skirts into which Jean-Paul Gaultier put young men in the early 1980s (a direct display of anomaly, in which the style worked by presenting a contradiction for the beholder to resolve).

When convention governed behaviour, public scrutiny was less intense or less stereotyped; either people did not notice differences in detail as we do today, or they were less disposed to ascribe characteristics on gender lines. Traditional ballads tell of women dressing as pageboys, soldiers and sailors. A manager of the Hudson Bay Company in Rupertsland in 1806, when employees were forbidden to bring their wives over from their native Orkneys or to have anything to do with local women, was surprised to come home one afternoon to learn from his lad that he was Isabelle Gunn, forced to reveal herself because she had gone into labour.[15] She did not merely state her case but offered evidence by opening her shirt (and shortly after, by having the baby), as if more confirmation of gender was needed than merely asking the beholder to reinterpret the image.

This suggests that the appearance of being a man had to be strongly contradicted by countervailing evidence to override conventional interpretations. This difference between appearance and reality which underlies clothing and costume has exercised a long fascination and is a device which has frequently been used in drama.

The idea that individuality was less to the fore in the past is supported by the writer and academic Elizabeth Wilson. 'Until the seventeenth or even the eighteenth century, sexual difference in dress was not strongly marked,' she remarks in her book on fashion and modernity,[16] describing how for riding and sports women wore similar clothes to men and habitually carried the same sorts of daggers and purses on their belt before the invention of pockets in the sixteenth century. Then 'mannerist styles' clothed both men and women in high hats, ruffs and ringlets, and put women into bodices that flattened their chests.

Convention in dress could disguise much of the personal from public view. At the same time, if dress then did not delineate people so much as individuals and by gender, it did so more by class and by occupation than it does now. Richard Sennett describes how tradesmen, including those in occupations we now think of as professional such as the law, wore clothing appropriate to their calling, and medieval sumptuary laws in England and France prohibiting wives of some classes wearing the decorations permitted those of higher classes remained on eighteenth-century statute books.[17]

The relationship between identity and clothing is close. Sennett points out that the new occupations which developed in the seventeenth century needed new clothing to signify them in the street; this they borrowed from the clothing of older trades. Thus the connection between clothing and impersonation was formed, though at first it was determined by convention, not idiosyncrasy: 'Whether people were in fact what they wore was less important than their desire to wear something recognizable in order to be someone on the street.'[18] At the same time, Sennett describes the difference between public and private dress: in the home people wore loose and simple garments in contrast to the elaborate clothing worn in public: 'At home, one's clothes suited one's body and its needs; on the street, one stepped into clothes whose purpose was to make it possible for other people to act as if they knew who you were.'[19]

This is the way today's subculture clothes act as badges of group membership which can be recognized only by those in the know. Just as the significance of tribal dress or embroidery may escape the untutored eye, so to the old the young may seem to dress in uniform because what is salient to them is not the differences which establish individual identity but the similarities which show membership. To the young, the styles used by the old can be similarly indistinct. As well as generational differences in the interpretation of style, however, there are also sex differences. Val Hey comments:

Generally it's true that more women are sensitized to what is fashion. I can't think of any woman of my acquaintance who isn't interested in clothes. All the women I know are interested in their appearance. By contrast, lots of men couldn't care less about what they look like. There are two ways to read that: one is that they are completely abstracted from all these pressures to be commodities – that's a very noble position; otherwise, they are so wretchedly self-centred they don't think it's important to attract people. They think they're intrinsically wonderful; they don't need to disguise themselves, to wrap themselves up to attract people.

Private dress became associated with the real, personal self, which in relation to a mass society is the individual self. It is now read as more sincere and authentic than anonymous conventional clothing, which it has displaced. There is now much less demand for rigorously prescribed formal clothing, but much more use for leisure clothing. There are also many more varieties of dress appropriate for public use, so that the issue of self-presentation is more complex and more in evidence.

Fashion and face-painting

Concepts like power-dressing or 'dressing for success', which developed in America, prescribe in detail which items of clothing are appropriate to which status, social and professional, and hence what the female aspirant for achievement at work should wear to improve her chances. It is the correlative of the behavioural training which teaches women to act in a manner appropriate to the role they aim to occupy.

For women (as we saw in chapter four) cosmetics are just as important as clothes as a means of achieving an image, but they have slightly different connotations. Women have been castigated for wearing make-up, first by purists who decried cosmetics as artificial and therefore unfeminine (stressing the connection with prostitution, where 'natural' sexuality was seen as sullied by commercial use, and artifice and deception were seen as paramount) and then by purist feminists who interpreted make-up as a collaboration, conscious or unconscious, with patriarchy. The latter account is possibly a misinterpretation carried over from patriarchy, for it is equally arguable that the use of cosmetics constituted a revolt against patriarchal authority in which women asserted not only their power to attract and to deceive but their individual differences.[20] But like dress, cosmetics also offer their own pleasures and satisfactions, as Val Hey was reminded when she once objected to her sister spending three-quarters of an hour each day putting on her make-up. Her sister replied: 'It's probably the most creative thing I do in the day.'

Plainness

The feminists of the 1960s and 1970s passed through an era of puritan plainness in their self-presentation by which they were popularly identified and which lingers still, since in the public imagination feminist clothing is unisex and utilitarian. The use of cosmetics was an important issue as one of the clearest outward signs of women's collusion with men's visual interest in them. Unpainted eyes, lips and nails represented unvarnished womanhood eschewing the artifices marketed as means of snaring men.

But plainness is a difficult style for women. It puts them in a direct, unmediated relationship with the world, with which – particularly in the public realm – they are accustomed to deal through the media of image, self-presentation, persona, dress, gesture and make-up. Women who abandon the stratagems of femininity in favour of naturalness are in a vulnerable position, having laid aside their conventional defences without the reassurance of reciprocal gestures from the public realm – the (masculine) domain of strangers. Like plain speech compared to eloquence, plain rather than elaborate self-presentation is a difficult way to achieve its intended ends, for it demands greater skill to select the minimum functional information than to elaborate on a theme. The more often a message is repeated – in speech, in dress, in behaviour or in other ways – the more likely it is to be understood, whereas minimalist communication relies on getting the message across on a once-only shot. Plainness also offers fewer refuges than the multiplicity of elaborateness.

Plainness, however, is seen as the appropriate medium for the truth, and simplicity is strongly associated with honesty and truthfulness in Protestant countries (the countries which were formerly Protestant: only fifteen per cent of people in contemporary Britain now describe themselves as Christian, but heritage is still a major influence). As plain thought and plain speech are elevated and associated with practicality and democracy as the best media to convey ideas, so plain dress is thought the most honest of appearances.

In fact, plainness of dress is as open to Machiavellian purposes as any other style. Minimalist dressing – for instance the black clothing promoted by the designer Joseph Ettedgui in the mid-1980s – is just as much a guise, in which appearance does not necessarily correspond directly with reality, as any other. But in confronting the constraints of femininity, feminists first chose plainness, not only because they wanted to make apparent their rejection of artifice; nor just to lay claim to an honesty unavailable to others; nor only to proclaim a new truth (though all these were incorporated into feminist dress, with its utilitarian boiler suits symbolizing the rejection of professional aspirations in favour of honest manual trades); but also because they wanted to demonstrate the importance of the personal over the public. So they abandoned conventional feminine appearance, with its highly individuated dress in which complex codes and conventions were at work, and its make-up to camouflage the private self, just as they rejected the elaborate speech of the highly educated in favour of the plain speech of the street in order to assert the ascendancy of the private and personal over the public, formal and conventional.

The appearance of reality

The paradox of the imperative to catch and keep men – in which tools like cosmetics and dress, skills like being a good listener and devices like not being too available were employed – was the necessity of feigning naturalism. However artificial the favoured face and figure of the day; however arch and designing conventional feminine behaviour; however divergent the feminine ideal from prevailing body-types; these facts of life were to be disguised and denied. Femininity, like beauty, had to be a natural acquisition. Contradictions like body hair, bulges, imperfect complexions, uneven teeth, unconventional proportions, bespectacled eyes, self-assertion, body odours, physical strength and self-esteem were to be corrected mechanically, surgically, chemically, physically and behaviourally. Anomalies were eradicated.

Sex and destiny

At the core of the romantic ideal betokened by the image of femininity is the notion of destiny and perfection. It is evident in traditional dynastic aspirations, and the contemporary model for sexual relations is a gigantic dating system preordaining perfect matches: for each woman, a mate. This idea suggests that each individually incomplete person, when united with her or his predestined intended, is made whole and given access to a fulfilment unavailable to the single or the mismatched. In this Noah's Ark conception of human relations the notion of an arranged marriage is an anomaly and anathema, and the greater success rate of arranged marriages over love matches is explained away by reference to the coercion implied by the social sanctions applied to refusniks.[21] Arranged marriage is interpreted as a violation of the individual's potential for fulfilment through self-determination, the most centrally sacred area of a society which elevates individualism to cult status.

The idea of individual choice in personal matters is a species of consumerism and applies to the private world a transaction generated by the public, the world of commerce, particularly in the matter of selecting a partner. Marriage has a long history as a commercial transaction, but love has been opposed to commerce and dissociated from its values though its relationship to private virtues like candour, honour and chivalry. This relationship goes back a long way, at least to the time when these were public virtues and love was established on a public basis in the late medieval courts of love. The notion of romance as an element of love also goes back at least that far.

The commercial world is essentially loveless – or heartless, as Jessie Bernard calls it. It is mechanical, open to vice (avarice and slothfulness) and fundamentally exploitative. It is therefore opposed to what the personal realm (notionally) stands for.

The suggestion that the two spheres are interrelated and that the standards and expectations of the public world impinge upon the private sphere to introduce transactions into relationships and to put intimacy on to a footing demanding reciprocation is one that has been developing since Engels first identified the relationship between family, private property and state.

What is given should be freely given; love is described as the greatest gift both in its universal aspect (religious passion) and as personal and sexual love, and contemporary as well as traditional ideologies hold that it should be offered without strings. In practice, however, it is offered if (and sometimes only if) it is returned, and the demand for gratitude lessens the degree to which it is offered freely. The need for reassurance about being valued is an indication that in many relationships, love given is subordinate to love received.

Love is conceived of as free and enfranchising, but it does not really work that way. The conditions in which love has to operate have been blamed for its failure in this respect. Marcuse suggested that sexual relations are organized on the performance principle, which consigns some instincts to subservience to genital supremacy. An alternative social and political order, he suggested, would enable personal relationships to work differently:

The body in its entirety would become an object of cathexis, a thing to be enjoyed – an instrument of pleasure. This change in the value and scope of libidinal relations would lead to a disintegration of the institutions in which the private interpersonal relations have been organized, particularly the monogamic and patriarchal family.[22]

Sexual liberation, then, heralded the transformation of society from a dichotomized state of public values in conflict with private interests into a unified and harmonious utopia. This was the cultural environment from which contemporary feminism also sprang, for unlike feminism in preceding generations, which focused on public issues like equal rights, women's liberation was organized around personal and sexual politics.

These adumbrations of the transformed sexuality that

would obtain under a new social order proved too theoretical and distant for a great majority of women. The sexual revolution failed to achieve its political objectives, although it did play a part in altering sexual and hence gender relations and in modifying social organizations like the patriarchal and monogamous family. But, more conspicuously than it liberated the repressed masses, it operated to women's detriment by constraining them to enter sexual relationships because sex became fashionable; unreformed sexual relations – fragmented, heterosexual, obedient to convention and imperfect – persist.

So do their discontents. Belief in the ideal that each individual, gifted with a particular configuration of talents, is complemented perfectly by some other individual configuration and that, unified, the two will achieve a personal fulfilment beyond the scope of each separately, continues unabated in the face of divorce statistics. These do not contradict the belief in romantic destiny; rather, they reinforce it by showing what adversity marks the path of true love in modern society and charting the numbers of true believers who, finding they have contracted themselves to a partner who falls below par, interpret the partnership as a case of mistaken identity: they thought they had found their perfect match, but on closer inspection find they have not.

This notion of the individual and her romantic destiny has been discussed by psychoanalyst Karen Horney in terms of 'the overvaluation of love'. The patients she diagnosed as overvaluing love were characteristically middle-class, in paid employment and dissatisfied with their lot. Not only was love central to their lives; it totally dominated them. Imperfections and failures in their (heterosexual, monogamous) relationships engendered disproportionate despair. Horney saw in women the dependency described by traditional Freudian analysts, but she viewed it not as normal but as neurotic.

Change

> Out flew the web and floated wide;
> The mirror crack'd from side to side;
> 'The curse is come upon me,' cried
> The Lady of Shalott.

Tennyson's romantic heroine the Lady of Shalott was condemned to view the world outside her magic tower through a looking glass only. When she came face to face with it, the illusion that sustained her died and she died with it. The social construction of femininity, from which sex stereotypes are drawn and which shapes the identity of many women, is a collective generalization from past experience. Not surprisingly, therefore, it does not prove a good fit in radically and rapidly changing circumstances such as the social, economic and technological changes within a society in transition from an industrial to a post-industrial state.

The romantic confabulation about an essential feminine mystery is hard for women to come to terms with, particularly because it is as unwritten as the British constitution. Romance offers many solaces in a world which sometimes fails to deliver the satisfactions it promises and certainly short-changes women on the success it offers.

At the same time, feminine traits have positive values and it would be a shame for women to have to reject them in order to validate themselves in the public world and earn its success. Some men, too, are now valuing feminine characteristics. But femininity, under the strong gravitational pull of the private, remains difficult to reconcile with achievement and the public world.

It is an imperative dictated by femininity and patriarchy to live in a private world and deal with the public world only at a remove, through the medium of mirrors and masks, which creates in women self-consciousness and distancing and impels the mechanisms of displacement, inhibition and lack of confidence which are the inner obstacles to achievement.

6

Barrier Zone

'Tell me how I can be successful too,' demanded a woman of the panel of speakers at a women's network group meeting on the subject of success. It made the rest of the audience uncomfortable because it bluntly exposed the real reason they had chosen to attend, focusing on the fact that each felt unsuccessful enough to want to find out how to be more successful.

Success has a cult following in the Western world: perhaps nowhere more so than in America, but increasingly in Britain too. None the less this remains largely unacknowledged, partly because naked ambition is considered vulgar but more because a great deal of magical thinking and superstitiousness attach to the idea of success, to which the notion of luck is intimately bound. To people who want to be more successful, declaring this interest seems dangerously hubristic.

Nevertheless, in response to this demand a great deal has been written and said about how to be successful, from guidance on social success to advice on how to make a lot of money, including advice on career strategies. But the central theme has been to meet the reader's search for an x-factor, a magical formula that people can acquire, learn or apply one night and wake up successful the next morning.

The answer given to the woman at the meeting was another question: What is it you want to do? In fact she wanted to get a book published, but she treated the response as if it were evading the issue. She wanted to get a book published because she wanted to be successful. It seemed not so much that she had a manuscript that had been rejected as that she wanted someone to tell her what to write about – what the sure-fire subject for a block-buster was going to be the following year.

If there were an x-factor in success to which all successful people were secretly party but unanimously refused to divulge, it would by now have been synthesized and mass marketed. The demand would be too large for the secret to be guarded. The truth is that there is no guaranteed route to success, because it is as various as the fields of human endeavour. A successful astronaut differs from a successful tycoon, and both differ from a successful artist.

But the fact that success is so earnestly sought is a clue to the way it is conceived of and why it is so highly prized. Understanding what is going on when people pursue success as an almost abstract ideal, and why they are so fascinated by it – evidenced not only explicitly in success manuals but through, for example, the market for autobiographies, a genre whose readership has grown massively this century, and also the persistent images of glossy soap opera – is as viable a route to the goal sought by the pursuit of success as anatomizing the careers of the successful or developing a typology of successful characteristics.

There are, it seems, certain characteristics that successful people in different occupations have in common, like being first-born in immigrant families. But these – besides being advantages which for the most part cannot be appropriated by those who find out, too late, what would probably have made them more ambitious – are identified by studies which, although replicated and extended over several decades, have concentrated on a narrow range of occupations. Managers, entrepreneurs, professionals in business-related occupations (like finance and law) and academics are over-researched, while there is little about people in other sorts of jobs: primary school teachers, sculptors or civil servants.

This is not, however, an oversight, because as a general description rather than a term qualifying a particular activity or event, 'success' connotes a certain way of life – a certain way of spending, money as much as time – and hence a certain image.

Success is not a term that can be applied to all occupations or activities equally: there are successful entrepreneurs but *senior* civil servants; successful designers but *head* teachers; successful managers but *loving* parents. And what is a successful doctor? The primary connotation is probably one who has a profitable private practice rather than one whose patients are conspicuously healthy. A doctor can advertise his success by his address, by his professional status, by the household he maintains and the car he drives; in rare circumstances, he may be a household name – Christiaan Barnaard or Patrick Steptoe. But his success rate in preventing or curing ill-health is not generally something which is publicly visible.

Success is a phenomenon solely of the public realm. It serves the function of a qualification in the small scale of individual career, for someone who can demonstrate successes in one job is in a good position to be offered wider scope. This is the practical reason for the interest success inspires. It is increasingly important that achievements be visible; hard work and a solid record of good decisions will not necessarily bring their own rewards, as Americans recognize in what they refer to as the 'po-po syndrome': pissed on and passed over. Publicity, having the right image, and being able to present yourself well are increasingly valuable credentials for the careerist.

Success as a general rather than specific concept is defined by a consensus, albeit unarticulated and unfixed. It is an exterior quality which adheres only to other people, to objects (like a successful product) or to activities (such as a successful conference). You can see a successful entrepreneur, or you can be an entrepreneur with a successful product or service, but you cannot apprehend yourself as a successful entrepreneur except by looking at yourself through others' eyes.

Satisfaction, on the other hand, is something which is felt by the subject more than it is perceived by others. You can tell that you are successful only from external evidence, never by reference to your own responses alone. You can tell that you are fulfilled only from subjective evidence.

It may be satisfying to be perceived as successful; it is certainly satisfying to be involved in a successful activity or responsible for a successful product or service. But applied to the private realm, success is an uncertain term. To call people 'successful' parents or spouses is an absolute rather than a comparative measure, for it implies that the alternative is failure. A 'successful' marriage is one which survives, compared with an unsuccessful marriage which ends in divorce; a 'successful' parent is one whose child survives temptations and dangers, rather than a parent with a given status, income or even a given number of children. (This does not apply in cultures less urban and industrialized than the West. Where children still confer status the exterior, commercial concept of success can be applied to parenting.)

For the most part success does not have much meaning applied to the private realm, for it is a measure of performance or output and essentially therefore quantitative rather than qualitative. In the public realm, success suggests unalloyed benefit deriving from special personal qualities – a particular success which others could not reproduce; a quality special to the successful individual. It strongly connotes luck.

Fortune

But it is luck well aspected by destiny rather than mere happy chance, and although the elements of fate and fortuity have always been inextricably present in ideas of success, the more we strive to rationalize the fascination success exerts over us, the more our superstitious traits are revealed.

Attitudes to success have probably never been simple, and they are certainly not so now. It is both admired as a goal and seen as a heartless pursuit. But views of success change over time. In the last century – still a potent influence on contemporary attitudes – success was considered the reward for hard work, which was also a duty to be discharged without necessarily seeking reward. Success then meant definable material gain. The transformation of the ordinary person into the successful person was concomitant with a movement up a social class or two and was signified by the acquisition of a grander house and household, a better-educated family with more leisure and higher aspirations. However, to subvert the proper order through personal social mobility was also a temptation to fate. At the very least, the stigma of class origins lay heavy on the socially mobile, whose new peers vigilantly scanned them for telltale pretensions. The underlying idea was that social position was, as it were, genetically determined: that people's origins were indelibly registered in their blood, and that to leave their roots was to deny their heritage and subvert the course of nature. Conversely, it was considered natural to be content with the station in life to which you were born.

This idea of the relationship between success and destiny is quite different from the prevailing opinion today. The work ethic in the industrial West has declined over the twentieth century in the sense that hard work is no longer upheld as an unreasoning moral imperative, while at the same time success is increasingly perceived to be the reward of recognition.

In contrast to the Victorian magnate whose fortune was made out of his (and others') toil, the types of twentieth-century success are the film star and the rock musician, whose fame is not so much the reward of craft and practice as recognition of particular personal qualities. Though musical or acting ability and experience certainly show in stars who have long careers, it is not a necessary condition for fame. Originality is one of the key concepts here, although it is very loosely applied. Idiosyncrasy would stand in just as well for the most part, and on occasions novelty would do.

We live in the age of the personality cult when it is important to perceive, in any activity or product, human agency. It is necessary, in a mass society, to have a specific sense of the individual behind the artefact, the person using the skill or craft – to the point where the personality of the actor, craftsman or performer takes precedence over the skill, talent or experience represented in the artefact or performance. This is most apparent in those areas of life involving success in its most pronounced form – fame – but it extends into other jobs with the decline of manual work and the growth of service occupations. For instance, the term 'skill ownership', which has been current in training circles for about a decade, refers to the idea that someone who learns a skill in one job can translate it into another. It is a key concept in building a flexible work-force, which has been one of the predominant public administration projects of the 1980s. A flexible workforce is one that can adapt quickly to new technologies, new production processes and new products and services, without causing at one end of the scale a skill shortage and at the other massive unemployment.

But as well as being a simple economic remedy this also incorporates the pervading notion that people's skills and experience, like their talents, are special. It is part of the tendency to look at careers as customized to individual requirements rather than rolling off the production line, which is also expressed in the growth of self-employment and flexible ways of working. Jobs, like skills, are moving towards being fitted to people, rather than people having to fit into jobs.

The importance of personality and talent as qualities in success also expresses something which is a real condition of success: that it is not under the conscious control of individuals who pursue it.

Richard Branson, one of the pre-eminent entrepreneurs of the eighties, has said that he had always wanted to edit a newspaper and that he originally developed the independent record label out of which the Virgin empire grew as a by-product of his attempts to do this. He had found that in order to edit the paper, he had to attend first to the business side of publishing. Thus he came by accident into business.

The element of serendipity is at work in another paradox of entrepreneurialism remarked by Gifford Pinchot III, a business consultant who developed the idea of intrapreneuring, in which a company expands by encouraging employees to develop their own ideas even if they are for services or products outside its current activities. This, incidentally, is another indication of the way the world of work is beginning to turn itself into an environment more shaped by the individuals who happen to be around than demanding conformity to existing modes of organization.

Gifford Pinchot III commented:

I think a lot of the initial moves are made in the shower, or driving a car, or sailing a boat, or some activity. All of these activities . . . have something in common. They are times when there is no particular reason to feel that you ought to be doing something else, and at the same time you can't get your hands on paper, which are the times in which the imagination is most likely to flower, because you're thrown back [on your imagination] – you have nothing else that you can use aside from your imagination, to paint the picture on.[1]

This shows how formal organizational systems are divorced from the generation of ideas on which they depend and reveals the element of play. Paradoxically, as we shall see, one of the inhibitions to achievement is the tendency to take it too seriously.

Pinchot also stresses that entrepreneurs are not motivated by greed, but by an idea. They are enthusiasts, whom he calls 'the dreamers who do'. Here again is evidence for the fact that the pursuit of success is unlikely to produce it. Success is really the by-product of having a good idea and putting it into practice.

The pursuit of success, a contemporary passion, is filled with contradictions. First among them is the fact that success is an outcome, not an aim in itself. The woman who demanded that the speakers on success should tell her how to achieve it was expressing the sense that success is a commodity and that all successful people are party to a secret they withhold from the general public. She, and the others like her who look for a process to employ to become successful and want to analyse the behaviour that leads to success, is trying to mimic the successful, letting imitation take precedence over useful activity.

This sort of magical thinking shows how much success is conceived not as a result of specific activity and hard work but as a concomitant of talent and luck. This is what misleads fans of success into thinking that there is a successful personality, which they can acquire by altering their behaviour. Mimicking a successful style does not produce achievement, and the pursuit of success without a definite object is a hopeless quest.

Displacement activities

What makes people successful cannot be reduced to a concrete programme based on a simple description or a crucial element. The factors are too various: a good idea, the appropriate combination of skills, the right conditions (including a market receptive to the product or service) and the enthusiasm to carry the project through from conception to completion. Those general prescriptions are obviously very different when applied to starting a new business, writing a script for a film or composing a song, but the barriers to activity, and to success generally, are more easily defined.

I used to do crosswords and I used to work at night, I'd piddle about for three or four hours. Once I did a children's colouring competition in *Woman's Realm* . . . I felt dreadfully guilty. I gradually got more disciplined and realized that I prefer not to have that horrible feeling in the pit of my stomach. I used to spend hours digging out the holes in the telephone with a cotton bud. I spent a very happy hour sorting brass screws out. Not even ones we needed. I just sorted them out.

Victoria Wood's 'horrible feeling' did not finally stop her from working, and she has become successful and famous. But what was it? 'The barrier to work was that I thought I wouldn't be able to do it and it would be the end of the world. I thought – the gaffe will be blown.'

The crisis was the question of success. Victoria Wood achieved this in her early twenties, going from university revues to television. The problem was whether she could sustain it: whether she had deserved and had earned it by ability and work, or was just lucky.

Women are more prone than men to such doubts. Several studies have shown that success in women is more often attributed to luck than to ability,[2] and there is a neat double bind: where women are seen as successful because they have worked hard, this is interpreted by both men and women as indicating lack of ability. Therefore women are perceived as not deserving success and often suffer anxieties which can be disabling, as Victoria Wood has described. For women working on their own, either isolated in organizations or self-employed – work patterns which have emerged strongly in recent years – such problems can be particularly debilitating:

What had knocked my confidence was that all the television work had dried up. A friend who was a television director asked for a children's play and when she received it, said: 'It's not funny and we're not doing it.' She didn't say why. I had been pinning all my hopes on it, because I thought the singing and piano was finished. I had been waiting for the next stage.

She was twenty-three when this happened, and she felt 'over the hill':

I suffered a complete loss of confidence, and I had to come to terms with not making it. I rarely went out of the house for six months. It had been coming for a long time. I didn't work at all – I didn't have any self-discipline. I had always slept a lot, which I now know is a form of avoidance when people are mildly depressed. I used to wait for the phone to ring. Then it dawned on me that the phone wouldn't ring because I was not that good. I hadn't developed. I thought I'd blown my chance. I didn't know what to do.

As a new entrant to a competitive profession without experience, a long track record or wide contacts to fall back on, Victoria Wood's depression was realistically founded in external circumstances, and it was change here – small pieces of luck – which took her from a state of passive dejection back to an active working life:

Some months before I got depressed, I met a radio producer who asked: 'How about writing a radio sitcom?' He wrote to remind me. And I sat down and wrote it and sent it off. They didn't do it; he wrote back and said, 'I'm sorry . . .', but at least

I'd done something. But Denise Coffey at the National Youth Theatre liked the script. Everything started to roll from the time I had written that radio script. I was approached to work with someone else [the partnership with Julie Walters began], then I was asked to write a play and it won three awards. And I've never been out of work since then.

Choosing second-best

Victoria Wood says she never puts things off now. But she has recovered the motivation that deserted her when she lost confidence in her abilities, and she also has the stimulus of demand for her work. Her lack of discipline when she was depressed was not the cause, but the symptom of her problem.

Inhibiting interior barriers are most conspicuous when activity is directed from inside rather than out. 'Writer's block' is a widely known term, even if it is experienced only by the relatively small number of people who earn their living by writing. But if it is taken to mean something more than just a temporary paralysis when faced with a blank screen or sheet of paper – and it is not a condition with known time limits – then there are larger numbers of people with a more pronounced form of writer's block: those who want to be writers, but are not.

Jillie is an information officer with a good reputation and a responsible and rewarding job creating large public data bases. 'I wish I could do what you do – write,' she said, almost in the same breath in which she handed in a book review for a magazine. 'This doesn't count as writing. I wish it was my job, but I simply can't. I always make the excuse that I haven't the opportunity, that I can't write at home with the children . . . But really it's not that, it's because I can't write.' The fact that she had before her the disproof of her argument, something she had in fact just written, did not comfort her. She was measuring the distance between her occupation as it was and as she wanted it to be and judging that it would take a long time and a lot of effort to change her job description into 'full-time writer', and it was this that discouraged her. But what really stood in her way was the fact that she had chosen to work as an information scientist, a second-choice job, rather than try for an occupation she really wanted. She said she would have liked to be a lawyer, but she considered that, after a career break to have children, she was too late.

Liz Crossley is a painter and art historian who also runs support groups for women artists. Her personal strategies for avoiding work are, like Victoria Wood's, thrown into high relief because her work is her own and not dictated by an organization's demands:

I file papers and make lists of things to do. My thing has always been: I don't have the space, I don't have the money. And then I go out to earn the money, and then of course I don't have the time. I have an enormous number of separate compartments in my life, which dissipates energies.

The organizations Liz has set up for women artists show too that the strategies for avoiding work she – like Victoria Wood – uses are commonplace:

It comes down to this whole fear syndrome. You create for yourself all sorts of so-called obstacles that aren't really there. For instance, I've always said: I cannot paint in my room because of the oils and because of the space; and so, always the thing of needing another space or studio, and feeling you're not really professional, you're not really an artist until you've got a studio – all these bits and pieces that add together to make you a professional artist. But those are perhaps ways of avoiding things.

Sense of self, success and failure

The need to be validated by externalities, to acquire the image that goes with the activity before engaging in the activity itself, is a prime example of procrastination, and one which offers a clue to its origins.

First, the need for validation or for an activity to be sanctioned by some external agency shows lack of confidence, a problem central in training and in therapy for women. Lack of confidence is something on which women's groups, networks and trainers have focused closely (and it is discussed more in chapter seven) But it is not the root but another symptom of the condition inhibiting women from achievement.

Just as women are perceived as more likely to achieve something through luck rather than ability, so their lack of achievement is taken to reflect lack of ability rather than adverse exterior (social) conditions.

But the lack of confidence from which individual women suffer, which inhibits them from engaging in activities and pursuing occupations they are interested in and makes them feel guilty, is not something which arises in their separate, personal and private experience but a phenomenon so common that it clearly has a social, not a private, origin. It is the women who feel confident and are able to engage in activities without inhibiting self-consciousness who are the exceptions who prove the rule.

Research into the relationship between self-consciousness and explanations for success and failure illustrates the mechanism which undermines many women's confidence. For instance, one study found that people who were made self-conscious in a role-playing experiment (by sitting in front of a mirror or a camera, for example) felt more responsible for the outcome of the experiment than those who were not.[3] Further investigations showed that making people more self-aware also made them more defensive about failure. On the other hand, people who did well were more likely to take the credit themselves when they had been made self-aware. Another piece of research showed that people with low self-esteem were less defensive about failure and more likely to think it was their own fault than those with high self-esteem.[4]

Women expect failure more than men do and blame themselves more for it. At the same time, women seem to be more self-conscious; this is reinforced by the importance they attach to image and by their disposition to analyse character, including their own. This is indicated not only in the content of women's conversations, which social scientists have found contain more self-disclosure and discussion of family, friends, feelings and motivations;[5] it is also supported by the numbers of women drawn to psychology and associated fields like psychoanalysis, therapy, self-development and self-help, and their often-stated preference for jobs involving them in dealing with people. Fifty per cent of members of the British Psychological Society, the professional organization for psychologists, are women, which is a much higher proportion than in comparable professions: fourteen per cent of solicitors are women; twenty-eight per cent of doctors; thirty-eight per cent of health administrators and forty per cent of personnel managers.

Features in women's magazines often meet exactly this human interest, while Jacqui Bianchi comments on the prevalence of the 'But I thought . . .' session, the dénouement in love stories where the hero and heroine analyse each other's motives earlier in the plot and the ensuing misunderstandings.

Self-esteem is positively related to masculine but not feminine character traits;[6] and there is a large body of evidence to show that women are less confident than men about their abilities.[7] Because women expect failure more, they are more vulnerable to it. Moreover, opportunities for women to achieve success in the public realm – for instance at work or in politics – are in reality limited by comparison with those for men. Fewer women than men occupy top jobs, women earn less, work in a narrower range of occupations, are more subject to sexual discrimination and have fewer opportunities, and here the lessons of the public world reinforce personal disposition. Consequently women have more reason than men to fear failure and to take it badly. And as Liz Crossley and Victoria Wood both mentioned, the foundation of the obstacles to achievement is fear.

Procrastination

Activities displacing work take many and varied forms in addition to cleaning telephone receivers, sorting nails and making lists. Some amount to little more than hesitations or settling in before beginning work, like making a cup of coffee or having a chat with colleagues. Others are more insidious and pervasive, like taking on too many commitments. Displacement activities are often masked as useful occupations, but anything done voluntarily which replaces the activity which has to be undertaken in order to achieve the required and desired outcome is a displacement activity.

Making lists is a preparatory habit many women adopt. Planning and organizing are obviously intended to facilitate more effective use of time, but sometimes the planning and list-making replace the activity, as Liz says they sometimes have for her.

A common form of procrastination is disorganization, so one type of training to increase women's effectiveness at work is time management. Women taking part in time-management exercises keep a detailed record of how they spend their time and why they do things the way they do – who they report to, what their responsibilities are – and then analyse it with the trainer's help to see if there are better ways to organize themselves.

But in a different vein, even training can become a means of procrastinating. Women often see training as a solution to obstacles at work – in surveys of attitudes to work they usually place it high on their list of preferences or, conversely, name lack of training opportunities as something with which they are dissatisfied.

Generally, training is obviously a very useful tool indeed, but sometimes it can displace the goal in view. For instance, at a planning meeting for a national campaign to increase the number of women appointed to public bodies like royal and government commissions, advisory committees and committees of inquiry, one woman's suggestion that the first step for the lobby was to provide training for women wanting public appointments was discussed for some minutes before the meeting collectively realized that the campaign was about women who were already qualified for public appointments. Thinking of training as a necessary preliminary to any activity seemed to be a reflex action; in this context it illustrates how even such an apparently positive step can in fact function as a block.

In cases like this women seem to view training as a means of supplying a validation for an activity which, untrained, they do not feel permitted to undertake. For instance, women are often described – by trainers and also by employers justifying the lack of women in certain areas of their workforce – as reluctant to apply for promotions for which their male colleagues would try without a second thought.

Training here is a means to promotion in a world where expertise is considered more important as work becomes increasingly specialized. Women's greater emphasis on training may also reflect the greater degree to which they find the public world intimidating with its specializations, networks of contacts and codes of behaviour different from those in the private sphere, like 'professionalism'. Women's sense of the world as a more complicated, less comprehensible place is a different aspect of their generally lower confidence in their abilities.

Being late

Rebecca, a regional manager in a large service organization, is permanently late for meetings and appointments, sometimes arriving hours after the arranged time. She has a busy job, but so do the other regional managers against whom her performance can be compared. She was aggrieved when her application for a promotion did not even get her an interview and the job went to a younger man, but her poor timekeeping and obvious disorganization outweighed her good points, such as speaking well at meetings.

Superficially she is committed to her job – for example, she took little maternity leave – but although she has a daily nanny for her baby she is still torn about leaving him, and the conflict of interests undermines her effectiveness at work. Rebecca was late and disorganized, though, before she was ever pregnant; having a baby has exacerbated, not created, the problem.

Rebecca has a permanently harassed air about her; the fact of her habitual lateness and lack of organization is obscured from her by the mass of circumstantial detail surrounding it. She is always late for perfectly good reasons – traffic, overrunning meetings, last-minute claims on her attention – but underlying her inability to organize claims on her attention, which is the immediate cause, is a nervousness about changing from one activity or state to another. Rebecca may feel safe doing whatever she is doing at any given time, but uncertain about how she will perform under changed circumstances. If she is coping in her office but has to go to a meeting she is anxious – albeit unconsciously – that she will not do well there, so she stays in the office; but if she is in the meeting and feels she is surviving all right, she does not want to go back to her office, so even if she has an appointment she delays until – or beyond – the last possible moment.

For people like Rebecca, it is not so much a particular

circumstance that is scaring so much as the whole question of the unknown. Even when that includes familiar elements like routine meetings or going into their own offices, there are still random possibilities to make them feel uncomfortable. They feel insecure because they can never know, in complete detail, in advance, what the day will bring and what challenges they will be subject to. They fear to be caught out, because they do not feel that they are personally responsible for what success they seem to have achieved. They see luck as responsible; therefore fate can take away the benefits it has bestowed. So they feel that they have 'got away with it' so far. But they also do not believe their good fortune can last for ever; hence they fear the unknown circumstances that will unmask them . . . and seek to put off the moment of truth as long as possible.

That frame of mind is the result of an embattled self, where the public world in all its manifestations seems threatening. Its logic is that if you feel you have no control over your circumstances, then any change threatens your ability to cope. It is an attitude which overestimates the dangers of change and the difficulties involved in changing, because it derives from a sense of having very little power over circumstances. Change is seen as an external force, not as something which the self initiates and controls.

For all their apparent confidence and ability and despite their achievements, women like Rebecca can feel hopelessly at the mercy of every event; they therefore prolong as far as possible circumstances in which they are safe, because they feel they will be tested to the limits of their limited ability by even very small changes. They are exemplars of what Christopher Lasch has called 'the minimal self' – his notion of an embattled selfhood with few resources, reduced to this condition by the depredations of a mass consumer society which has eroded people's confidence in their own judgement and abilities by setting up expert opinion in their place and at the same time increasing the sense of danger to the self in a competitive and apocalyptic social order.[8]

Rebecca does not admit, possibly even to herself, that she feels insecure, untalented and unconfident; she does admit to feeling undervalued and unsupported at work. But her behaviour suggests that she is anxious and feels she is struggling more to survive than to succeed.

In the mood

Shirley used to like painting and drawing. She thought of going to art college after school, but instead went into secretarial work. She did not like it much because it was second-best and she was always half-thinking of trying for another sort of occupation, although she was not sure enough about what she wanted to do to take any training.

Her friends and family tried to encourage her; one suggestion was that she should try to put together a portfolio of drawings to see if she could get work. Shirley seemed enthusiastic about the idea, but did very little drawing. When friends and family asked, she excused herself from work on the grounds that she was not in the mood for it.

Shirley did not really feel entitled to draw because she had not been to art college and she felt it would show in her work. She rightly sensed that this would be a very competitive field, and felt that to justify trying to get work without professional qualifications she would have to be able to produce art of unparalleled brilliance. But she was so daunted by this thought that she could not even think of subjects to draw. She could not start; therefore she could not practise and overcome the deficiencies she recognized in her drawing style.

The fact that she phrased it as 'not being in the mood' suggested that she felt there had to be certain exterior circumstances to enable her to begin work. Everything had to be just right, because she felt that what she drew had to be perfect; but she knew this was impossible and that she would inevitably fail. Therefore, because things were never 'just right', she never started.

This sort of thinking is only an exaggeration of the way some people have to have everything perfectly tidy before they can begin work. The critical difference is that where the one is a precondition for work, the other prevents it.

Under scrutiny

In part this is a superstitious behaviour, for it is founded in a sense that by arranging conditions a desired outcome can be attained, despite the fact that the two are not apparently causally related – like conducting a ceremony for rain in a drought. The fact that Shirley treats a matter of volition as a question of destiny or luck, waiting for a propitious occasion to begin an important task like putting together a portfolio of drawings, shows how little control she feels she has over her own life.

Studies of superstition generally find that women are more prone to it than men, which is unsurprising since women feel that luck plays a bigger part than ability in their successes. The only field in which men are as superstitious as women is in sports, where clearly luck does play a major role, and sports players' superstitions often revolve around re-creating circumstances in which they were previously successful – by always taking the same route, always following the same routine or wearing a lucky piece of clothing.[9]

Such behaviour may work by putting the players into the same frame of mind as when they were last successful. Studies of memory and attention show that people recall information better in the circumstances in which they learned it ('state dependence'), so players are probably well advised to psyche themselves up for an event by imaginatively re-creating successes from the past. But the distinction between state dependence and magical thinking blurs in everyday life.

Playing the part by presenting the appropriate image is a case in point. Power-dressing, for example, operates at many levels; a superstitious belief in the efficacy of powerful clothing may be one. A woman may feel that she puts on authority with her business suit.

Performance is a growing element in many areas of life. It implies an audience, but it is a concept which extends beyond the conventional performance occupations – sports, acting and political debate, for instance – to other jobs which at first sight might seem to be judged solely on outcome or effectiveness and not at all on appearance.

As Erving Goffman demonstrated in the 1950s, people are increasingly conscious of themselves playing a role when they are doing a job. They identify with and display the recognizable attributes of the task or occupation. Goffman suggests that this is true even, for instance, when a plumber is working for someone who cannot judge his or her competence in detail – he or she varies the performance if another person is watching; this element of acting in a job also applies to team efforts.[10]

The sense people have of being scrutinized increases self-awareness. The idea that you are being watched by other people while you are engaged in a performance – whether of a job of work or a social function like going out shopping – means that you are less absorbed in what you are doing and more aware of how you seem. It brings real activities closer to fantasy activities and disposes us to judge our performance from an exterior point of view and hence to think of extrinsic factors, like success.

But this increasing self-awareness in public activities as commonplace as routine work means that the type of self-consciousness engendered by femininity is now becoming a factor in the lives of men too, reducing women's disadvantage in the public world.

Fear of success

The cult of success venerates achievement and abhors failure. Among women, however, there are signs of a third factor complicating attitudes to success and failure. As well as fearing failure for substantive reasons – like calculating that it is a more likely outcome than success and feeling that achievement is due more to luck than to ability – there is evidence that women also fear success. That, at least, is the popular phraseology for a theory which is rather more sophisticated than the name suggests.

In the late 1960s, Matina Horner found that women used negative images to describe a woman being successful (coming top of her examination lists).[11] She suggested that they saw success as entailing certain social costs because it contradicts conventional constructs of a feminine role. Specifically, the women students Horner surveyed seemed anxious that women who came top of examination lists were likely to become unpopular, both generally and with their boyfriends. She pointed out that such imagery was not necessarily the result of pathological fantasies but arguably had a perfectly real basis. High-achieving women do constitute a threat and an anomaly in an order where women are subordinate.

The motivation to avoid success has been attributed to women showing a noticeable pattern of underachievement and dissatisfaction, and is termed 'work inhibition'.[12]

Adrienne Applegarth, a psychoanalyst who studied work-inhibited women, characterized them as pulling out of a challenge before the moment of truth; for instance they applied to prestigious universities but then withdrew their applications; they failed to finish papers and dissertations, or just did not sit their exams: 'Most often the action seemed to them to be motivated by a sudden and puzzling loss of interest in what had seemed up till then to be a most engrossing pursuit.'[13] Typically this interest which had so mysteriously evaporated was inspired more by the desire for success itself than the wish to succeed at a specific job or task: what they wanted was 'an illustrious career, being admired, etc.' rather than to exercise a particular ability or skill.

These women believed more in innate talent than in acquired skills. They therefore interpreted difficulties with work as evidence of a basic and irremediable defect in themselves and not as something which could be overcome by perseverance, training or help. They saw themselves as flawed.

At the same time they resented the setbacks they suffered and responded to them with rage and a sense of injustice. Since they believed there was no practical remedy, they appealed to the agency of fate, or to someone else to intervene on their behalf, or they looked for tricks – in the sense of employing some sympathetic magic – to make their difficulties disappear.

The women exhibiting the work-inhibition syndrome came from a wide variety of backgrounds. One was the only child of a single-parent mother who idolized her daughter, who 'was never able to carry any project past the point to which unpractised talent would take her' because having to develop a skill meant that her talent was imperfect. Other sufferers had mothers who expected nothing of their daughters and who, if they noticed their daughters' abilities at all, derided them. Where one sort of mother needed to feel she had produced a perfect being, the other perceived herself as defective and incapable of producing anything not similarly flawed.

One typical patient came from a family which expected her to achieve very little; she had grown up very attached to her family and then became powerfully attached to a man, because she saw herself as intrinsically worthless and felt she needed other people in order to function. Because of this low self-esteem, she could not cope with any problems at work.

Another problematic family background proved to be that in which the child was the tool for the mother's frustrated ambitions. Traditionally this has been seen as a problem for sons, since they were the ones to whom the achievement option was more obviously available, but it seems that gifted daughters can play a similar role; they may refuse to use their talents later as a means of both individuating themselves from and having revenge on their mothers.

Lack of confidence was a serious obstacle for many women. Some felt it so strongly that they expressed it as a physical problem (as psychosomatic symptoms can be a manifestation of ambivalence). They complained that they felt they had something missing, and specifically that they lacked certain intellectual abilities possessed by men: 'No matter what success they achieve academically or at work, they tend to think of themselves as having fooled people or gained their position through some fraudulent means.' This misgiving was noted among women managers from a range of industries in the UK by Judi Marshall, a lecturer and author on women managers, who found it was associated with feeling that women had to use feminine wiles to get things done at work.[14]

These feelings are not always inhibiting. Sometimes they act as an incentive, but the women motivated by them often share with those inhibited by them a sense of fraudulence or illegitimacy. Just as among men ambivalence towards success is often centred around a guilty feeling that competitiveness is destructive, so some women also feel this way.

The psychoanalytic view sees work inhibition in women

as often accompanied by a strong sense of deprivation and injury. Applegarth represents women in this syndrome as contemptuous of other women but admiring men, though often this admiration is masked by anger and hostility, signalled by disparaging things with masculine connotations like sport and cars. Like women who overvalue love,[15] work-inhibited women overvalue men enormously and imagine that they do not suffer difficulties and uncertainties like their own.

The interpretation of work inhibition in women is in line with the thinking on achievement motivation. Applegarth takes Horner's point about the masculine connotations for success which threaten femininity (a social, not a genetic trait). Some women had difficulty in learning because they were preoccupied with the threat not just of ultimate failure but of making any mistake, so they avoided any circumstance in which they might make fools of themselves. Impelled by unrealistically high expectations and ambitions, they were at the same time full of bitter self-reproach for their failure.

In trying to help women suffering from work inhibition Applegarth found, as earlier psychoanalysts had noted of hysterics, that they resented her efforts. She thought they preferred the hope of redress to giving up their sense of injustice, but she did recognize that there are substantial grounds for this. Their feelings are not imaginary but are heavily reinforced in a world where their efforts and abilities are, one way or another, more likely to be disparaged than recognized. And, overvaluing achievement as they do, they are more sensitive to criticism.

So the work-inhibition syndrome is an exaggeration of the commoner lack of confidence women report. It is an extreme example of how a sense of invalidity or anomalousness in the public world manifests itself in individual lives.

Another writer on this subject, David W. Krueger,

broadens fear of success to a wider range of circumstances than paid work.[16] He also sees it as affecting a wider range of women than those with the personality disorders Applegarth describes:

A fear of success – recoiling from what one is constantly striving for and values – seems paradoxical . . . None the less this fear is quite prevalent among contemporary women. Conflicts manifest themselves in social, career or familial arenas to preclude opportunity, creativity and achievement. As we witness more opportunity for women in roles formerly seen as the exclusive domain of men, there is also an unveiling of the issues which inhibit their striving.[17]

Although he does not deny exterior obstacles to women's success, he thinks women feel these less than the internal obstacles: 'The external restraints and pressures militating against achievement for women in general are secondary to the perception of these restrictions and their effect on character formation and self-definition.'[18]

He suggests that career success, which implies striving and independence, may be engendered via media images and work through the desire to conform to socially accepted standards and to win approval, quoting a professor at a women's college who found that while a generation before it had been the women who wanted to follow a career who sought advice, now it was those who wanted only to marry and have children who felt 'peculiar and vaguely unjustified'. Krueger, like Applegarth, also suggests that the frustrations of being blocked by indefinable internal as well as tangible external obstacles can produce psychosomatic symptoms or psychological problems within a marriage.

The cases of pathological work inhibition of which Applegarth writes and the more general fear of success which Krueger describes both illustrate these inner obstacles to achievement. They are parts of the continuum of experience which in ordinary life appear also as lack of confidence and procrastination or displacement activities.

As women's magazines often recognize, many would join the demand voiced by the woman in the anecdote at the beginning of this chapter for a simple route to guaranteed success. Magazines are among the media from which women derive the ideology of success; their careers coverage tends to be fairly upbeat, focusing on opportunities and routes to the top, illustrated with plenty of human interest from women who have achieved success in various fields, this serves two purposes. On the one hand it is strongly supportive of women's aspirations and buoys up their confidence in their abilities to get to the top. On the other hand it emphasizes the glamour of success and stresses the role of luck and individual talent rather than the mundane realities of career development; this reinforces the gulf between fantasy and reality.

A writer for *Cosmopolitan* interviewed the editor of a journal for women managers about what jobs there would be for women in the 1990s. The point he was pursuing was really the same one raised by the woman at the meeting on success: What is the formula for success? Which jobs will offer women success in the 1990s? Which jobs will carry high salaries and high status, and can women get them?

But the trick is not to locate the high salaries and wide opportunities, but to decide what you want to do. An interest in success *per se* is self-defeating for two reasons: first, it does not provide its own means for realization; secondly, it can too easily assume a disproportionate importance which inhibits practical achievement. At this juncture fear of success or work inhibition can set in.

One of the motives for the generalized interest in being successful, detached from specific roles and activities, is that it offers what seems like a complete role. To women who feel uncertain it promises to eradicate uncertainty by supplying a sense of self constructed out of other people's high regard. The next chapter shows how this lack of confidence affects their decisions about their careers, in the context of initiatives to supply the confidence women need.

The kernel of the question about women and success in the future is not really whether there will be an increase in job opportunities but whether there will be an increase in the number of women who can grasp them. So, as Dale Spender's response to Melissa Benn showed, the question: 'How can I be successful?' has to be answered with: 'What's stopping you?'

7

Confidence Tricks

Confidence is a crucial factor in success and is increasingly valued in a public culture where at work, in politics, in the media and in society people are judged according to the way they present themselves. The era of the reclusive tycoon is past; high profile is rapidly becoming as important in the corporation as it has always been in politics or in acting.[1]

As we have seen, self-presentation, the construction and management of an image, is crucially important now in the public realm. It is an area in which feminine conditioning gives women something of a lead, for they create and maintain the images other people hold of them in many complex and subtle ways besides the use of cosmetics and clothing.

But the problems of work inhibition and fear of success show that for many women the barrier to achievement is the fact that they idealize and overvalue success, making it remote and unattainable, because their self-esteem is so low.

So the advantage of being able to project an image and style is cancelled out by lack of self-esteem. Indeed, in some senses women's facility in shaping and maintaining the simulacrum of confidence worsens the situation: it masks their difficulties from the outside world and may also confuse the issues for women themselves by making them feel at a distance from their real lack of confidence.

It ensures that these problems are felt to be private and individual rather than part of a general social condition, and therefore an embarrassment to be further disguised.

This, however well masked, is a chronic condition for many women. And lack of confidence cannot be remedied simply by achievement, for it afflicts successful women just as much as those who are so overawed by the idea of success that they dare not even try it themselves. Successful women's confidence is tested more than that of those who remain secure in obscurity, for women who have achieved some eminence are often also isolated in a competitive environment.

In training

Ruth Poppleton runs courses for women doing well in their careers; she also leads courses to help women get into management. She is interested in their career development and the difficulties they encounter in fulfilling their potential. She thinks it is important to see these problems as not only to do with work: 'I run another course called A Women's Development course; and that's about trying to help women to improve their effectiveness at work. Although it's work-focused, it really becomes a life skills and family focus.'

The women she sees on her career-development courses range from secretaries to solicitors; from clerical officers to tax inspectors; but although there are differences between women in different sorts of jobs, as there are in individual personalities, they all have something in common:

Some women from the Women in Senior Posts course are quite clear about their careers. They're more used to examining themselves and their lives and making plans, while a lot of the women on courses for women in lower-level jobs in local authorities are more or less stuck ... and have never thought they might be capable of anything else ...

There's never any problem about finding things that everybody's got in common to talk about . . . things like confidence and dealing with criticism come up very strongly. Course participants find that a very inhibiting factor in their own work and compare themselves with their male colleagues, who are quite impervious to criticism. A lot of that is self-image; that usually comes up: how can we come over, how can we present ourselves more effectively?

This point is corroborated by Jane Conniff, whose courses help women already in management and women manual workers who want to gain supervisory and management positions. She has also participated in two groups for women managers and professionals to look at issues in their own working lives, one of which is a small group for very senior women.

She too identifies lack of confidence as a crucial barrier to women taking the first steps in career development:

They say 'I could be a cleaner'; they never think: 'I could run a cleaning company.' Women tend to think at a low level . . . That is a first indicator of the sort of lack of confidence and expectation. The next thing is, everybody has difficulty saying 'No' to a male colleague or superior . . .

There's another area where I've picked up women feeling their confidence is really chipped away at: we ran a pilot course specially for women managers, and one of the things a lot of women said was that they were always being tripped up by their male colleagues and that women had to perform that much better than men in the same position, and so their confidence was always being knocked, or always in question. It was really quite unpleasant – some of the stories were really quite tense-making; you could see how the stress was being formed by male colleagues resenting their female counterparts. The men would typically comment: 'You're not doing that the right way, you should do this' when in fact they were doing a perfectly good job.

One senior woman was given no assistance at all; she was promoted from quite a low grade to a high management position responsible for 450 people and a department with very high service delivery – and no one gave her any training. It never occurred to them. And she floundered for six months; she did her best and she's a very talented woman, but no one dreamed of giving her any management training. At the end of six months she went and demanded training.

Not all women are in the same position in the public world, but even for those with authority and power uncertainties and difficulties remain.

Sarajane Harris-Richard, one of the new breed of civil servants – not a lifetime administrator but an entrant from the business world – is herself very successful, competitive, competent and confident, but remains sensitive to the issues of confidence to which women are vulnerable. She describes herself as:

On the heavy end of export promotions – chemical plants, steel plants, power plants, that sort of stuff. We are trying to make the system a bit more entrepreneurial. Not a conventional civil service job.

She is a practising believer in the value of management training, convinced both by the results it has produced in her staff and from her own experience. She sent a woman member of her staff, whom she had inherited with the comment that she was 'useless', on a women's management development course and finds she is now much more able to work on her own initiative because she is more confident of her own abilities. She herself attended a Henley Management Centre course on a scholarship for women and felt she benefited greatly:

What happened to me at Henley was that, in a group of people who were used to dealing in any sort of senior management position at all, I established myself as arguably the lead figure, but certainly as one of two in the syndicate in the ten-week period. And I thought: 'Well, if I can do that, I can do anything.' It's slightly phoney, but it's the sort of thing you hug to yourself.

And I think that that's one of the things that good management training can do for women, because it places them in an environment where you can take risks without the prospects of long-term repercussions.

Career planning

Perhaps surprisingly, for all her competitiveness, drive and achievements, Sarajane Harris-Richard did not enter upon her career with a clear plan before her:

It was 1965, when jobs just fell off trees. I had no vocational drive at all. I got myself a job as a programmer at ICL through the university recruitment round, which I made a hash of. I'd gone in for all the Unilevers and Shells and all that kind of stuff and I guess I didn't want to do it. Then I went off to America and hung around for a while. I wrote ICL a letter saying I wasn't going to turn up on the first of October after all. Then I did this and that, and it got to the point where I was going to have to start tangling with American bureaucracy and get a proper job or go home, and I decided to go home. So I fetched up in England at the end of November with absolutely no job at all. The CBI was the first advertised job that looked remotely suitable so I answered it and they offered me the job. It was economic research assistant. I had a PPE degree with an economics specialization. I had no desire to do this at all; I simply wanted a pay packet and I thought: this'll suit me while I look for something better to do. And I stayed for seven years.

She ended up setting up the CBI's Brussels office before joining the civil service, where she is now an Assistant Secretary, a grade in which only five per cent are women.

This lack of 'vocational drive' is something on which Ruth Poppleton comments: 'What I perceive generally is that more women drift around, particularly at the beginning of their careers. A lot of women just don't quite know where they're going.' She thinks that the trouble many women have in assessing their abilities and planning their careers is associated with women's habitual altruism.

This value of the private world is invalid in the public world:

A lot of them do see planning as a bit cold and calculating and almost as if they're not entitled because of this thing of always putting themselves second, putting other people first.

Women are probably more frightened of change than men. Maybe women come to believe that it's other people who can make plans, but not them: that women's role is to encourage other people's development but not to look after their own.

I think an awful lot of us believe that we're lumbered at the age of twenty-one, when we're grown up, and we don't expect a change and that somehow it's all set out for us. And I believe in quite the opposite: that it's infinitely possible to change.

Wanting to be discovered

Women's irresolution and lack of vocational clarity are to do with an image of self which is inconsistent, with different private and public selves and uncertainty about how to integrate the two ways of being.

Ruth Poppleton relates the way some women sabotage their own chances to the desire many share of wanting to be discovered: to be offered the job they want rather than having to apply for it. In its purest, most extreme form this was the motivation that attracted so many young women and men to low-status jobs in Hollywood – they hoped to be spotted by a talent scout, a casting director or a film director. In everyday life, the same sort of motivation is at work:

There's the question of a lot of women obviously being competent and having a lot to offer and yet perhaps being too scared to apply for senior posts, or not assessing their capabilities really very well; having some idea that they could do an advertised job but not really having got it together to actually sum up their situation and do something about it. For instance, a woman who is competent, she would like to be promoted – she has a particular job in mind – and yet she doesn't seem to be capable at the moment of putting herself over in any way that would lead to her being considered seriously for that job. She is the sort of woman who gets her head down, gets on with her job, does a very competent job, and it's a kind of waiting-to-be-recognized syndrome. She expects that other people will appreciate her work and that other people will perhaps pick her up. She feels bitter. But she presents herself as a timid little mouse, frankly, and an irritable timid little mouse. I think she sees herself as put upon, as not being recognized, as sort of a bit pathetic because she hasn't achieved the same things as her husband. She thinks he's senior; he's always had a very clear idea about his career and he's achieved what he wanted to achieve, but she has not achieved what she wanted to achieve.

This attitude stems from feeling invalid and illegitimate. Public – hence 'objective' – recognition for the individual woman contradicts her personal self-doubt and provides her with the authority she needs to act and to be, which the private world does not generate for her. In the obscurity and invisibility of the private world she is a non-entity, an unindividuated provider of others' needs. In the glare of publicity, however, she exists in a different and more valid way: if other people know she's there, then even if she does not believe it herself, she believes other people. The problem is that deriving reassurance from living and working as a reflection in other people's eyes means that when other people are not there, her sense of self disintegrates. But the sense of self which comes from others' approval is also untrustworthy because it refers only to the public persona, which the private self does not control and which does not correspond to the private inadequacy women feel; therefore the support supplied by the outside world is unsatisfactory.

This is why women hunger after success separately from desiring to fulfil particular abilities and exercise certain skills; and why, too, jobs which are particularly public displays – air hostess, photographic model, film actress – are highly valued by girl school leavers:[2]

Isn't that to do with really what we're brought up to want as girls and young women: to have men admiring us for our looks? For most girls and women still, I think, that's the number one priority, to find ourselves a suitable man. Maybe there's more emphasis on the legitimacy of women getting good jobs, but I still perceive that that comes second, whereas there's no question that with boys, they're still brought up to see work as central. I was struck in my own study of the under-representation of women in management that success at work and family life were seen as entirely compatible for men but they clearly aren't for women, because all the time women have conflicts. They tend either to find a real conflict between work and home life in terms of the pressures being too great, or the other side of that coin is that women who perhaps don't live in families feel that in some way they're deprived, and certainly they're not getting any support for their work role. Which of course they wouldn't anyway. They seem to lose out both ways.

Support groups

One source of exterior support is groups where a few women, not necessarily from the same employer, occupation or industry, meet to discuss their problems and to help each other. This is an idea originally developed for men managers and for men and women together from earlier management development ideas like T-groups and sensitivity training, but in the early 1980s women-only groups started. They also bear some relationship to the consciousness-raising groups of the early 1970s, which were a more political project aiming to help women solve the contradictions in their lives through feminism. But like all solutions, this has its drawbacks. From her experience running support groups for women artists, Liz Crossley calls it an 'underworld mentality'. She notes that they create a small culture of negativity in which failure is the norm and possibly even the goal, as a badge of group membership; hence the dynamic of the group insidiously counteracts its ostensible *raison d'être*. She saw one group ostracize a member whose career began to take off, not

out of simple jealousy but because although notionally
their aim was just such an outcome, in practice they felt it
was not part of their world and that the successful woman
was not one of them. Her success made them feel like
failures, when they had joined the group for the reassurance that they were average in their lack of pre-eminence.

But although women's need for support may sometimes
be counterproductive, it is clearly widespread enough to
dismiss any argument that it should not be remedied for
fear of indulging it. It is an expression of a real enough
disadvantage. Ruth Poppleton did some research into
women and support:

A very interesting thing that came out of my study was that the
men in very senior positions were married and so presumably
they had some sort of support at home, and probably in most
cases a lot of support at home, in terms of being looked after
physically and emotionally. But for the women in senior posts it
was exactly the opposite way round and virtually none of them
was married; they were either separated or single. They didn't
have that sort of support; they were on their own. And looking
at the sort of jobs that I deal with in the course for women in
senior posts, I cannot see how a woman who is expected to
make a significant contribution, in her home life, to another
person could possibly hold down a job like that.

Working mothers – torn in two

One of the great contemporary icons for the ambivalence
women feel towards the public world is the dilemma over
whether and when to have children. The issue is emblem-
atic not because it is not a real problem, since the
opportunity costs of taking some time off work to have a
baby and the attendant doubt among traditional-minded
employers about a mother's commitment to paid employment are considerable,[3] but because it concentrates the
issues underlying the opposition of home and work, public
and private realms.

First, the question of if and when to have children which

besets many women developing a career throws into relief the problems of time management and organization which are chief among the indicators of women's conflict between the public and private realms.

Again this is rooted in the real, intransigent problems inherent in a dual role, but it also has a psychological dimension. The decision to have children is often the focal issue for uncertainty about how to integrate the worlds of family and of work, which is how the difference between the public and the private realms is often conceptualized. Jane Conniff comments on a support group for very senior women managers of which she is a member:

Three of us in the group have children, the rest of them would obviously like children. But you don't have time if you're going to get on in a major employer organization, because you sell your soul to it. At the age of thirty-three they've suddenly realized that they've had a pretty bloody awful social life. They've been moved from pillar to post around the country. They've formed very few relationships at all. And if they don't look sharp, they're not going to get those children.

Similarly the conflict for many working mothers is reinforced by the guilt engendered by 1950s concepts of maternal deprivation, which suggested that children who are not the constant subject of their mothers' ministrations will suffer some psychological damage. In fact, there is evidence that children who are the chief object of their mothers' concern day after day are likely to suffer problems.[4]

But those anxieties are also an expression of conflict founded in the sense that the values of the two realms, public and private, are often in direct opposition and that to participate in one sphere reduces the degree to which participation in the other is possible, not because of the practical limitations of time and energy alone but also because of their different ethos. Ruth Poppleton also counsels women in this dilemma:

I'm reminded of at least one woman who has been at work for a number of years, really enjoys her work and is interested in promotion, but she also wants to have children. She'd previously seen it in terms of either/or, but through the course she was able to see there might be some middle way in which she could do both.

Making the decision to have a baby can be difficult for women who have focused on the public side of life. It means developing parts of their personalities that may have lain fallow for years, and it is particularly difficult for those who see the public and private worlds as mutually exclusive.

Closing the gap between the two realms and showing that they can be integrated in one person's life reduces the sense of an absolute either/or choice and enables women to hope that they can feel both more valid and established in the public realm and at the same time fulfilled in their private lives.

This is the position nine out of ten women reach now.[5] But although there are now fewer childless women than in earlier generations, the greater numbers who postpone having children reveal the dilemma, particularly for women interested in careers. In particular, women with higher educational qualifications and women in social classes I and II (covering couples and families in which the men are in management, professional and executive jobs) are having babies later. Their average age when they first give birth is twenty-eight, four years older than women in classes IV and V, whose partners work in semi-skilled or unskilled jobs. Women past child-bearing age (whose families were therefore completed) who had O-level and above qualifications had fewer children than the less qualified, which also suggests that more of the more

educated women have children later than the less educated. Similarly by the age of twenty-five, whereas seven
in ten women with few educational qualifications had
children, exactly the same number of their highly qualified
sisters had none.[6]

Economic factors play a big role in the decision about
when to have a child, but they are not the only determi-
nants. They are, however, easier to articulate and so to
draw a conclusion over than the less coherent problems of
being pulled between public success and private satisfaction. The question for women who want a rewarding
working life as well as a fulfilling family life is not just at
what point they can afford to have a baby but at what
point they can afford the childcare provision which in the
UK, unlike neighbouring countries, is not a state concern.

Reliable and satisfactory childcare arrangements are
important for a woman who hopes to continue with
rewarding work after childbirth, but even though more
women are delaying having babies until they can hope to
pay for good childcare, one in three women who go back
to work after having a baby return to a much lower-level
job than they left, while of those who return to work on a
part-time basis nearly half find themselves in lower-level
jobs. Maternity leave, a statutory right for full-time
women employees who have been with one employer for
more than two years, is taken by only four per cent, but
half of all pregnant women are not in any case eligible for
it. One study found that more than one in four women
who did not return to their jobs after maternity leave said
it was because there was no job with suitable hours.[7]

In fact, a 1984 judgement from an Employment Appeal
Tribunal, the next recourse up from industrial tribunals,
found that employers must offer women returning from
maternity leave part-time work if they need it. But as with
so much equal opportunities and pay legislation, the
procedures are so complex that many women do not

consider taking legal action, even when they have a good case. Many lawyers are unsure about the law in these areas because they are not used to dealing with such cases. And even for those who know what the law can do for them and how to use it, the cost of taking a case is usually prohibitive, not only in money but also in time and perseverance.

The public remedy for this problem is to improve the law and to make sure women know their rights. But the UK government has a strong incentive to encourage women to be attached to family life and the home more than to work, not only because it can then offload the responsibilities for caring for children, the ill, infirm and elderly – assumed, particularly after the Second World War, by the welfare state – but also because as the proportion of elderly people in the population rises and the number of people of working age shrinks, the financial base for paying for pensions will be overburdened, so it becomes necessary to reduce the number of people who can claim full pension rights. Since pension rights are calculated on the basis of years in employment, and since many part-time workers, most of whom are women, are excluded from these rights, it is in the interests of state solvency in the next century to keep down the number of women to whom more than the basic old-age pension will be due by not facilitating women's re-entry to full-time work and by maintaining a status quo in which part-time workers are attractive to employers; they do not have to pay the same rates or offer the same benefits to part-timers, who are also not covered by employment protection legislation. If employers had to treat part-timers as they treat full-time workers, the difference between the two sorts of work would be eroded – indeed it is in some senses illusory, for there is in fact no definition of part-time work in the UK; it is a relative concept, largely determined by prevailing local employment conditions, although employment law distinguishes between three categories of people: those working fewer than eight hours a week, those working fewer than sixteen hours a week and those working over sixteen hours.

Childcare is not the only critical consideration when women have to choose between the public and the private realms. Among women between forty and sixty years old, one in five looks after a dependent adult. In one sense the ambivalence entailed by this sort of caring is less than in making the decision to have a baby, for it is determined by uncontrollable circumstances such as family members falling ill or becoming unable to live alone. But there are still choices to be made over how to meet the needs of adult and elderly dependants: many adult children agonize over consigning their parents to the care of strangers.

In all these different circumstances, the division that presents itself in women's lives is between the contradictory demands of home and work, which includes the difference between public and private modes of behaviour, and one of the factors involved in the solution reached by individual women is the degree to which they are committed to and fulfilled by their paid employment. Their uncertainties in this respect complicate the decision-making processes involved in having children or coping with dependent family members.

Work as helping others

One way of balancing the extreme lack of confidence shown in work inhibition is by having confidence in work itself, rather than principally in the individual's ability to do it. Belief that what one does is important to others confers a legitimacy which counteracts self-doubt. People whose work is directly involved with people, as many women's tends to be, can benefit from this.

Victoria Wood, for instance, although a solo performer using her own material, says she sees herself as a means for people to enjoy themselves; her role as entertainer is therefore legitimized by altruism, which provides a more acceptable motivation than egotism. Women work with most conviction when they are working not for their own private satisfaction and needs but because their work is important and helps others. This is partly because it is congruent with the selflessness built into femininity, but partly also because working in this way is much less self-conscious than perpetually referring to an interior configuration of talents which lacks standards and goals. Working for others counteracts the problems which lead to work inhibition. This is why so many women are in the caring professions and want to work with people.

Modesty forbids

Another common difficulty, related to the question of placing self centrally, is women's problem with assessing themselves positively. Ruth Poppleton designs her courses to remedy this:

It's very difficult for them to talk about strengths. It is really very common that, if a woman's asked to describe herself, she will produce far more negative comments than positive, and some women just really can't produce any positive adjectives to describe themselves. A number of women have to keep reassuring themselves that they do have positive aspects. A woman solicitor who's visibly really competent: it emerged that she really just could not believe that she had any good points. One of the things that we did was, all the other course members wrote little notes about her to say what they'd observed about her during the course of the weekend and thus provided some sort of tangible evidence that she could refer to when she was feeling useless and hopeless. And that's by no means uncommon.

I do find it among men, but more commonly that's to do with men who are going through a temporary period of professional uncertainty.

You do get some women who don't exhibit such self-doubt, but they're very much in the minority of women on management or career-development courses. Most women tend towards the lacking-in-confidence side.

As well as lacking initial confidence, women are more easily discouraged:

Some of them have put themselves forward for promotion but haven't got it and are feeling very discouraged and not knowing what to do next. And of course, with men, that wouldn't worry them. They'd just go on applying for jobs. But women, if they apply for one or two jobs and they don't get them, they tend to become discouraged.

Research into teachers' careers, for example, showed that when people applied for headships the men would put in umpteen applications, in some cases over a hundred, and they'd just keep pegging on. But with the women, they became discouraged after relatively few applications. Women probably see being turned down as a personal rejection.

Women are very often aware of their hypersensitivity to criticism. The problem is often: 'I know I'm oversensitive, and what can I do about it?' Or feeling angry with themselves for being oversensitive. Although there's an ambivalence there, because they also feel: 'Well, to hell with it: men are far too much the other way'; the feeling that men ought to be more aware of other people's feelings.

Learning from experience is still hard

Displacement activities and procrastination are two ways in which lack of self-confidence becomes work inhibition, and they are also areas in which training can help. Jane Conniff is aware that time management is an important issue not only at work but in private life too. She thinks women are devoted to meeting other people's demands at the expense of their own needs, and ironically she has first-hand experience of the difference between knowing something to be the case and acting on it: 'I teach time management all the time and don't adopt it myself.'

Ruth Poppleton confirms this problem among the

women she trains. Knowing the answer is not the same thing as putting it into practice:

I do think that women find it really very difficult, having prioritized their aims, to concentrate on the number one priority. Whether it's a sex difference I don't know, because after all, number one priority is often the most difficult to achieve.

There seems to be no stage of seniority at which women's problems suddenly vanish, but they are refined as careers develop. In the first stages of management training the issues are to do with general lack of confidence, which becomes more specific and particularized as a woman rises through the ranks. In response to this, an offshoot of support groups and networks has been created for women wanting to resolve career issues. The self-development group, taken up first particularly by public-sector managers, helps participants to integrate experience at work with the rest of their lives. Jane Conniff comments that for women managers in such groups it is as if the message from the world of work to them is:

'There you are in a management position, you've got the confidence and the responsibility: now you've got to cope with a lot of male colleagues who are tripping you up.'
    And in a support network for very senior women managers for people who are very high-powered – in jobs earning £40,000 a year, which is not peanuts – they have different problems again. One woman high income earner, they wouldn't give her the title that goes with that job when she got it – because you couldn't give it to a woman all at once. She could have the money, but she had to earn the title by proving herself. And then it's less embarrassing, of course, if you don't make it; you haven't actually got the executive title so it doesn't have to be removed.

The interior barriers to achievement can seem just as intractable as the stagnation of public remedies to inequality. They are less immediately identifiable than the exterior obstacles like sex discrimination and they do not yield hard data which, as we have noted, is often taken in the public realm as proof of existence.

There are real, exterior obstacles for women in the world of work and in other areas of public life. The inner difficulties reproduce and reinforce the public problems, both in their acute form as work inhibition or in the more widespread form of general lack of confidence in its different guises – from seeming to be productively occupied while at the same time sabotaging the outcome, to excluding the possibility of more rewarding work; from pursuing an image of success while disregarding the means of attaining it, to wanting to be discovered and refusing to plan a career.

All these are traits encouraged by the overvaluation of success and individualism in contemporary society, which also influences men. The reasons it affects women more than men concern the question of what the public world is, what it can offer women and what women must do to succeed in it.

8

In Public

Women have to try harder

'I meet a lot of women managers,' said Donald, who worked in the printing industry, 'and one thing I have noticed is the number of them who duck responsibility when things go wrong. They'll blame anybody rather than take it on themselves. But that's what you've got to do. Things do go wrong, but with women it's emotion, tears, where men just [he shrugs] and accept it. Water off a duck's back.'

'How many women managers do you think refuse to accept responsibility when things go wrong?'

'Over thirty per cent, I would estimate.'

'And are the women completely different in this from the men? Or do you find any men managers who don't want to take the blame?'

'Well, they're more used to management. They've been at it longer. They're more inclined just to shrug it off and not to care. I should say about thirty per cent refuse to take responsibility.'

'The same proportion as women managers?'

'Yes, I should think about the same.'

'Isn't that all right then?'

'No, because the women who won't take responsibility are letting the others down. Women have got to struggle hard to get there, and they've got to be better than the men. So the ones who won't take the responsibility when things go wrong, tears and everything, they're spoiling the others' chances.'

'But what about the same proportion of men who duck responsibility: aren't they spoiling it for other men?'

'No, because they don't have to be so good.'

'But women have to be better managers?'

'Yes, because work is men's prerogative.'

Women have to struggle harder than men for achievement and against residual, institutionalized obstacles as well as inner conflicts about leaving the traditionally feminine private sphere and entering the harsher environment of the public realm. For instance, even recruitment and promotion systems ostensibly based on objective and rational judgements, which would suggest that they preclude sex discrimination, can be biased in favour of men candidates.[1]

Nice work for women

Not all parts of the public world are uncongenial to women. As we saw in the last chapter, some jobs intrinsically fit what some women want and others fit in with the way women are socialized or with the demands of their private lives – caring for homes, people or animals or literary and artistic occupations. However, these tend to be low-paid jobs precisely because they are seen to be closer to (unpaid) private-realm activities.

In literary and artistic work, the traditional genteel occupations of middle-class women, two out of three writers and journalists are men, with an even higher proportion in management jobs; the more junior jobs – editorial assistant, magazine subeditor or, in broadcasting, production assistant or secretary – are predominantly female, while peripheral arts and literary jobs such as library and information work are two-thirds female.[2] These are jobs for women graduates, who are the majority of arts, literature and language graduates and forty-five per cent of social science graduates.[3] These are also the jobs with the dimmest career prospects, as the exact inversion in these careers shows: men take two-thirds of the creative jobs while two-thirds of the support services are provided by women.

This is reinforced in assessing the value of a degree, calculated on the difference between earnings lost as an undergraduate and increased earnings gained by having a degree, which shows that social science graduates on average earn eight to twelve per cent more than if they did not have degrees, with engineering and science graduates earning a little less. Arts graduates, however, lose out compared with what they would have got had they gone straight from school to work, taking into account the cost of tuition.[4]

Even graduate women's jobs are overall less well paid and have fewer career development prospects. In the arts, salaries are held down by the demand for the entry-level jobs and by the assumption that they do not constitute the only – or the major – source of income. It is both custom and practice in many commercial arts and literary jobs to work for more than one employer at once, since freelancing is a recognized activity even for full-time employees and career paths are less established than in other industries. This is often a better strategy than loyalty to a single employer, but it contributes to the fragmentation of labour interests in the industry.

Arty jobs
Freelancing also represents the ideology that attracts so many women to jobs in the arts: the promise of freedom and individuality. This is why they are often willing to overlook the low pay: they work for love more than for money. 'Women tend to define power as the ability to use their own talents and control their own lives,' according to two commentators on women as managers.[5]

Correspondingly, women are supposed to care for people for love rather than money, so a wage in that sort of work is considered a bonus for doing what comes naturally or what it is a woman's duty to do for others. Nursing, home help and cleaning are examples of jobs where the pay is low. The fact that the work can be arduous does not count because it looks like housework and however hard that may be, it is entirely unpaid.

So low pay and work as a labour of love obtain in both manual and non-manual work for women. Manual work is declining as Britain's manufacturing base shrinks: two and a half million jobs have been lost since the beginning of the 1970s, while over the same period the number of jobs in the service sector (which covers personal services like catering, cleaning and hairdressing as well as banking, government and business services) grew by 2.3 million. In 1971 one person in three worked in a manual job with little or no skill involved, but now half of all jobs are classified as non-manual, and manual work increasingly demands not only one skill but multiskilling.

Women have not suffered most from the decline in lower-level industrial skilled work but twice as many women as men work in the lower-level service occupations, in which the biggest group is clerical (2.5 million) and personal services like catering and cleaning (2 million). Part-time work is a major feature of employment in these industries, with half a million part-time cleaners, the same number of part-time shop assistants and three-quarters of a million part-timers working in catering, as school dinner ladies, waitresses, barmaids or cooks. Part-time work acounts for most of the jobs created since 1971, and most part-timers are women.

These figures compare with about three million jobs in the professions and management, including two hundred thousand jobs in literary, artistic and sports occupations, which include fast-growing categories like leisure centre

management. About thirty thousand people work as actors
and entertainers, about the same as the number of women
working in publishing, journalism, broadcasting and
writing.[6]

Where women work

So most women, like most men, are not working in
professional, managerial, executive or graduate occupations. Only three occupations account for seven in ten of
all women's jobs, a third of them office jobs, nearly a
quarter in catering, cleaning and hairdressing and thirteen
per cent in teaching, social work and health care. By
comparison, the three top employment categories for men
account for only four in ten of all men's jobs, showing
that opportunities for men are much wider.[7] Although sex
discrimination legislation has removed some barriers,
women working in predominantly male occupations
report high levels of harassment and discrimination[8] and
this is an effective deterrent to others. Women also claim
that the society of other women is an important factor in
job satisfaction.

In addition, even in predominantly women's occupations men occupy more of the top jobs, as managers and
executives. The opportunities for women to pursue a
career that parallels that of the self-made man going from
office boy to chief executive are limited. The few women
who start as secretaries and end up as directors are
generally in small or medium-sized companies and many
women on company boards are there because they married
into or inherited a position in the company – for instance
Lady Porter, the only woman on the board of the Tesco
supermarket chain, is the daughter of the founder, while
the winner of the 1986 Veuve Clicquot Businesswoman of
the Year Award worked alongside her electrical engineer
husband in building up Norfrost, the refrigeration equipment company. This is not to say that such women are

less able or deserving than other directors of their companies: it shows that there is a large unexploited pool of talented women without the family connections which may give them boardroom positions.

Only in the more rarefied, graduate professional, managerial, commercial literary and artistic occupations is the emphasis strongly on individual talent. This is what prompts people to sense a split between the public and the personal worlds and fosters the fears leading to the work-inhibition syndrome.

In lower-level jobs, people have to be less autonomous at work and have simple skills whose performance standards are much clearer than those of more self-determined roles. It is, for example, easier to show that a woman working on a production line is achieving the same output as a man than to argue that a softer managerial style is as effective as a traditional hierarchical, authoritarian one. (This is why it is even harder to remedy pay disparity for higher-level, more individuated roles than in routine jobs.[9])

Presentation is a less important issue in non-managerial, professional or individual jobs. Even where a smart appearance is important – for example in work as a sales assistant – this means a conventional appearance and does not involve projecting a persona to the extent demanded in higher-level occupations. One difference between higher- and lower-level occupations is in the sort of clothes appropriate to each. In lower-level occupations clothes serve a protective function, like overalls or safety wear, or constitute a uniform identifying the employee as a public servant. In higher-level occupations clothes show status. They reflect fashions: the quality of cut and cloth is important and so is use of colour. It is the clothing of higher-level occupations that is discussed in terms of power-dressing or dressing for success, and clothes or image consultants work exclusively for high-powered and highly paid men and women who recognize the importance of projecting the right image in supporting their status at work.

Work that fits less well

Although some jobs suit women even if they do not remunerate them well, others are less accommodating to their needs, demanding for instance a demonstration of commitment (often through working long hours), high qualifications or expertise acquired through experience. Typically, these are the sorts of jobs that do not fit in with the claims of family life. But the more insidious barriers to these jobs are not the practical difficulties of balancing different demands on time and attention but the perhaps subliminal discomfort of operating in an environment designed for and run by men. Sarajane Harris-Richard says:

You need to be competitive to be successful in a fast-stream civil service job. People drop out. I think they go through periods of self-questioning. But I honestly don't think that's confined to women.

In industry, even people who are not really particularly ambitious have to make a lot of commitment, in that their companies are not going to be able to function unless they do make that commitment.

These qualities – neither belonging to the private sphere nor fostered by femininity – can prove as solid a barrier as discriminatory attitudes. For instance, a seminal study of successful American women found that the major difference between the few women who gained board-level jobs and those who got no higher than middle or senior management was that the most successful group had taken stock of the relationship between work and the rest of their lives in their mid- to late thirties and had then integrated the feminine, personal characteristics which they had until then played down. The women who did not break through were those who conceived of the management role as a masculine one which would not admit anomalies like being a woman. They separated their work and personal lives, and their work lives came first. They did not think they had the right to adjust their jobs to allow themselves more personal freedom of expression. Ironically, their simple devotion did not bring the rewards they sought.

Adverse attitudes

Not only do women have to struggle with doubts about their own abilities, reinforced by the misgivings of men even as kindly and well-meaning as Donald; they also have to deal with the problem of women's attitudes to women. Women's attitudes to achievement are shaped by men's and the values of the male world, and women who absorb these can come to dismiss the idea that women have special needs.

'I don't think women really can ask for favours. We can't afford it,' comments Sarajane Harris-Richard, highlighting the problem of persuading commercial organizations that there is profit in promoting women. Significantly, the public sector was first to espouse the concept of equality, establishing equal opportunities policies, officers and training. The private sector, with its shorter time scales, need for quicker returns and more concrete arguments for investment than for social and ethical concerns, is slow to make use of the wasted human resources its women employees represent. But the different basis from which women operate does entitle them to ask for different conditions, and this is supported by the fact that conditions are changing.

Sarajane Harris-Richard recognizes that there are certain conditions, both personal and circumstantial, which have to be met in order to achieve success: 'One thing that's very alive and well in terms of being a success in the senior echelons of the civil service is the concept of having a patron.' A patron or mentor is someone in a senior position who develops and nurtures a junior's career.

Many employers think of themselves as particularly benevolent towards women: a campaign to ask about the position of women in different companies at their annual general meetings often elicited the response that the company was not discriminatory, and directors and chairmen often express interest in the position of women.[10] At the same time it is not their major concern and they are often unaware of the circumstances that do discriminate against women working for them, in practice even if not obviously.

Similarly, women engaged in carving out a career are not necessarily more able than men to put women's general interests ahead of their own particular interests, and often do not identify institutionalized barriers as serious obstacles to progress. This is partly because they have themselves overcome them, but partly also because they identify more with their role as managers or professionals than with women in other occupations and at different levels. This was illustrated when a group of women lawyers and other professionals working in the City set up the City Women's Network and encountered strong initial resistance from some of the women they asked to join, who were not only unconvinced that they needed a network but were not sure that they could afford to be seen to make a move towards what could be construed as a ghetto. They had to stress their normalcy in their jobs and disguise their differences from their male colleagues, even to the extent of disguising it from themselves. It was, ironically, because it was an all-female activity that its future members were suspicious, despite the preponderance of all-male organizations in the City.

Similarly, women managers and professionals have often shown that they are aware of the problems women

encounter in the workplace but feel personally exempt
from them, even if they have had first-hand experience of
sexual discrimination and harassment.[11]

Women do not form a coherent and homogeneous
interest group but are divided by role and occupation. So
the presence of some women in senior positions in
employer organizations – which might show the organization's lack of effective bad intentions rather than a
systematic approach to getting the best out of the women
they hire – does not mean that women's interests are
adequately represented or that they have the same mechanism for developing a career as men of the same age,
experience and qualifications.

Good practice
Some employers, particularly large organizations in the
public sector like national and local government, have
tried to improve women's working environment. Sarajane
Harris-Richard sees her organization as an example of
good employment practice:

Certainly it is pretty unusual for me to go to a civil service
meeting and be the only woman, while it is invariable in all my
meetings with the private sector. There are one or two exceptions in banks, but I've never been to a meeting with an
industrial company or a contractor where there was another
woman present, other than secretaries. And that is an enormous
difference. In my immediate area of work there are two women,
who are among the people I work with most frequently. On one
absolutely wonderful occasion we were talking about doing a
project jointly with a British company and a German company
in India; the Germans all came over with senior people. They
walked into my office to find that their interlocutors from Her
Majesty's Government were three women! I think to begin with
they weren't sure whether to take it seriously or not, but once
they saw we could deliver . . .

The civil service represents itself as a conscientious equal
opportunities employer, yet the distribution of women and

their rates of promotion compared with men's shows that good intentions have not bred strict equality. While the vast proportion of bottom-grade jobs are filled by women, there is not one woman at the top. In 1984 Anne Mueller attained the highest position currently held by a woman in the civil service when she was appointed Second Permanent Secretary in the personnel side of the organization – a traditionally female sphere. A review of how well equal opportunities functioned in the civil service found that women achieved only sixty-five per cent of men's promotion rates from Principal to Assistant Secretary. This review suggested that the civil service should appoint equality officers to establish that the principles of equal opportunity were put into practice, but although the recommendation was accepted, no new posts were created. The responsibility was merely tacked on to existing jobs.

There is a good deal of evidence to show that direct sex discrimination remains widespread. One study of women in traditionally male areas of work showed that half of those questioned had been sexually harassed at work and even more had been directly discriminated against: being told, for example, that their application for a promotion or a job had been rejected on sex grounds. Although this is illegal, none had taken the question either of harassment or of sex discrimination any further because they simply were not aware of the law, or did not know how to proceed, or because it seemed too difficult.[12]

In the first ten years of operation for the laws prohibiting sexual discrimination in pay or opportunities, fewer than 6,100 people applied to industrial tribunals and these included groups of women – up to forty – bringing one case against the same employer.[13] Of these, something less than half (about forty-five per cent) in fact went to tribunal, the rest being settled out of court. The outcomes for latter are unrecorded, but in only one in ten did the tribunal find in the individual's favour.[14]

Even for those few women who won cases, there remained the problem of enforcing the judgement in their favour. Also, in addition to the heavy odds against winning, the cost, time and effort involved were enormous. There are complex procedures governing applications to industrial tribunals and, so far from being a people's court, they not only require that forms are correctly completed and submitted within fixed time limits but the 'informal' hearing involves several hours of making the case, presenting the evidence and questioning witnesses; the chances of winning for people bringing a case to an industrial tribunal without an expert representative was slim indeed, but only £50 was available in legal aid – this bought approximately an hour and a half of a solicitor's time.

Finally, an Equal Opportunities Commission study found that many of the people sitting on industrial tribunal panels were not themselves expert in the law they were interpreting. The work of industrial tribunals concerns other aspects of employment protection law; knowledge of the Sex Discrimination and Equal Pay Acts is rare even in the legal profession, since it is not – by comparison, for instance, with conveyancing or family law – a major money earner. And even epoch-making cases like the first taken under the amended Equal Pay for Work of Equal Value legislation – in which Julie Hayward, a cook with Cammell Laird, won equal pay with a man in a comparable job – can be overturned at higher tribunals. In Julie Hayward's case the Employment Appeal Tribunal decided that she had benefits which made up for being paid less, and cancelled her equal earnings.

So the law does not provide real redress and even though attitudes among employers have shifted, reflecting social changes, discrimination is still a real obstacle to advancement.

Talent

Even highly successful women like Marianne are aware of
operating in some ways differently from men:

There seems to be a category of successful men who just relax
their way to the top, who are extremely able in terms of
achieving the objectives of whatever organization they work for.
They have a very relaxed, laid-back attitude, never actually seem
to be pushing, but the right things happen around them, they
get the early promotion, very quiet, very relaxed. Successful
women rarely, if ever, fall into this category.

This has been verified by psychologists who determined
experimentally that men and women alike interpret the
causes of achievement for men and women differently.
Women are perceived as achieving through conscientious
hard work while men are seen to rise by virtue of talent
and opportunity. These deserve reward, while effort is
disparaged as a poor substitute for innate ability. So when
men work hard, this augments their natural rights to
achievement and is seen as doubly deserving, but when
women work hard it is taken as further evidence of lack
of natural ability.[15]

These perceptions tie in with the work-inhibition syndrome and more broadly with the attitude discussed in
chapter six, which disposes people to feel that they should
not have to struggle to achieve a goal. Yet women, with
other disadvantaged groups like ethnic minorities and the
disabled, are struggling against real, systemic but hidden
obstacles, all the more difficult to cope with because they
are invisible and even denied by some women.

Under these conditions, women must make the best use
of the resources they have. Their better social skills,
particularly in observing other people and managing their
public personae, can be marshalled against discrimination,
although they do nothing to diminish internal inhibitions.

Playing up feminine characteristics might exacerbate the disadvantages, and relying on them has been construed as collaborating with the adverse attitudes of the public world at large. Women who are overtly feminine in public can look to other women like Uncle Toms.

But women can use charm and present positive images of themselves which do not exclude traits usually described as feminine, without losing their integrity. When they use these traditional routes for dealing with the public realm confidently and consciously, they are less vulnerable to being consigned to a conventionally feminine and marginal role than when they adopt such strategies unthinkingly. Using feminine traits for support depends on selecting those which are appropriate, and again it is crucial that these give the impression of a coherent and integrated persona. By these means women are defended from the isolated position of being conspicuously unfeminine in a masculine public realm. Feminine behaviour is still a social norm for women; hence unfeminine women are anomalous. Sarajane Harris-Richard recognizes the value of turning traditional restrictions to their best advantage: 'I'm tempted to think that women have some advantages in that area and that traditional female wiles and charm and so on can be quite useful and should be made use of. Why not get an advantage for once?'

Distinctions

It is feminists who have fought the campaign to reduce inequality between the sexes; they have always acknowledged the distinction between the public and private worlds, though they have tended to see it in terms of male/ female difference. The division between public and private experience, however, exists in everyone's life, though the effect of being brought up feminine is that personal values and private experiences are accorded more importance than public or objective issues.

The gender gap is still here, and in areas like pay may even be widening. But it is possible now to look at the public/private distinction without fudging the issue of sex differences in society because, marginalized as women's issues tend to be, their roles – and men's too – have changed over past decades.

The way the world views and treats women has been investigated and argued over in depth and at length by many people and from many points of view, far more than the way women see the world. The way women distinguish between public and private realm is just as important for its consequences on their achievement as the way the public realm distinguishes between men and women.

It has been quite clearly shown, were reference to common sense not proof enough, that women have not chosen relative poverty or deprivation but have had to accept it as a consequence of powerlessness in the public world and often as the price of fulfilment in the private world. An analysis of the poor shows that the biggest group is single old people, the majority of whom are women.[16] Single-parent families are also significantly represented among the poor, and most single parents are women.

First socialist and then feminist writings have looked at the public/private split as an essentially social and political issue, and to collective action as the appropriate remedy. Unfortunately this does not speak to personal experience, as it generally subordinates private solutions to social change, which has a much longer time frame.

The tradition of presenting the difference between private and public experience and the unfairness of public necessity bearing on private desires in the general truths of an 'objective' public-realm style does not concern itself with the details of individual cases, except as brief illustration.

Now, however, individual experience and attitudes can

be put first without undermining the case for social change, partly because the private realm – growing in importance, like the private sector – is taking over much that was formerly public, but mainly because the socialist and feminist vanguard has established that there are real inequalities. The opposition between work and the family, self and society, the individual and the state had to be clearly established before an investigation of ambivalence to the public realm could be undertaken, otherwise this ambivalence would have been read as a sign of women's unfitness for public roles. Recognizing the contradictions in personal experience between public and private is not a justification for driving the ambivalent out of public roles but clarifies how the two realms can more comfortably coexist in individual experience, and in particular how otherwise paralysing doubt can be dealt with.

Men's preference for personal fulfilment

One index of the social change that enables women's ambivalence to the public world to be considered is the different attitudes men now take to their positions in relation to women.[17] They seem increasingly prepared to reconsider stereotypes and are less willing to sacrifice themselves to their careers and more interested in pursuing personal interests and responsibilities: their role as parents, for example. Melvyn Bragg, who as a novelist, television producer and presenter and arts critic has not lacked public success, speaks for a generation of men for whom it is not an imperative:

A lot of men, like myself, decided after a certain point not to have a career. I don't want a ladder career. I want to do what I'm doing and write books. Now, a lot of men of my age decided that about middle age; so we swerve away from a conventional career path in a different way to women, who swerve away when they have children. It's much more clearly defined and much more obvious and much more definite for women. But there is a similarity.

A lot of guys I know here and at the BBC, who are film directors, television directors, want to stay doing that. They don't want to become head of a group, then head of a department, then head of a channel.

Anthony Clare, a professor of psychiatry who as a writer and broadcaster has investigated the price paid for success in personal lives, corroborates this view of changing attitudes:

I know people who've backed away from the ultimate in success – there are many more men who are doing that now, it seems to me; who say: 'It's not worth it.' I am interested in the extent to which people are beginning to say: 'There are other values.'

Some men are prepared to refuse promotion, opt for job-sharing and try to negotiate parental leave.[18] Roy Close, when director-general of the British Institute of Management, commented that surveys by the organization showed that senior managers were sometimes at a loss to know how to motivate and deal with younger managers who were not interested in promotion.

Out of six positive 'candidates' for my job (should I die or leave) not one of them would actually take the job if a final offer was made. 'They say the price is too high to pay,' commented one male manager of the rising managerial generation.[19]

This phenomenon is reflected in a growing literature on managing the 'new managers' or 'new leaders', to whom the attractions of conventional rewards like salary rises and promotions are subordinate to criteria like personal satisfaction and freedom.[20]

Interestingly, this reluctance was identified earlier among women than among men. A 1980 study of why more women did not go into management found that one of the reasons – apart from lack of opportunity – was that they had rejected the idea because they wanted to remain doing the work that made them happy: this was, for instance, articulated particularly by women in television, who said they preferred to retain creative jobs rather than move into management, which they saw as a mainly administrative function.[21]

Change

Another area of change is in concepts of what is appropriate for women, and in the larger concept of changing sex roles and stereotypes.

There is a difference between sex and gender, between the sex to which most people are assigned from birth and retain throughout their lives and the learned attributes of femininity and masculinity they acquire as they grow up; these concepts of masculine and feminine are not immutable. Gender is differently defined not only in different cultures, but in the same culture at different times. Compare, for instance, the idea of femininity portrayed variously by Rubens, Titian or Renoir with the women in paintings by Modigliani, Picasso or Julian Schnabel; compare the lip-rings and scarifications some contemporary peoples consider enhance femininity with the partly shaven heads and electric cosmetic colourways of European sub-culture women, and contrast them with the discreet charm of bourgeois make-up on older contemporary urban women.

Just as the presentation of femininity in public changes with time and place, so do attitudes about women and their appropriate roles. Large-scale opinion polls reveal differences in attitudes to men and women according to age group, which show both how attitudes change generally and specifically how feminist ideas filter out into a wider population.[22]

Psychologists testing how far people subscribe to sex stereotypes have found evidence that these weakened their hold in the 1970s,[23] while in a survey of European men and women's attitudes to each other, themselves and life, only the over-sixties' attitudes corresponded with traditional stereotypes of women and women's roles.[24] Countries in the survey varied in how traditionally they viewed women, with attitudes in Britain more polarized than in countries like Greece and Denmark, where attitudes were distributed in a broader way; or in Belgium, Ireland and Luxembourg, where the traditional view of women as housewives and mothers predominated. This survey also indicated that a very large proportion of women would preface a comment with: 'I'm not a feminist, but . . .' and then go on to make a feminist point.

Feminism

Naming is an important tool in changing attitudes and thus in changing society. Without a name, an issue cannot be readily identified or effectively acted upon. Feminists' concern with enshrining the principle of equality in language, to point up and push out sexist language and counter sexism, has not been an obsessional displacement of real objectives but a valid point of departure. The women's-movement arguments about whether the person who controls a debate was a chair, a chairperson, a chairwoman or a chairman were no mere sidetrack. Changing the language was a revolutionary project because it entailed changing the way people thought: whenever 'men' is used to mean 'men and women', women are effectively obscured. In such innocuous ways language upholds the principle that women are by definition also-rans; men are frontrunners.

Obscuring women linguistically and in the public world means that token women are correspondingly conspicuous. In their turn, because they command disproportionate attention, they obscure the lack of other women around them. A Tory backbencher, Anthony Marlowe, illustrated this when he commented that no woman could claim that discrimination holds women back from achievement since we now have a woman prime minister, forgetting that one swallow does not make a summer.[25]

Taking care not to subsume women under headings primarily denoting men and identifying them separately is an effective means of making women visible, as is promotion to positions of eminence. But women's lack of visible achievement is not only attributable to terminological inexactitude. It also reflects the fact that the heights of public achievement are commanded almost exclusively by men.[26]

The fact that the public world is strongly masculine is recognized in its language – both in the magisterial, impersonal, objective style appropriate to it (exemplified, for instance, in official documents and reports rather than extempore political speeches, where personal values make themselves more felt) and in the use of male norms, like the common default to the pronoun 'he'. In itself this is a trivial point, but it signifies a habit of mind which has serious consequences for women's aspirations. An Equal Opportunities Commission booklet on job evaluation schemes, which are used to set rates of pay and are therefore crucial to equal pay claims, gives a list of contrasting names for similar sorts of work: men are described as assistant managers, women as managers' assistants; men are technicians while women are operators; men are salesmen but women are shop assistants.[27]

Women at work

The notion that women going out to work is a new phenomenon is both incorrect and pernicious because it suggests that the lack of parity between the sexes in the labour force is due to women's recent arrival in substantial numbers and will be redressed in time. In fact, despite the sudden increase in the numbers of women going out to work, the number of those climbing up through the ranks or otherwise gaining eminence is declining.

The argument that the effect of being newcomers will soon wear off is advanced, for instance, in management education, where it is sometimes claimed that the growth of women in management schools, from three per cent when they started in the 1960s to fifty per cent now, is an indication of the fact that in future management will consist of men and women in equal proportion. Against that, however, there is evidence that within management women work in specializations and very few occupy top jobs, even in organizations with a reasonable proportion of women at lower management levels. It is also widely claimed that 'feminine' values are increasingly recognized and rewarded in managers: however, as Judi Marshall points out in her book on British women managers, feminine values and attitudes are still not considered consonant with managerial success.

Dr Susan Vinnicombe of the Cranfield School of Management found that women managers in Britain did indeed have a different approach to work from men. Using five personality types, she noted that over half of men managers can be described as 'traditionalists': dependable, realistic, practical and methodical: 'Their priority is to reach a decision . . . [they like] clarity and order, dislike ambiguity and are concerned with resolving issues.'

Only a quarter of women managers are traditionalists. Whereas the majority of men follow one managerial style, women are more evenly spread across different ways of managing people and problems, but three to four times as many women as men managers are 'visionaries' and 'catalysts'. 'Visionaries' are logical and rational, intellectual and creative, excellent decision-makers, but may be insensitive to others. They 'are supposed to be the "natural" strategic managers', while 'catalysts' are strong in personal charisma, excel in working with people and are comfortable in unstructured, complicated situations.[28]

Even more telling evidence that women's position is declining, in contrast to the claims that it is improving, is the fact that in the mid-1980s the Institute of Directors reported a fall in the number of women managers over the past decade, from nearly ten per cent to six per cent.

Earnings are another means of showing the disparity between men and women. In 1970 women's average hourly earnings as a proportion of men's stood at 63 per cent. Between 1975 – when the Equal Pay Act was introduced – and 1979 their proportional earnings rose from 72 to 75 per cent, but since then they have dropped back and currently stand at 74 per cent. The comparison of weekly earnings shows a bigger disparity, since women do less overtime: in 1970 women full-time employees earned an average of 54.5 per cent of men's weekly earnings, which had risen to 61.5 per cent by 1975 and peaked in 1981 at 66.7 per cent. Subsequently it also slid back and now stands at 64 per cent.

Women's earnings also peak earlier than men's, and consequently at a lower level. Where men's pay rises over their working lives to peak for non-manual workers in their forties, women full-time employees, who peak at thirty, average in their forties just over half of what their male colleagues get. Women come nearest to earnings parity with men as full-time manual workers under eighteen, when they are paid at a rate of 93.6 per cent of men's average weekly earnings. Between the ages of eighteen and fifty-nine, women's earnings steadily decrease as a proportion of men's.[29]

The culture of professionalism

That corner of the public world which is for ever professional and managerial does not offer much room for women. A survey of UK men managers' careers compared with women's confirmed the indications of women's lower

pay and status, showing that they changed jobs for different reasons.[30] Women more often left a managerial role in
an organization to become self-employed consultants
because they had reached the top of the career ladder,
while for men further promotion prospects remained. So
even in the rarefied ranks of management, women have
lower career ceilings and the only way to escape is to step
off the ladder and into the uncharted areas of self-
employment.

There were other differences between men and women
managers, notably in attitudes to their careers. The men
were concerned about autonomy at work. In some cases
this was associated with job security – some managers
were frustrated by feeling like pawns in vast corporate
struggles, mergers and takeovers, which could mean that
their jobs were 'rationalized' – while in others they simply
felt unappreciated or stifled. The women were frustrated
with lack of management training, but were particularly
sharply defined from their male colleagues in that for them
gender at work was a major issue, while men did not
mention it.

The women were aware of two main problem areas: the
tensions between family and work commitments, and the
problem of being female in a male-dominated world. A
number also identified a need for counselling. A woman
who switched from being a civil engineer to work in
personnel and remarked on the lack of counselling available to her said:

My personal motivation did not 'fit in' with the motivation to
be successful and fulfilled in my first choice of career. For a
considerable period of time I felt guilty about my 'inadequate'
personality before I realized this.

Other professional and managerial women knew that they
doubted their abilities to a much greater extent than their
male colleagues:

When I did get the job I was after, I worried a great deal about whether I was living up to the expectation and doing the job well enough.

I was very lacking in confidence in my ability in a managerial career.

And the sense of being different effectively undermined some women managers' chances of assessing and redressing their disadvantages. Typical remarks showing this include:

I was lucky enough to find a company that thought women were often better and more conscientious workers than men and they gave me the opportunity of employment, although not equal pay/perks with the men.

There is no discrimination in my company, but they advertised for a man and current colleagues were astounded when I got the job.

I have never felt discriminated against because I am female, although it is undoubtedly true in this organization that women have to prove themselves beyond reasonable doubt more than men.

The ideology Donald expressed has clearly had a powerful – and not always benevolent – influence on women who want careers.

Better off by comparison with other women, yet relatively deprived in relation to similar men, are the professional and managerial women, including those in 'intermediate non-manual' occupations like commercial literary and artistic jobs. For these career women the goal, often established unthinkingly because it is the obvious reward of the public world, is success. But they have also to contend with uncertainties over the price they will have to pay in personal fulfilment. At the same time it is perhaps more difficult for them to articulate the dilemma than for the men who are turning away from the conventional career path, because their position is relatively tenuous. If men like Donald feel that all women have to perform well if any wish to hold career positions, then the women who get those jobs cannot afford to voice the doubts their male colleagues express over 'the price' they have to pay for success.

Bringing private values into public

The importance of humanizing work has been recognized for a number of years: the economic reasons are good, but the means do not appear to be conveniently at hand. Public and private, however, are fundamentally opposed in many ways and the nearest the public realm can come is to reproduce social relations – by organizing work into smaller units with more autonomy, providing a pleasant environment, sports facilities and leisure activities. But this remains a far cry from the private realm.

The professional world is characterized by literal-mindedness, lack of humour, lack of colloquialism, the pre-eminence of track record, an innate conservatism and an inability to act or respond spontaneously. (Decisions can be made fast but they are impersonal, based on objective considerations and capable of justification even if this has to be *post hoc*, unlike the subjective responsiveness of the personal realm, which can be unexpected or capricious.) This world aims to be functional, efficient and cost-effective and expresses this through the conventional clothing, impersonal offices and passive constructions in the language of official reports and documents, an argot sometimes almost incomprehensible to the plain-English speaker.[31]

By comparison, the values of the private realm include humour, complexity, subtlety, sophistication, dissimulation and ambivalence. This variety makes it much more interesting.

For some time it has been acknowledged that the dour public world must accommodate qualities of the private realm to remain competitive. It needs imagination in order to devise and to market products, to solve the problems entailed in development and manufacturing and to manage and motivate the people involved in these projects.

Management critics like Alistair Mant have pointed to the need for leaders with wit, humour, irony and the serious playfulness which is an important element of creativity. But it has also been noticed that these bright young minds prefer to stay away from commerce and to pursue 'purer' occupations – often, if they can, staying in the universities.

The distribution of talent between the sexes, measured in terms of IQ and ability, is even. But lack of confidence can appear to dull bright women's minds. The only area in which women have been targeted by professional bodies, government and its agent, the Equal Opportunities Commission, as recruits for industry is engineering. The critical shortfall in technicians and professional engineers has led to a publicly sponsored programme to persuade girls and young women to choose engineering as an occupation. The fact that such work is lower-paid and of lower status in the UK than in neighbouring countries may also be considered to bring it under the rubric of women's work.

The Women Into Science and Engineering (WISE) campaign is an illustration of the use of women as a secondary labour force, to be drafted in to make up a shortfall. It is not an attempt by government to rectify visible inequalities of opportunity and pay, and although a similar initiative, Industry Matters, includes a women's committee there is no wider context for the WISE campaign to fit women's skills to industry's needs, such as a co-ordinated official effort to match what business and industry offer with what women want.

Success: the desirable objective

Women have been associated with the domestic realm; this has stood for the private world, which has been obscured by the public domain. At the same time women have developed skills and abilities in responding to people, in being perceptive and empathic, which are at the core of the personal world. Now the public realm is coming to realize that these skills are valuable commodities, but it does not know how to import them. No bargain has yet been struck, nor is it certain that one can be.

Hitherto these personal skills were unwelcome in the public world and women were damned by association with them, accused of being emotional, unreliable and unprofessional. In practice the old guard, which remains dominant in business and industry (in the person, particularly, of the 'traditionalist' manager), still looks with disfavour on the softer qualities that the pundits – consultants and trainers – tell them they need. Hence the proportion of women who are managers falls.

Yet men managers are able to act on the rising value of personal qualities and consciously and carefully to choose career paths which do not demand increasing commitment but offer personal fulfilment. In this, perhaps ironically, they are showing women the way. Women are less likely to make such decisions clearly since, as Ruth Poppleton and other commentators have noticed, they plan their careers less than men, are often not secure enough to express ambivalence about their work and are more likely to separate the issues into positive beliefs but contradictory behaviour, undermining their avowed interests by the extreme of work inhibition or the more commonplace lack of confidence.

Success is an issue over which women are personally divided. The dilemma of whether to choose success or satisfaction clearly represents the alternatives presented in the public and private spheres.

Success is one of the chief aims of the public world in a society which places a high value on individualism. Inherent in the idea of individualism is that each person is in possession of a unique configuration of talents which success – which means public recognition – validates. The recognition recommended to the aspiring individual is not for her skills and abilities but for the distinguishing features of those abilities: in the personal configuration itself. It is the style, more than the substance, which is judged to be successful or not.

Success is largely recognition not so much of the meaning of an achievement as of the individuality behind it, because the development of increasingly narrow specializations renders one area of expertise obscure to experts in another.

Just as going out into the world of strangers makes women self-conscious, so moving into an unfamiliar world is likely to make them question their abilities more closely. One manifestation of this – apart from self-reported crises of confidence – is, as the writer Susan Brownmiller notes, the importance of image in women's ideas about work:

Unremarkably, the tiny handful of ambitious careers with certified feminine allure remain those glamorous big dreams with a slim chance for realization (actress, singer, model, interviewer on television) in which looking attractive is part of the performance, so the desire to be noticed can be partly excused.[32]

Similarly, a study of careers advice in women's magazines noted the stress on success, which the authors thought of as a male motive. They explained this as possibly because the editors of the features were men; or because they were aimed at atypical, 'mannish' readers; or because 'the harsh world of magazine publishing may attract a peculiarly competitive and power-hungry female . . .'[33] but they did not entertain the idea of the mainstream

reader sharing such an attitude. The authors also noted
that the careers features presented little information on the
jobs but concentrated on the personalities and background
of recruits to and successful women in the careers discussed, and concluded:

Identification with achievement and power-oriented girls in the
magazines might serve as a catharsis for motivational needs that
female readers are unlikely to satisfy in real life.

They remarked that such features were probably not
'taken seriously as advice. Magazine editors and writers
should be alert to the therapeutic possibilities.'

   These authors overlooked or misunderstood the complicated and subtle interrelation of fact and fantasy in
women's magazines. Glamour is an important element of
the package they present. Women's pages and women's
magazine editors know what their readers want. It is not
simply information.

What do women want from the media?
Journalism is attractive to women, although only half of
those who train manage to get a job.[34] It is competitive
because it has a strong public image, with journalists
featuring in fiction, plays and films as well as being visible
through their work. Even those who are not 'personalities'
have by-lines or credits and there is a strong association
between the worlds of journalism and entertainment,
which offers the same sort of validation for the individual
talent.

   The attraction of journalism is that it seems to be a
highly autonomous job in which individual talents like
investigative skills and news sense are to the fore. Journalists are often depicted in fiction as exempt from certain
restrictions in the public world – the flash of the press pass
admits one to realms from which the general public are

excluded. It seems to offer an opportunity for self-expression and in women's media it revolves around image and visual style (in fashion and beauty), personalities and human relationships (in interviews, features, agony columns, letters pages and show-business and gossip coverage).

In the media the separation of public from private is reproduced in the difference between news and features, and sometimes in fiction. There is also a distinction between men and women readers or audience, with men perceived to be interested in hard facts while women are supposed to be interested in the softer, more personal and discursive style of features and fiction.

This is mirrored in the way women are employed in the media, as well as the hotly disputed way they are portrayed. Women are employed on women's and features pages in newspapers and women's magazines (where nevertheless not all the editors are women) and on children's and health programmes in television.[35]

Campaigning and pressure groups have protested against the way women are portrayed in advertisements and against sexist reporting, and the National Union of Journalists has issued guidelines to its members on avoiding sexist language. But publishers and their managements' ideas about what is commercial greatly diminish the power of journalists and advertising executives to represent women in less stereotyped and sexist ways. In addition, as the fact that two out of three journalists are men indicates, the work culture is strongly male-biased.

One study of the position of women journalists reported that they were largely excluded from the pub culture which is a primary means for exchanging information. After the enactment of the Sex Discrimination Act in 1976, two women journalists implicitly challenged this in taking to court El Vino's, a prominent meeting and drinking place for journalists, for refusing to serve women.

One of them was Anna Coote, who has worked in newspapers, magazines and television both as a writer and an editor. She comments on the separation between women and men, public and private values, in the media:

Female news values: you think about the community, about children, about education perhaps, about seeing the world through the eyes of ordinary people and not through the eyes of politicians, and then of course all the things that directly affect women as opposed to men.

But you also have to think about where power lies in society, which in turn is created partly by news values and traditions inside the media; so power is constructed by that. We have to accept that power is something we are concerned about as women. How do you reinterpret the Tory Party conference as a woman reporter, who isn't just out to make feminist points but is simply seeing it through a woman's eyes, unaffected by her own knowledge of what is traditionally thought in the media to be acceptable? That is where you start.

Features are more about things women are concerned about. The difference between news and features is determined by stylistic traditions of creating newspapers. I'm sure where that comes from is that the tradition grew up that you put the shorter, topical stories on the front page and called them news. You then had inside longer stories. Why? All right, you want to see what's important, but I think that that isn't very problematic; you're only talking about the items there's probably little dispute about. It's just about design, which is again created by men. But if you were reading your news in a magazine instead of in a newspaper, you might put the features first, the news at the back ... And then the distinctions are broken down and you start thinking about news as features and features as news. Certainly in magazine journalism you get that; it's not so hard and fast.

The people who work on newspapers are by and large very narrow-minded; and so are the people who work in television.

She recognizes that competitiveness is a major element in determining why journalists work according to rigid conventions:

It's a restrictive practice in a way; when men took over health they said: 'This is the way to do it.' They laid down rules and they made sure that people who didn't follow the rules were kept out, and thereby kept it for themselves.

Well, it's the same process in journalism: 'We know how to do it, you don't know how to do it.' It's an unchallengeable position: 'We are telling you the truth.'

While the quality papers generally recognize the importance of distinguishing between matters of fact and matters of opinion – and to most of their readers, most of the time, it is clear which is which – the mass-circulation papers differentiate less sharply between news and entertainment, and reporting about women falls largely into the second category. Women adorn the pages of the tabloids as topless models and as the subjects of stories about sex. The other news value attaching to women is their anomalousness. It is still newsworthy if a woman does something men more usually do.

Images of women

The predominant images of women in the media are to do with sex and gender, which themselves are at the core of the private and the personal respectively. The media claim to reflect social attitudes, and also to shape them. Therefore the culture and attitudes of journalists have a bearing on the way women are perceived in the public realm and the way they see themselves. Even the apparently positive images presented in women's magazines can subtly distort expectations by presenting a glamorous ideal of womanhood which most cannot attain. This is one of the major sources of many women's conception of success.

Images of women are transmitted not only by magazine covers but in the tone and style of the features, fiction, letters and fashion spreads and in the captions, headings and text which create the magazine's personality.

Women's magazines show, with consummate artistry,

how women create their personae for public consumption. They survive and prosper, or lose readers and close, according to how precisely they pitch the image of their readers. More subtly than newspapers, which represent themselves as reporting the world and its affairs factually, women's magazines create a world. They are not in the business of crudely disseminating information, but of packaging an image.

Magazines are like clubs; they offer their readers a group identity. The fashion and beauty spreads demonstrate the visual image but it is in the features and articles, on the shopping pages and in the practicals like cookery and furnishing, that the identity of the magazine is sustained. The reader gets a whole package which must, like the individual woman's persona in the public realm, be consistent and attractive.

Newspapers rely on their features pages and leaders to create their identity, for their news is presented impersonally. They are therefore at a disadvantage by comparison with women's magazines in creating and sustaining a consistent identity. The more features material a newspaper carries, the more it is likely to seem to have an identifiable personality. In her advertisements for the *Guardian*, for example, Edna O'Brien treats the paper as a person with whom she has had a long-standing relationship.

With the rise of broadcasting, print journalism has lost ground as a primary source of news, while in-depth coverage becomes more important; so features gain at the expense of news in the quality press, or topless models in the tabloids, in line with the rising interest in the private side of life. But different media have different relationships with this: women's magazines create their own world; broadcast media carry drama and some fiction; newspapers, with their instrumental and objective approach and emphasis on information, are furthest from the subjective, personal and private world. Their approaches vary with the age of their target readership; those with older readers tend to stick to the facts, are more pragmatic and less sophisticated than publications for younger people, where opinion, features, controversy and campaigning journalism are more to the fore. Wit and satire feature more prominently in media for young people than the simpler humour of the more traditional media, where there are more stereotypes and more conventional assumptions about the reader's standpoint.

The uses of publicity

Women are under three pressures to look at the externalities of public achievement and to pursue them rather than personal fulfilment alone: success, public recognition of individual achievement, is desirable because it is rare, particularly for women; it is a source of validation for the individual, and women express a greater need for this than men do; and it satisfies the need to present a coherent image and personal style.

Uncertainty and internal contradictions belie a consistent performance while confidence is crucial to coming across well in the media, particularly in broadcasting, as it is for successful functioning in the public world as a whole. Business or political confidence entails gaining the backing and belief of others. Confidence has become a critical issue for women as they endeavour to acculturate to the public world in which they find themselves increasingly often and for increasingly long periods as their expectations of a working life lengthen and their participation in political institutions like trade unions grows.[36]

At the same time, the media are an important means of creating a reputation and sustaining business confidence. Being featured in the media is a principal way of becoming known in the public world and is sought by politicians and on behalf of businesses by their public relations staff. Media coverage is an acid test of success.

The paradox of display

There is an obvious relationship between privacy and invisibility, as there is between publicity and visibility. The private world lies behind closed doors, inside the home, in intimate terms and without an audience. The public world has an audience and generally entails publicity.[37] To be public, a person or an action usually has to be seen by other people.

The mass media – and broadcasting in particular – have vastly increased the size of audiences. But women are not as accustomed as men to being visible and this shows in many ways, for instance in their discomfort in addressing a public meeting. Political parties and organizations like the 300 Group train women in public speaking because they identify it as one of the chief obstacles to political life. Women are anxious about public speaking, not necessarily in anticipation of a difficult reception but because they feel exposed, anomalous and, above all, self-conscious.

Just as the images through which women present themselves change, so (more slowly) do their roles and (more slowly still) the stereotypes shaping expectations about them. At the same time, the context in which women change is itself subject to alteration.

The boundary between public and private is not fixed. It has been differently located at different periods in history, has been perhaps altogether lacking in some societies and is changing perceptibly with the transformation of Western society to a post-industrial economy. Consequently the inhibitions and ambivalence women face in entering the public realm can be changed.

As a primary means through which the individual learns about and communicates with society the media are instrumental in this change, and women's attraction to and fear of publicity is one example of the contradictions governing their entry to the public realm and their identity and validity in it.

9

The Defence of Identity

Honor
Honor was sent to school in England by her American
diplomatic family. In her teens she developed the idea that
she had to strengthen herself and adopted strict regimens
of exercise and eating, apparently with the aim of keeping
herself pure. She kept rather apart from the other girls,
whom she described as weak, and felt she had to be able
to rely wholly on her inner resources.

At college she became increasingly involved with religious activities and despised most of the other students for
what seemed to her their dissipation. In particular she felt
that they lacked the intellectual edge of a more ascetic life.
She read archaeology and worked very diligently at the
subject; she venerated T. E. Lawrence and practised stren-
uous daily exercises.

She refused to use a word processor because she saw it
as an artificial prop which made things too easy. She
generally found modern artefacts distasteful, as she felt
that the past was purer and closer to God than the present.
She pursued rigour in all aspects of her life, but tended to
confuse it with self-denial. She lived within a budget
smaller than her allowance and during term generally ate
only cabbage and boiled eggs because she did not like
being economically dependent; also probably because she
felt that her allowance was insufficient and insecure.

Her work was meticulous but it was hard for her to
come to terms with the fact that she was not perceived as

a gifted student since she worker harder than any of the others, and she saw her academic limitations as a weakness on her part. She felt that she was insufficiently inspired and hoped to increase her inspiration by reducing her attachment to the material world. She felt much more self-sufficient and hardy than her peers, particularly the girls, since although she disapproved of feminism she found femininity personally repugnant. On one occasion she invited a fellow-undergraduate to punch her in the stomach to demonstrate how tough her stomach wall was, explaining: 'I could hang by my fingertips for half an hour if I had to.'

The fantasy of having to save herself in desperate conditions was something that had persisted since her school days. It also symbolized the degree to which she felt that her material circumstances were insecure. Her frugal existence and ascetic habits – she slept for only a few hours at a time and sometimes woke herself to pray during the night – reduced her dependence upon and engagement with the outside world, from which she partly withdrew, probably because she felt intolerably vulnerable and disadvantaged in it.

Although she did not gain a good enough degree to win a research grant, she remained at the university and refused to consider working outside. Her dedication persuaded the department to accept her for first one and then a further degree and later to offer her some work, and because her needs were modest she was able to survive on the very limited income this yielded.

Through the church she gained a small circle of friends and as she was – despite privation and denial – an attractive woman, a series of admirers. Although she was flattered by their attention she found them all, in different ways, wanting. As a staunch traditionalist she supported the idea that women found fulfilment in home and family, but she excepted herself from this rule as she felt privately that she was not like other women. She rationalized this by saying that she hoped one day to marry and have children, but that the right man for her had not yet come along.

Puritan, old-fashioned and rugged, she heavily rejected modernity and aspired to a classical or antique purity. She was in her own way competitive and ambitious, qualities she despised in others. She saw the academic world as morally better than the rest of the world and as the domain of the brightest and best people. However, since she was flawed by a relatively poor academic performance she could not view herself, as she would have wished, as *primus inter pares* so instead pictured herself as a person apart. Without the support and validation academic success and fame would bring, she considered that the price of being true to herself might be lack of personal fulfilment.

Purity and danger

From her school days, Honor had made a separation between inside and out that diversified as she grew older. As an adult she tended to divide people into clear categories and to attach to these comparisons of moral worth: people within the church were better than those outside; academics were better than other people; her family was special, other people were not so lucky; the past was better than the present; she was purer and stronger than others.

She devoted a great deal of time to strengthening and purifying herself, not because by the law of opposites she felt in fact unclean and weak by comparison with others, but because she felt she needed to be absolutely the best in some sense. That absolute position represented a clear distinction between herself and others, which was something she needed to establish and struggled to maintain. Conversely, without feeling that she was the best, she had trouble in knowing what she was. Purity – asceticism –

and strength defended her from the danger of losing her identity.

Honor saw things very much in simple and clear-cut either/ors, and could not come to terms with the complexity and subtleties of contemporary experience – hence in part, perhaps, her rejection of the present in favour of the distant past.

Contemporary society is much more complex and demands levels of sophistication and self-awareness beyond those called for in earlier generations. Comparing developing with traditional cultures shows this clearly. For instance, there are distinct cultural differences in the degree to which people see themselves as able to manipulate others, those from modern societies scoring much higher than those from traditional, non-industrial cultures.[1]

Comparisons across cultures at different stages of development show that the more institutions and systems in a culture, the more egocentric are its children[2] and the more urban, more educated, more industrialized and socially mobile a society, the more competitive its children.[3] Rural children are more co-operative than city kids;[4] urban middle-class children are more assertive than poor rural children.[5]

Town and country
Ninety per cent of us now live in cities, where the size, sophistication and complexity of contemporary architecture mirror complex social structures (it is interesting to note the development towards transparency and revelation as post-modern architectural values, with formerly hidden functions like lifts, generators and even the skeleton of the building being put on public display). Correspondingly, living in cities stresses the individual, personal resources, subtlety and complexity.

These traits contradict simplicity, directness and trust,

the nostalgia for which is evidenced in a shift back to the countryside, with the growth during the 1970s of smaller towns at the expense of the major industrial conurbations.

Innocence, once lost, cannot – unfortunately – be restored. The populations of the new and recently grown towns have not lost their sophistication, emphasis on the individual or habit of thinking in more complex terms than their parents and grandparents. They remain more self-aware, for instance in sensing provincialisms, a consciousness which is reinforced by the metropolitan orientation of the mass media. With the massive expansion of the lower middle class and the corresponding shrinkage in other classes, the chief differences between people now are less class- than generation-based. The older generations seem less sophisticated than the young, less able to accommodate social change and less technologically proficient. The skills appropriate to the smokestack industries are no longer passed on from parent to child; instead children are differentiated from their parents by computer literacy, affiliation to youth subcultures which specifically exclude older people and an expectation of joblessness which exceeds even the much-vaunted miseries of their grandparents' depressed childhoods.

Simple or complex?

To simple people those who are complex may seem incomprehensible, complicated, duplicitous or prone to sophistry. To complex people those who are simple may seem enviably untroubled and able to act on clear choices; but they also seem easy to manipulate, to live narrow and uninteresting lives and to lack sensitivity. For this reason they seem relatively impersonal and incapable of refined and responsive intimacy.

For simple personalities, much is dictated by external organizations: morals are learned from their parents or religion; in their style of dress and manner they conform to the social norms with which they identify, and by comparison with a complex personality they question little. Simple personalities do not grapple with the regular questions of identity or image which beset others. The complex personality, however, as we saw in chapter three, is by contrast both tolerant of and prone to ambiguity and ambivalence; the choices apparent to it are more varied and more numerous than the either/or decisions presenting themselves to the simple personality. Consequently it can be harder for the complex personality to act, given that there are more variables to consider.

Honor found the idea of personal complexity confusing and threatening. She liked clear choices but correspondingly could not easily adapt to changing circumstances: despite her poor degree, she refused to consider work outside the university. Her persistence paid off, and she was therefore able to maintain a consistent idea of herself. However, since she will probably not attain eminence in her field, as a long-term strategy it may not prove beneficial.

Louise

Louise, unlike Honor, is complicated and unsure. Where Honor is doggedly persistent, Louise says of herself that she always runs away from anything hard.

She had a military family background and describes herself as having been 'a very strange little girl', an imaginative child whom her parents found difficult to understand. After the age of eleven she was continually in conflict with her parents and finally at nineteen left home for London, where she first worked as a secretary to the editor of a national quality paper, and this association with the media continued as her career developed.

She recalls that during this period the discrepancy between self and image, inner and outer realities, became heightened:

I used to wear a lot of make-up. One day I was feeling ill and I went in without any make-up and no one recognized me. One woman said to me in the corridor: 'Hello, Louise,' and when I lifted my head, she said: 'Oh, it's not Louise.'

Louise had always wanted to study art but her parents insisted on a secretarial training. After a couple of years' secretarial work, she went to art college and then returned to work in the media as a magazine art editor. She found the work extremely stressful and after a move to her second job, which was better paid, more responsible and represented a career advance, she left the media and went to work as a shop assistant for a year, during which time she was also seeing a psychotherapist.

She felt that she had

a hateful little demon, something chipping away inside. I get to a point where something says inside my head: 'You can't do it.' It's not the work. It's my ability to cope with work and deadlines and my ability to cope with blocks.

Where do ideas come from?
Although creative work allows the individual more free-dom and opportunity than other kinds to express and investigate the self, it also carries with it equal and opposite dangers: in particular, the danger of the creative block.

Autonomy and lack of routine, even if there are rituals surrounding it, divest work of an automatic structure and momentum. Teamwork can carry people who have run out of ideas over a barren patch, but even more import-antly the collective will provides each member with struc-ture, stimulus and momentum.

But where the source of ideas is wholly internal, where the product of work is completely identified with person-ality and depends on inspiration, the danger of creative block is increased because all the ideas come from the self rather than from outside, with the self as an organizing or expressive medium, and there is no fallback when the ideas stop coming. This was Louise's position when she gave up her new job, abandoned the career she had struggled for and became a shop assistant.

She returned to the media by taking on part-time art and design work for a studio, where she later began to do copywriting and then whole campaigns. She has subsequently moved into advertising, where her verbal and visual skills are integrated.

Of the doubts which led her to leave magazines, she said:

It was not my work I didn't have confidence in, it was myself. I remember I had done nine front covers and I thought: 'It's been nine now. Will there be any more?' And I knew that eventually I would run out of ideas. But it didn't occur to me then that there were other ways of coming up with ideas.

I never thought of working on an idea, that there were other ways than simply expecting them to pop into my head. But that's not what happens at all. You work from an idea and follow all sorts of paths away from it and around it and then you come back to it and work on it again. You use stimuli from outside on it. You *make* the idea.

In describing the doubts that undermined her she said that she felt her brainpower was limited, a comment common to people in a similar position, as Applegarth reported on her work-inhibited patients.

The imposter syndrome

This sense of operating at the limits of ability is also a factor in the imposter syndrome. It is partly a misconception of intentionality, suggesting that others achieve more easily what people who feel like imposters in their career know takes hard work and partly a misconception of inspiration, seeing it as the only legitimate source of ideas and hence devaluing ideas from other sources.

Louise's problem with feeling that her flow of ideas was going to dry up, which involved the notion that things can flow only in one direction – from within to the outside – also entailed a sense of inner emptiness or lack. She reproached herself bitterly for lacking inner resources, and this is what the specific sensation of lacking brainpower represented.

Louise accused herself of incompetence in the face of normal difficulties and felt that she was not resilient. Conversely she felt she was too dependent, that she ought to be more self-reliant and self-sufficient and that her output was inadequate, which illustrates how an extremely individualistic society can distort people's expectations of themselves. In her self-determined, creative job Louise felt that she was working at or beyond the limit of her ability to generate a constant flow of ideas and that her inner resources were insufficient to meet the demands of the outside world.

The clash between the inside and the outside, self and others, is one of the chief conflicts between the public and private realms in contemporary personal experience. The simple personality reduces the clash by denial or rejection, but the complex personality, with less field dependence and conformity, a greater tolerance of ambivalence and ambiguity and more self-awareness and empathy, cannot adopt these strategies to cope with the conflict. Instead, the complex personality must try to synthesize contradictory areas into integrated personal experience.

Two worlds

We all live in two different realms, but in a complicated, sophisticated society individual experience of this is discontinuous and fragmented. Yet the public culture demands a consistent performance, and so, by inference, values the integrated personality and denies the duality of experience. The private realm can be realized in the public world only via 'objective' methods like psychological research or 'personal' political issues like family and housing. Subjective experience is therefore masked – and hence invalidated – in the public realm.

The split between public and personal experience is not necessarily at all clear to the individual – particularly if she feels it should not be there or does not really exist for other people. Yet it is real and has an impact on how well people can function in each sphere. The fact that the two are separate suggests that people have to choose between them, opting for either attainment or fulfilment.

It also makes people feel comparatively unreal and fraudulent in one or the other domain, according to which is real and valid for them. For women femininity, with its strong associations with the private realm, means that they are likely to feel less real, less valid and more fraudulent in the public world.

Consistency is important in the public realm, where reliable performance is a measure of ability; this produces a matching emphasis on being internally consistent, which can be taken as a sign of an integrated personality. In fact, an integrated personality is not one which merely performs consistently but one which can integrate disparate experiences and cope with contradictions. Different roles place different demands on people and therefore require different behaviour and responses.

The private world admits inconsistency and anomaly. In personal relationships, for example, it is important to be responsive and flexible to meet changing circumstances. In the private realm, therefore, people can reveal more of themselves and so are more interesting. The private sphere is correspondingly more open and exploratory, more conditional and less absolute.

Sensible and sensitive

Just as the activities and aims of the private and public domains differ, so do the forms of behaviour most likely to achieve these different goals. Complex perceptions and behaviour produce concrete results more slowly than simpler views, are less amenable to control and regulation, can be less clear and are more demanding and interesting.

Simplicity is therefore generally a strategy fostered in the public world even though it has a less straightforward political dimension, both in government and in the world of work as a whole. Yet the political senses operant in the public world, even though they resemble the private world's values of perceptiveness and responsiveness, are at a far remove from these. In personal relationships the objective is to understand and action is secondary, but in the public world action is necessary and understanding only the determinant of the appropriate course of action.

People who are accustomed to thinking in concrete and practical terms are inclined to treat reductively things they find complex. For instance, a successful male manager responded to the idea that women might be deflected from participating equally in the public domain by their greater connection with the private sphere with his experience of the recruitment practice of a major brewery, which puts candidates for running a public house through psycho-metric ability and aptitude tests. 'And if,' he said, 'they say they like to keep home and work separate, they don't get the job. Because you can't do that if you're running a pub.' His response, which was a little offbeam in terms of developing an understanding of how work can generate ambivalence in career women, was to simplify the abstract idea into a concrete example and to translate it, by the association of 'public' and 'home', into 'public house'.

This sort of concrete, literal thinking is not very useful in dealing with personal and psychological issues but is well adapted to the job of manager in a large organization. It illustrates how the pragmatic person who thinks in concrete terms distorts a complex notion. The idea of ambivalence is antipathetic to people who like to be highly structured and hierarchical.

This way of thinking answers the question of women's ambivalence positively by training them to fit in better with the existing order, or negatively by denying the problem or suggesting that ambivalent people are unsuited to their jobs.

Training aims to change people rather than circumstances, but because the obstacle to wholehearted engagement in the public realm is diverse and not unitary it is not amenable to a single, practical solution. It is not a problem which can be solved at a stroke, though employers can ameliorate women's difficulties by taking them into account. Training can at best be only a partial remedy; changes in working practices – and above all in corporate cultures – are much more effective, but only within the context of general social change. Fortunately, there is a lot of that about in the latter part of the twentieth century.

Inadmissible evidence

In a competitive culture, as commerce and industry pre-eminently are (though this ethos permeates the whole of the public realm), the admission of uncertainty is an immediate disbarment. The public realm cannot admit ambiguity, ambivalence and self-doubt, though it can allow duplicity and dissimulation, which are equally complex.

In questions of private sensibility, the tools – like training or counselling – available to organizations are generally too blunt for the purpose. There is no programme or system for solving problems arising from a disjunction in experience apart from the slow process of therapy, the personal remedy, which is borrowed in some forms of training.

The failure of public-realm mechanisms to deal with – or even to recognize – such difficulties disguises the degree to which they are a common element of contemporary experience, one which is particularly salient for women and, most acutely, for women in professional, executive and managerial jobs. In refusing to recognize a problem which it cannot effectively solve and in consigning it to the private realm, the public world effectively invalidates the experience of fragmentation which troubles many women.

The distinction between the public and the private ethos can be represented, too, in the different sensibilities appropriate to each. In the public world sense and being sensible are important values; in the private world sensitivity takes priority.

An integral part of sensitive response is the ability to admit contradiction and ambivalence. But the disposition towards complexity and ambivalence is not particularly useful in most sorts of work. It is the idea that things are not to be taken literally that acts on many perfectionist or work-inhibited women. They think that whatever they do is not difficult or clever enough and assume that more is always being asked of them. The discrepancy between the inner and outer reappears here, for it increases the sense that inner resources are insufficient to meet the demands of the world.

So there is a value to simplicity and literalness if the goal is public, material achievement, just as there is a value to complexity, sophistication and tolerance of ambiguities and ambivalence if the goal is interpersonal or private. While the public sphere is the realm of the literal, the private domain is the realm of contradiction and possibility.

The personal factors that determine how people distinguish between public and private and how they manage the transition from one to the other are useful in changing the inequalities inherent in the way sex roles dispose people to distinguish public from private differently.

People cope in very different ways with this dichotomy: some are shy; some are efficient; some are ambitious; some are sensitive; some are agoraphobic; some are unwell; some are successful.

One of the basic ways of organizing experience is by distinguishing between me and not-me. Applying theories of artificial intelligence to human behaviour, some personality and social psychologists suggest that we aim to reduce discrepancies in what we expect and what we perceive.[6]

Self-monitoring

The idea that we constantly monitor ourselves has been mentioned in chapter three in relation to self-attention. The idea is that we have a model of the world which provides us with standards for behaviour; although this is continuously updated and modified by experience, it works fundamentally by checking if a piece of information fits into an existing conceptual category. We categorize on an analogue principle, deciding whether the information is this or not-this on its resemblance to the definition established by past experience.

For instance, you might decide that a person you have just met is a bit like someone else you know and categorize them accordingly, even though in so doing you miss or deny some important characteristics of the new person. With closer acquaintance you build up a more accurate and detailed picture, but the information is processed using the same model: this and not-this.

If this description of human thought and behaviour is true, rather than a falsely mechanistic analogy, it also suggests that we aim to reduce discrepancies in our experience by refining our perceptions of the world so that it creates a coherently ordered whole. The antithesis of this is dissonance, anomaly and ambiguity, which we try to reduce.

The ability to tolerate ambiguities

Different cultures and individuals tolerate ambiguity to different degrees, as we saw earlier. One modern typology starts with the description of the authoritarian personality as being disposed to categorical, simplistic thinking, patriarchal and supporting convention and traditional institutions and with little tolerance for ambiguity and anomaly.[7]

But the more complex and diverse life is, the more the individual must be able to incorporate ambiguities and to work with information that will not conform to existing categories. Writing about personal identity in terms of the way people use personae, the social scientist Anselm Strauss commented:

It is precisely this continual necessity for reassessment that permits the innovation and novelty of human life. If expectations were always fulfilled – if present situations and events were exactly as anticipated from experiences with past ones – then actions would be thoroughly ritualistic, and conceptions eternally static. Innovation, in fact, rests upon ambiguous, confused, not wholly defined situations.[8]

This is an optimistic view of the good that can come from uncertainty. Translated into public terms, it describes current prevailing ideas about entrepreneurial culture which derive from technical and economic change. It is corroborated, in another context, by psychological definitions of the creative personality, one of the attributes of which is, again, a high tolerance of ambiguity (and of disorder, including a messy environment).[9]

Creativity

Creativity is accorded a high value in an individualistic society because it manifests, more enduringly and more publicly than for instance eye- or fingerprints or genetic markers in the blood, the unique configuration of individual personality attributes. It is better respected than skill and experience, since these do not inhere in the individual, and is thought of as innate and mysterious.

Studies of creativity have looked for personality and aptitude indicators and have considered sex differences, asking whether it is because women are less creatively gifted than men that they are under-represented in the annals of achievement and in primary creative occupations as distinct from secondary roles like public relations, information and editorial work.

Women are strongly represented in the secondary creative roles: two-thirds of members of the NUJ Book Branch, which covers editors and assistants in publishing, are women, compared with writers, where the proportion of women to men is reversed. In managerial roles, the majority of posts are held by men.[10] This has an impact on the opportunities for women to write. Although authors like Edna O'Brien have argued that writing fiction is particularly suited to women with domestic responsibilities because the necessary – if not sufficient – conditions are simply the corner of a kitchen table, paper and pen, Dale Spender has found that getting books published is another matter. Of all books published, the number written by women is one in five, a proportion which includes books both by and for women in such specialist categories as romantic fiction, cookery and beauty. She also reports that only six per cent of space given to book reviews is allocated to women's books, and less than seven per cent of authors studied in literary courses are women.[11]

Gifted women

Beside women's inequality in an area which is often perceived as one where women are well represented, and consonant with femininity, stand investigations into female creativity. First, it has been established that creativity is not the same thing as intelligence: no highly creative people are of low intelligence, whereas plenty of highly intelligent people are uncreative.[12] The distribution of intelligence between the sexes is the same; so is the distribution of creativity measured in psychological tests rather than achievement. The argument that creativity is a function of the right hemisphere of the brain, while girls tend to develop left-hemisphere dominance earlier than boys, is subject to a plethora of contradictory findings. A study begun in 1921 followed the lives of a group of gifted children and found that although the girls were the most artistically gifted, they were much less successful than the boys in adult life.[13]

Other studies suggest more detail about the causes: a survey of members of the American Association of Women in Mathematics found that although as children boys and girls were equally encouraged to pursue mathematics, the girls were also discouraged twice as often as the boys. The girls who subsequently worked as mathematicians despite the disincentives frequently came from families in which they had escaped the usual male dominance, either because they had no father or because their fathers had treated them as sons. Compared with other women they were more independent, more introverted and less tied down in their daily lives. A comparison of the personalities of creative mathematicians and creative writers showed that the women in both groups were similar: they tended to be unconventional, individualistic, non-social and to have an engrossing inner life.[14]

Stereotypical femininity is thus in opposition to creativity, and stereotypes of women result in discouragement from creative endeavour and in women's creative achievements being rewarded less often. Just as fewer books by and for women are published, so too women mathematicians published fewer papers than their male counterparts.

But factors like high private self-awareness, or high self/

non-self segregation, are strongly associated with creativity. Again, this is in opposition to the sort of self-awareness which John Berger attributed to women in all their actions – a public self-awareness fostered by femininity.

Creativity is a value which is imported into many areas of life with which its association, in the strict sense, is tenuous. Creative management, for instance, even creativity in advertising, is not the same thing as creativity in the fine arts because it operates under the constraining necessities of commerce and hence detracts from the sole authorship implied in artistic creativity: it is as industrial a process as manufacturing.[15] But the concept is borrowed to make the production process more palatable, because the term 'creative' is so attractive in contemporary society.

Inner and outer

Psychologists use creativity in another sense: to refer to an integrated and active rather than merely artistic personality. This reveals the extent to which psychologists (and psychiatrists, analysts and therapists) conceive of themselves as remedying disorders for which the idea of a creative block is a metaphor. They are engaged in the effort to heal the split between public and private which for some people becomes an impassable chasm.

Implicit in this is a dualism of self and other, the in- and the outside. For example, the psychoanalyst D. W. Winnicott wrote about:

the inner psychic reality, the personal property of each individual in so far as a degree of mature integration has been reached which includes the establishment of a unit self, with the implied evidence of an inside and an outside, and a joining membrane.[16]

The joining membrane is literally the skin, by extension the frontier between the inside and outside, the me and not-me, the private and the public. Psychosomatic symptoms illuminate the way the body is seen as a symbol of self: stress, hysterical symptoms and phobias are all indications of the importance of this basic distinction of me and not-me, inner and outer, self and non-self and, ultimately, public and private.

Home and family

The home is also intimately connected with the definition of the private world. At home, in private, the individual is released from the self-consciousness of being in public where, to a greater or lesser degree, she or he is permanently on show.

Erving Goffman studied behaviour in a small hotel in the Shetland Islands, where he noticed things like how differently the staff behaved when they were not in view of the guests. For instance, they jumped up from their seats and put on a great display of busyness about the kitchen when a guest put his head round the door. From this observation Goffman developed the idea that most jobs have an element of theatrical performance about them, with people outside the work group as the audience and colleagues and workmates as the team putting on a show of competence for them; this element of display, self-consciousness and performance is central to all ways of being in the public world.[17]

But in private, at home, unless there is an audience such as a visitor, none of this performance need take place, and this is perhaps one of the most recognizable and valuable features of privacy in an industrial society.

Engels was one of the first modern thinkers to offer an account of the family and the state, women's role and the division of labour, and although some parts of his analysis have not continued in the canon of feminist thought, he has inspired much further work.

Jessie Bernard comments on the way the private realm

of the family and home are opposed to the public world
of work:

The home came to be seen as a protection against the harshness
of the outside world . . . One of the major functions of women's
sphere, therefore, was to . . . [supply] the balm needed to heal
the wounds inflicted by the outside world. It made life in the
male world tolerable.[18]

Changes in this conception of public and private, with
women no longer universally bearing exclusive responsibility for emotional support, are an index of the transition
from an industrial to a post-industrial economy.[19]

Boundary markers

The change in the boundaries between public and private
is similarly charted in the decline of formality in everyday
life: for example, although less than one per cent of the
population now has live-in domestic help, market
researchers notice that larger numbers of people are now
interested in gourmet food and entertaining.[20] Dinner
parties, formerly held only by the middle and upper
classes, are now part of most people's everyday life.

But the home remains primarily a female realm, just as –
or by virtue of the fact that – it largely embodies the
private sphere. It meets the needs of those who go out
from it into the public world, providing food, clean
clothes, rest and recreation both for families and for the
increasing number of single-person households. It is the
inner realm where emotional needs are sanctioned and,
ideally, met.

The family, however, is not the same thing as the private
inner world, for it assigns to its members roles which can
override or even contradict personalities. The idea that the
family is the personal and private sphere is a misconception based on the public world's construction of the
private sphere, which cannot distinguish between different

realms outside political and economic activity. In these areas family, domestic, social and personal interests are conflated, because they all fall outside the public realm.

But from the perspective of the personal realm it is clear that the family is in some ways modelled on the public world, not just in the roles taken by each member but in the sometimes stringent and explicit rules in the household and in the amount of work involved. The family and domestic realms are not for everyone equally a haven from the necessity of the public world, because for the most part they are serviced and managed by women's unpaid labour – on average twenty-eight hours per week for women with full-time paid jobs as well. Where the family and home represent leisure for men and children, it offers much less to women.

Again the social realm, although it falls outside the public world, is not the same thing as the private domain. People enter into social activities in their personal rather than their professional capacity, but precisely because these are activities they do not permit the responsiveness and freedom characteristic of personal relations. The social realm also assigns roles to people and sometimes borrows power relations from the public world, from which in some instances – like the business dinner or works outing – it is not far removed.

Intimacy
Richard Sennett argues that intimate relations are themselves contaminated by being modelled on public exchange relationships. He gives as an example the way inexperienced interviewers often offer information about their own personal lives in compensation for the information their respondents give them, and points out that in intimate relationships this habit devalues the exchange by treating self-disclosure as a commodity. Sennett explains this as the interviewers' desire to reassure their respond-

ents that they see them as real people and not just as data sources, and notes that with experience they find that they learn more about the other person by listening and not interrupting. He does not say – although this, even more than the notion of exchange, is a borrowing from the public realm – that there is something competitive in such apparent reciprocity. The literal idea of equality between people, requiring some demonstration of even-handedness, is replaced by a more complex way of affirming the importance of others.

This is also a broad-brush, working description of the development of personal relationships, which start with frequent exchanges of information from both parties to establish common ground and their relation to each other, and then move on to cater for the different needs of each. Between close friends the exchanges are never equal in terms of the amount of time allocated to each in conversation, who determines the direction of the relationship, who gives and who takes. Nevertheless, close friendships are entirely mutual. They change with the changing needs and interests of the people involved, and confer as much benefit on the giver as on the recipient.

Family roles, however, often suffer by comparison with friendships from lack of freedom of choice. Children do not choose their parents and siblings, nor do parents consciously and freely choose the people their children turn out to be. There are also power relationships at work in the family – parental authority, patriarchal rule and sibling rivalries, for instance. Families also suffer from the transposition of consumer expectations into circumstances where freedom of choice is in reality limited, for family relationships are supposed to be close and intimate since the family is, in the eyes of the public world, the seat of the private realm. Since the private realm is all about choice and freedom, family relationships suffer from expectations of the intimacy, understanding and satisfaction which friendships provide. But the family is not able to legitimize its members in the same way as friends can because it is more constrained by necessity, work and roles than are freely chosen relationships. Yet still the ideology of the family as the heartland of the private world raises expectations which are rarely met; consequently people often feel more disappointed with their family life – partnership, parents and children – than with areas of life where they can see that they must compromise and that their personal needs are not going to be fully met.

Paradoxically, there is evidence for women deriving satisfaction from parts of the public world which would, at first sight, seem to offer them very little. Several studies have investigated the anomaly of why women, confined to less interesting work, worse remuneration and more limited prospects for improvement than men, nevertheless report that they are in general just as happy, or even happier.[21]

Personnel experts strongly recommend a close fit between job-holder and job for the satisfaction of both employee and employer, to whom they suggest that job satisfaction increases productivity. The pursuit of job satisfaction has meant that jobs have been redesigned to simulate and stimulate entrepreneurial activity, under the guidance of authorities like Gifford Pinchot III. The idea is to fit work round people and to encourage self-determination and autonomy in the workplace, as these are seen to be associated with commitment and innovation. At the same time, the number of people changing from unemployment to self-employment has risen markedly during the 1980s. Eleven per cent of working people are now self-employed, three-quarters of them men. But there has also been a big rise in the number of women working for themselves. Between 1981 and 1984 alone, the numbers went up by forty-one per cent.[22]

The distinction between work and leisure may well

change even more with the introduction of new ways of working. Flexible work, with core hours agreed on a daily, weekly or monthly basis or by working, for instance, a nine-day week and taking a proportional break between working 'weeks', job-sharing, part-time work, freelancing, consultancy and teleworking are all becoming more common.

Kristoff is an example of the way the construction of work can change to fit individual aspirations more closely. He is the first doctor in Switzerland to share a job at a Basel general hospital. He works full-time for six weeks before handing over to his job-share and taking the next month to six weeks off. Every other month, Kristoff, who has no relationship or family responsibilities to tie him down, is able to fly to a different part of the world for a holiday. This form of job-sharing was his reaction to the shock of returning from Africa, where he practised in the field with a high degree of inventiveness for lack of standard supplies and equipment, dealing with any and every medical condition. He found life in a big modern general hospital bureaucratic and removed from the realities of medicine from which he had come, and instigated the job-share to counteract this. He plans next to study tropical medicine in London. In this he also exemplifies the new lack of attachment to a career ladder among younger professionals and managerial employees, which creates the conditions for developing different ways of organizing work to fit individual needs better.

For more than a decade, predictions have been issued from all sorts of forecasting organizations about the imminence of the shift from workplace-based to home-based employment.[23] Information technology is the means; with electronic communications there is a decreasing need to gather people together to co-ordinate activities. Whether the new way of working will resolve itself as home-work, with people working individually and meeting intermittently mainly for social purposes, or whether it will be organized round neighbourhood work centres, is open to debate. Experiments with neighbourhood work centres have not proved conclusively that this is a usable option, and so far home-working remains largely the province of women on low-paid piecework.

But the infrastructure for the new ways of working is now being developed, and at the same time there are indications that the rise in part-time and home-working, in which men are beginning to participate, is changing the demarcation of public from private, home from work. The difference between home-working and self-employment is increasingly elusive. So far the rise of these adaptations of the conventions of paid work is hard to quantify, since the statistics are not collected and the black economy obscures it.[24]

On the one hand the spread of home computers is an indication of the ease with which the transition from industrial to post-industrial ways of working could be accomplished. Developments like satellite and cable telecommunications mean that the electronic highways, facilitating new ways of working, which import public activities into private, are now being built. On the other hand, movements like self-development groups and support groups point the ways in which the values and behaviour of the private world are being introduced to and applied to the world of work. Such initiatives are focused on work but operate on a personal basis, with people discussing their lives without necessarily making the distinction between what belongs to work and what is a private matter.

Sex

Another indication of the shifting boundary between public and private is the degree to which women – and men too – are now prepared to discuss sex in public. Sex has conventionally been a secret subject for many cultures, and women – who in many societies, including those of Western Europe, are the politer sex – were therefore less likely than men to broach it.[25]

But there has been a change in recent decades and sexual habits have altered with easier access to contraception. Although that in turn is moderated by the fear of AIDS, women have had to learn to chart their own courses and rely less on received behaviour than in earlier generations, and so have opened up the subject for debate.

Rosalind Coward, an academic, writer and social critic, discusses the purpose served by the agony columns of women's magazines:

Women have been encouraged to write to magazines for a long time, asking for beauty or home advice; but it is only since the Second World War that they have been exhorted to reveal to all the intimate doings of their sex lives. Problem pages believe they are dealing with timeless human emotions. In fact, problem pages are themselves a historically specific symptom of the way in which sexuality and its emotional consequences have been catapulted to the foreground in our culture as the true expression of our most intimate selves.[26]

She remarks too on the importance to the writer not merely of writing but of sending the confessional letter. The process of this sort of intimate confession requires that it is made public, that it is read by someone else:

The implication behind this is clear. Speak out. It will make you feel better. Organize your crisis into a narrative, be honest and perhaps then you will see the causes . . . Indeed, sexual relations generally are under a discursive injunction. These are the secrets that must be told. There has been an increase in the ways in which sexuality is talked about, medically, sociologically, statistically and legally. And with this increase in discussion there's also been an elevation of the significance of sexuality . . . We are enjoined to confess our innermost feelings and thoughts about sexuality because they seem to be, in this society, the key to our personalities.[27]

Along with increased verbalizing there has been increased visual representation of sexual matters, which has drawn fire from the rearguard of suburban propriety. Feminists also protest against pornography on the grounds that it incites men to violence against women. For lack of mass support, both fail to proscribe the images they find offensive.

Rosalind Coward thinks that the injunction to speak about sex is directed primarily at women and that it is an indication of their continuing greater responsibility for the emotional workings of relationships. She thinks this encourages them to drop their defences in sexual relationships: to be, in their self-revelations, utterly transparent in a sexual system in which women are often vulnerable and powerless. She is concerned that while on the one hand the social fiat to explore sexual responses, and thence the whole personality, is positive and healthy for women in that it identifies the dynamics of sexual relations (which for most means relationships with men), it also exposes them to more potential abuse by lowering their guard.

This parallels the arguments advanced by feminist psychotherapists, analysts and psychiatrists about the possible dangers to women of being treated by men, particularly by patriarchal and older men drawn to authoritarian structures, exemplified by the traditional relationship between the omniscient doctor and the ignorant and passive patient. Just as women practitioners questioned psychology's construction of women as inadequate measured by male standards, so they feared that women would be encouraged to confess themselves to men who would imperfectly understand their patients and would therefore, unwittingly, mistreat them.

In America the injunction to confess has found expression in particular through the reliance in many sectors of society on therapists, analysts and psychiatrists, and it was this feature of the American way of life which particularly drew the attention of social critics in the seventies who commented on what Tom Wolfe christened the 'me-generation'.

But the forms of self-disclosure which are a central function of friendship serve positive purposes. They can legitimate women's subjective selves by establishing a normalcy for intimate experiences, thereby authenticating them. Rosalind Coward says that women are effectively dramatizing their own experiences through turning them into a narrative; paradoxically, this serves not to distance them from what they feel but to reassure them that what they feel is real and justified by reference to what others feel. Conversely, one of the important functions of women's fiction, particularly romantic fiction, is to present to women feelings they have in common which they might otherwise find ephemeral and unbelievable.

So agony columns provide their readers with an external confirmation of their own inner feelings and thus support their sense of self. People who do not read for this sort of support might wrongly construe this voracious interest in intimate details, both in problem page letters and in romantic fiction, as a displaced sexual appetite or as merely a lurid extension of a taste for gossip. But gossip itself has the same basis; it is not idle or malicious but motivated by women's search for a solid sense of self, for validity and authenticity for their subjective experience so contradicted by the public world, which underlies the need to measure themselves against other women. This is sometimes misrepresented as evidence of competition between women, but research has found that women are generally not competitive but supportive of each other.[28]

Needing support, lacking confidence, feeling fraudulent and therefore working extra hard to stave off being unmasked conflict with the injunction to confess because of the necessity of preserving credibility, dictated by a competitive environment. The one implies that there is no solution without self-revelation, the other that such self-indulgence deserves no place among the successful.

Decline and rise

Richard Sennett shares Rosalind Coward's suspicions about the confessional mode, but for different reasons. He suggests that our model of sex is an act not of communion but of self-discovery, the aim of which is self-gratification. He argues that confusion of inner and outer is replicated in the gradual encroachment of the private, intimate sphere on the outside, public sphere, which means that the private domain loses its boundaries:

> It is no longer restrained by a public world in which people make alternative and countervailing investment of themselves. The erosion of the public life therefore deforms the intimate relations which seize people's wholehearted interest.[29]

His view is formed by the American context, but it has some wider relevance.

> The psychic life is seen as so precious and so delicate that it will wither if exposed to the harsh realities of the social world, and will flower only to the extent that it is protected and isolated. Each person's self has become his principal burden . . . [He is thinking of self-obsessed individuals in interminable therapy – the 'me-generation'.] The more privatized the psyche, the less it is stimulated, and the more difficult it is for us to feel or to express feelings.[30]

Although he may be confusing social isolation, which is widely thought to be conducive to depression, with the growing importance of privacy he clarifies the disadvantages of an intense inner life and a distortion of relationships between the self and others.

The evidence for the growth of the private realm is not indicated only in the rise of the confessional mode: the number of people in analysis, the increase in chat shows where guests are supposed to be sincere and natural, as distinct from the roles by which they are known to the public, the frankness of problem pages and of ordinary conversations between people. It is also indicated by the growth of the markets servicing it.

Attitudes to leisure have changed as the time devoted to it has increased; the working week has shortened not only over the last century but within a generation and now stands at under forty hours in the UK, while in neighbouring countries employee representatives, employers and governments are negotiating a thirty-two-hour working week to increase the number of jobs.[31]

Many of the growth industries in the service sector involve leisure activities; entertainment is growing through the increasing number of radio channels, satellite stations and cable networks. The major increase in employment in the 'literary, arts, sport and related' category is in the growth in leisure centre staff. Public companies run by women are almost exclusively in the personal services sector – Debbie Moore's Pineapple dance studios and Anita Roddick's Body Shop, for example. The fashion industry has grown and the garment industry has allied itself with the health products industry to meet the growing interest in health and fitness over the past decade. Travel and tourism have boomed, with an increase from six million Britons taking holidays abroad in the mid-1970s to sixteen million by the mid-1980s.

Richard Sennett sees the public world as increasingly cast in the image of the private – for instance, in the way that

We may understand that a politician's job is to draft or execute legislation, but that work does not interest us until we perceive the play of personality in political struggle. A political leader running for office is spoken of as 'credible' or 'legitimate' in

terms of what kind of man he is rather than in terms of the
actions or programmes he espouses.[32]

Similarly much pro-women activity in Britain has been
aimed at making women visible by publicizing individual
achievements: the Businesswoman of the Year Award run
by the Institute of Directors is one instance. The whole
project of many women's organizations, where network-
ing has been chosen as the way forward, also elevates
individual women as role models, as powerful contacts for
others and as exemplars to the rest of the world of what
women can achieve. In this respect the personal and the
individual take precedence over the collectivity but are
transformed by the public presentation.

   Sennett argues that our increasing emphasis on the
private side of life at the expense of the public drains the
public of attractiveness. By contrast with the private realm,
which he identifies with 'warmth and openness of vision',
he sees the public realm as rendered 'impersonal . . . stale
and empty'. To the extent that this polarity is sustained in
the individual's imagination, the public world is less
attractive and people are reluctant to engage in it.

   But the changes between public and private now going
on hold out the possibility of introducing the fulfilling
qualities of the private realm into the impoverished public
sphere – a process, in effect, of feminizing the realms of
work and politics. Women are already pioneering the
change.

10

Integration

I was my own worst enemy. I was sabotaging myself – but I think it suited me to sabotage myself. That makes it sound very extreme. Also, you don't like to advertise the fact that you're sabotaging yourself, because it sounds like making an excuse. If you're aware of sabotaging yourself, then you must be aware enough not to sabotage yourself. So it's Catch-22.

Moira Goodall started to design clothes when she was ten years old. In contrast to Dale Spender, the firm message she absorbed was that she could not pursue her ambitions. She was dissuaded from going to college to study fashion and believed that without a professional training she would not be taken seriously as a dress designer. So she went to work as a temporary secretary, and confined her interest in clothes to making her own.

But first friends, then friends of friends, noticed the designs and asked her for copies. Even so, it took years for her to accept that she was entitled to work as a designer, her lifelong ambition, because of the barrier that lacking an art college background represented to her: 'I thought that if I hadn't had a formal training, I wasn't good enough. I couldn't do it.' Even when she was finally convinced by other people that she was good enough and could do it, she remained very tentative: 'I knew I was good, that people liked the clothes. But I always would undercharge. I never had the confidence to say: "This is what it's worth. Take it or leave it." Now I regularly price myself out of people's pockets.' Now she is established she is clear in other ways too: about what she does and what she wants to do. Although large fashion organizations have asked for her pattern book, which is obviously gratifying, Moira has decided to retain control of her clothes herself:

Before, I wanted an image, I wanted people to know about me and what I was doing. But now, as far as I'm concerned, if I do good work and enjoy doing it, they're going to get to know about me anyway, which is what is happening.
   A design doesn't come out of nothing, it's a progression. People say: 'My God, how have you thought of that?' But it's not something you've just thought up in the dead of night.

The learning years

Of the years she spent coming to terms with the contradiction between her desire to design and her need for permission to do so she now says:

I don't regret, now that I'm past that stage, that sabotage, because during that time I developed other skills and enjoyed other things, which means once you come through, you've got more going for you. I find I can understand people, for instance in the therapy I do with ex-alcoholics; and in business, I can relate to a buyer or customer without having to put on my professional hat. Before, I always used to put on a 'hat' because I worried that I wasn't good enough. When I started I had to set up this 'business space', so when customers came round they would have a certain impression. I'd spend quite a long time setting up my work space, rearranging it – taking up my work time, in fact.

So for Moira, in retrospect, the struggle was worth it. It was personal and intense but it resulted in a certainty and resilience she feels she would not otherwise have achieved. Along with the personal achievements came the professional ones:

Confidence means you can state things more clearly. I feel much more organized now. What happened before was, I used to get depressed. I wasn't doing so much work as now and I used to feel things weren't going as well as they should and I was very much an adjunct of whatever boyfriend I was with. I used to be scared of ageing. I'm far happier now. Since I started taking a correct pride in my work, my work has got better and my self-image has got better, and I'm much happier.

When I was a temporary secretary, I had to invent things and construct a future – for instance, I planned to do A-levels and go to college to validate what I wanted to do. Also, one of the reasons I didn't go to art college to begin with was that I was too embarrassed to put up my work for general consumption. The thought of people criticizing something so personal as a drawing or design was more than I could think about.

This is a valid fear. It is not true that, confronted with someone's work, critics will turn out to be really nice people, as Sally A. Davies's experience testifies.

Keeping something in reserve

Sally is a freelance illustrator. She makes a good living, with a reputation for consistent work of a high quality.

Freelance illustration is a highly competitive arena in which illustrators not only compete against each other but are also suspicious of their clients, often art directors in agencies or in publishing, whose interest can lie in reducing prices by derogating the work they commission. In addition, because the work is based on a brief from the client, clients may be dissatisfied with it because it somehow fails to convey the idea they had in mind, or because their minds have changed since they originally discussed the brief with artist or agent. The illustrator's job is to interpret an idea which may have passed through the medium of several different minds before it reaches her. This alone is a delicate task.

The illustrator is therefore vulnerable to criticism on many different grounds, and it can be very destructive:

I have only ever given, say, eighty per cent to illustration, because I didn't think it was worth any more from me. But I also think that underlying this is the fear that if you give a hundred per cent and that is messed about with or not accepted, you've got nothing else.

The area she reserves for herself – the work to which she does devote herself a hundred per cent – is painting privately, apart from her commercial work. This was something she found it very hard to embark on:

I was reluctant to start on my own concepts or topics, using my own style, because I felt my style had been sullied. It was the only voice I had and, using that on subjects that were really important to me, I didn't want to go through the routine, not of having it criticized but having it trampled on.

Of her career success as an illustrator, she says:

It's been like climbing a mountain and I'd got three-quarters of the way up and it had been quite arduous. And I'd found a crevice and just slipped into it. I was too afraid to do the other twenty-five per cent. Because I thought at the time, once you get to the top, there's only one way: down. Whereas if I stopped just short of that, I might be able to stay in the same place, and descent from there would be less painful.

Having established herself as an illustrator, Sally has now formalized that part of her which she keeps separate from her abrasive commercial working environment. In addition to her personal work she teaches in an art college, which is personally and creatively important to her. For one thing it is an antidote to the isolated and enclosed existence of an illustrator, who works at home and whose contact with the outside world is limited largely to meetings with agents and clients to pick up, deliver or discuss work. Before she taught, she found: 'I wouldn't leave the house during the day. I found that very difficult. Even going to the shops to buy fags.'

In the role of teacher, in which she nurtures other

people's talents and offers them her experience, the act of giving has proved more enriching than the limited, self-involved world of illustrating, which had gradually drained Sally's creativity in requiring her to be defensively able to cope with criticism, suspicion and competition. She was progressively thrown back on her own inner resources in an environment which did not replenish them:

I lost all feeling. I don't know, sort of dead really. Maybe I thought I hadn't got a voice any longer. Apart from illustration, I threw myself into decorating, doing all kinds of things which were really a displacement activity, a way of not getting down to some proper work.

By 'proper work' Sally means her own personal painting. In coming to terms with the limited satisfaction of success as an illustrator and broadening her base in response, formally recognizing that she was prepared to give illustration only so much of herself and no more, she was able to reintegrate her creative abilities.

Being a successful illustrator is not a source of undiluted satisfaction, and paradoxically Sally's success is founded on a degree of self-sabotage. It is the extent to which she is cavalier about her work that helps her function successfully. Work is not ultimately and overwhelmingly important to her: 'Personal achievement has absolutely nothing to do with outside applause or with cash benefits. It's a very separate thing from being a success in one field.'

The importance of being in earnest
Just as Sally's success is related to her confidence in dealing with clients, which is itself a product of the fact that the work does not matter too much to her, so Moira found the same solution to the obstacles that beset her in following her métier as a clothes designer:

I just realized a few years ago that this was what I wanted to do and there was no big deal about it. As long as I could support myself, then it was valuable. It's not just something I'm doing on the side, which was what I used to put out. I didn't take myself seriously, so why the hell should anybody else?

The paradox in what Moira is saying – realizing that it was 'no big deal' to do what she had always wanted to do, but that at the same time what stopped her was 'not taking herself seriously' – is crucial to breaking the circle of fear which dams up private aspiration and directs it more towards a fantasy existence than towards realization in the public sphere. It is in both taking aspirations seriously and not taking them too seriously that escape from the vicious circle lies, for overvaluing achievement leads to overestimating the difficulty it involves.

Just as businesses need the creative values of wit and humour, so do individuals. Taking oneself too seriously can be counterproductive if it is tied to the sense of inadequacy that perennially dogs some women. Yet although the problem is common it is not, ultimately, something that can be solved by an external agency. Moira Goodall sums it up: 'I think the great learning thing is for women to have confidence of their own. And there's no way it's going to come from society. It's just not. It's got to come from themselves.'

Integrity as achievement

The problem of the contradiction between public and private, as it is played out in the way the glamour of success intimidates some to the point of inhibiting them from even undertaking an apparently epic project, is that as a personal experience it shares the private characteristics of complexity and ambiguity, so there is no simple solution. For this reason external agencies like legislation, training and networks can only facilitate the process of reconciling the conflict; they cannot deliver the solution.

Although the problem derives from external sources like

social attitudes which invalidate private senses, public and political solutions cannot and will not solve it. The issue does not appear near the top of any political agenda, for which it is in any case too complex and too diverse, and the steps that have been taken to reduce the practical aspects of the contradiction between people's public and private lives, such as attempts to legislate for parental leave from work and leave for family reasons (in addition to responsibility for children), have been rejected in the public – parliamentary – arena.

Yet this is not a matter for serious regret. For the answer lies, properly, in the hands of the individual. Political will can ease women's transition, but the crucial factor is personal will. Qualities like resolve, fortitude, honesty and percipience are finally much more important than legislative change. The dichotomy of success and satisfaction is a moral and personal issue, and its resolution lies in the hands of the individuals who most acutely sense its conflicts. Those who feel the schism between the public and the private realms most strongly stand, by that very token, the best chance of resolving and integrating the disparities.

Integrity is a moral value, and one which is much admired in a world where naturalness and reality, sincerity and authenticity are prized – and rare. The dichotomy of public and private spheres is the problem of achieving and maintaining that oneness. All the women who have spoken directly in the previous pages about their acute discomfort at the split between public and private, between their real and their ideal selves, between their desire for achievement and their fear of its cost or of failure, have arrived at a synthesis of their disparate public and private selves and have attained a measure of working integrity. A common factor between these women who speak directly of their difficulties and doubts about their working lives is that in articulating their ambivalence they crystallized it, and this seems to be a first step towards resolution.

Raising the barriers

It may seem wasteful that so many women must struggle so hard, apparently against themselves, in order to realize their own abilities. It may even seem unfair when one thinks not only of men but of women like Dale Spender who have not been blocked by the reproduction of the schism between public and private in their internal, personal experience.

But women like Dale, who feel that they have never been told they 'can't', are rare beacons to others. Femininity conditions many more into unwilling passivity but this is not, as the struggles recounted in the preceding pages show, immutable.

Those women in whom the sense of the duality of existence is acute and painful, who feel their real, inner selves to be besieged by an unsympathetic and impoverished public realm and who feel invalid in the domain of strangers even in the everyday experience of going out to work, can learn from others that this can change.

There are two external sources of support for the task of raising the barriers dividing many women from performing to their best of their abilities. One is the shift in the frontier between public and private. The rise of private values has been widely decried because it denudes the public world of fulfilment, leaving only thin, exterior values like success. But as the masculinized public realm declines, so opportunities for private sensibilities rise, welcomed by men as well as women.

The other source of support is the news that this isolating experience of invalidity is a common phenomenon. The fact that the feeling is so widespread itself contradicts its most crippling effect, for perceiving it as shared transforms it from a disintegrative into a unifying experience.

The most effective help for women is their own. One of the reasons there are so few women at the top in the public world is that there are so many preventing themselves from getting there. But the pinnacles of public achievement are not the only ends to which women – and men – should aspire. The pursuits of both success and satisfaction are equally legitimate; the choice between them should be informed and free.

Notes

1: *Starting Point*
 1. Dr Yves Bennet and Dawn Carter, *Sidetracked? A look at the careers advice given to fifth form girls* (Equal Opportunities Commission, 1982).
 2. Mant, *Leaders We Deserve*, paper to the World Congress on Management Development (1986) referring to his book of the same title (Blackwell, 1985) in which he charts the rise of 'raiders' as leaders compared with 'builders'. Raiders are motivated by power, builders by altruistic interests; builders depend on external structures, raiders are self-sufficient. Builders are capable of abstract and creative thought and of reaching compromises rather than ruled by power relations. 'Raiders' are occupied with survival, an idea which parallels those put forward by Christopher Lasch in *The Minimal Self* (Picador, 1985), which discusses the encroachment on the potent, free-ranging psyche of the vast, chaotic, uncontrollable – and therefore dangerous – public world.
 3. Wilde, *The Critic as Artist: A Dialogue*; Part II of *The Artist as Critic*.
 4. Goffman, *Interaction Ritual: Essays on Face-to-Face Behaviour* (Anchor, 1967) p. 6.
 5. Ibid., p. 8.
 6. Ibid., pp. 9, 10.
 7. Helen Bright, personal communication.

8. Spender, *Learning to Fail* (Routledge & Kegan Paul, 1978).

9. By the early 1980s nearly 50 per cent of students at some business schools were women, from a tiny 3 per cent when these schools first started in Britain in the latter part of the 1960s. As managers, however, the proportion of women dropped from 8 per cent at the start of the decade to 6 per cent at its midpoint.

10. In 1911 18.8 per cent of employers and proprietors were women, compared with 24.9 per cent by 1971; 19.8 per cent of managers and administrators compared with 21.6; 6 per cent of higher professionals compared with 9.9; 62.9 per cent of lower professionals and technicians compared with 52.1; 15.5 per cent of unskilled manual workers compared with 37.5 (excerpted from Hakim, *Occupational Segregation* [Department of Employment, 1979] p. 28, table). This shows that while some gains have been made, working women have also suffered considerable losses. 'The proportion of women in managerial and administrative positions or in lower professional and technical occupations actually declined between 1911 and 1961, although figures for 1971 suggest that women are now regaining some of the ground lost. In manual work the trend is towards greater segregation, with men increasingly over-represented in skilled work and women contributing an increasing share of unskilled and semi-skilled workers' (ibid., p. 27).

11. See Allin and Hunt, 'Women In Official Statistics', in *The Changing Experience of Women* (Martin Robertson, 1982), on how government statistics fail to give a true picture of women's participation in the labour force. Employers are not required to return employment census details of domestic employees even though this seems to be a significant source of employment for women; similarly this excludes home-workers,

although a 1981 survey of England and Wales found 1 million people, or 4 per cent of the labour force, working from home (*Social Trends 1985* [HMSO, 1985] p. 61) and it is estimated that over half a million women, equivalent to 6 per cent of the UK female labour force, work at home (*The Changing Experience of Women, Units 10 and 11* [Open University, 1984] p. 30). A government survey (Cragg and Dawson, *Qualitative Research Among Homeworkers* [Department of Employment, 1981]) estimates that 1.5 million people – 6 per cent of the total UK labour force – work at home but found only one man among all the home-workers interviewed.

As 'snapshots', government surveys generally exclude from the picture of the working population all those who are not in employment during the reference week of the survey – for instance, mothers who work only during the school terms. See also the account of the failings of official statistics to represent the true position of women in *Women in Statistics*, EOC Research Bulletin No. 10 (EOC, 1987).

12. In 1851, 40 per cent of the workforce was female compared with 42 per cent in 1981.

13. The 1851 Census showed that 40 per cent of women employees were servants, with the next largest number employed in textiles, clothing and agricultural labour. There were no female clerical workers in this census (*British Labour Statistics Historical Abstract 1886–1968*, quoted in Beechey [ed.], *The Changing Experience of Women* [Open University, 1984]). In 1911 most working women were in domestic or other personal services: 35 per cent were servants (including laundresses), 19.5 per cent were textile workers and 15.6 per cent were in the dressmaking trades (Scott and Tilley, 'Women's Work and the Family', in Rosenberg [ed.] *The Family in History*

[University of Pennsylvania, 1975] p. 148). By the middle of the century just under 2 million women were domestic servants in Great Britain (Sheila Lewenhak, quoting the 1939 ILO *Yearbook of Labour Statistics* in *Women and Work* [Fontana, 1980] p. 208). As mentioned in note 11 above, statistics on domestic servants are now not customarily collected; this is one index of occupational change. However, in 1984 four in ten part-time and one in ten full-time women employees worked in personal service occupations, including hairdressing, catering and cleaning (*New Earnings Survey*, Department of Employment, 1984) and in 1981 736,000 people in England and Wales were living at their place of work (*Social Trends 1985* [HMSO, 1985] p. 61).

14. Bell, McKee and Priestley, *Fathers, Childbirth and Work* (EOC, 1983); Helen Franks, *Goodbye Tarzan*: *Men after Feminism* (Allen & Unwin, 1984) which, though it shows the tenacity with which men resist feminist ideas, also reveals their impact and the expectations some men have about what they are prepared to do in the house.

15. Between 1961 and 1980 the number of part-time workers in the UK doubled (*Working Women* [TUC, 1983] p. 27); in the seven years to 1978 the number of women part-timers rose by more than a third (Table: *Employment in the 70s* in *Women in the 80s* [CIS, 1981] p. 10). Of all OECD countries the UK has the highest proportion of women as part-time employees: Table 3 (p. 15) in Sivard, *Women . . . A World Survey* (World Priorities, 1985).

16. In 1974 a Post Office Social Forecast (Joan Glover, *Working from Home*) predicted that some 13 million jobs could be done at home instead of the workplace. The estimated time of arrival at such a revolutionary state was given as 1980, but although with hindsight

such predictions seem a little Wellsian, the reasoning
remains sound.

17. Marshall, *Women Managers: Travellers in a Male
    World* (John Wiley, 1984).
18. See, for instance, Dr Elizabeth Vallance's analysis of
    voting behaviour in *Parliamentary Affairs*, June 1984.
19. *Women and Men of Europe* (Commission of the
    European Communities, 1984). Two-thirds of the
    women surveyed were not particularly interested in
    politics, significantly more than the 50 per cent of
    men. While 15 per cent of men described themselves
    as very interested, only 7 per cent of women said they
    were; 29 per cent of women and 18 per cent of men
    said they were not at all interested. Twenty per cent
    of men compared with 12 per cent of women said
    they often discussed politics with friends, while 37
    per cent of women (22 per cent of men) never
    mentioned it.
       By contrast, 23 per cent of women (24 per cent of
    men) said they often discussed 'important social prob-
    lems' with friends, and the survey found the increase
    in the number of women who were politically moti-
    vated enough to join a public demonstration marked
    enough '. . . to say that participation by women is
    beginning to approach the levels for men' (Sup-
    plement 16 to *Women of Europe* [European Commis-
    sion, 1984] p. 45). For a further discussion of the real
    and mythical differences between male and female
    political interests and practices see the section on
    'Women and Electoral Politics' in Siltanen and Stan-
    worth (eds) *Women and the Public Sphere* (Hutchin-
    son, 1984).
20. Reiter, 'Men and Women in The South of France:
    Public and Private Domains' in Reiter (ed.) *Towards
    an Anthropology of Women* (Monthly Review Press,
    1975) p. 258.

21. Although occupations remain very largely sex-segregated in Britain there are now more women in paid employment than in earlier decades of the century, the major factor being the number of married women in paid employment. As note 13 above indicates, personal services is a major category of employment for women (though not for men), with 58 per cent of all women manual workers. Of women non-manual workers, 55 per cent do typing or general clerical work (*Working Women* [TUC, 1983] p. 11). 'By the end of the 1970s, just over a quarter (27 per cent) of all women were working in occupations where they outnumbered men by nine to one, while over half (58 per cent) of men were in occupations where they outnumbered women to the same extent – a picture that hardly differed at all from that in 1971' (Hakim, 'Job Segregation: Trends in the 1970s', in *Employment Gazette* [Department of Employment, December 1981] p. 523). The *Women and Employment* survey (HMSO, 1984) shows much the same picture. However, it showed that occupational segregation markedly diminishes in social classes I and II (with the highest-level occupations) and is strongest for women in semi-skilled domestic jobs. Women in other semi-skilled work had lower levels of segregation at work; segregation was higher in manufacturing than in service industries (p. 27) and part-timers were more segregated than full-timers (p. 28).

22. Helen Franks, *Goodbye Tarzan*.

23. See, for example, Colette Dowling, *The Cinderella Complex* (Fontana, 1982).

24. The Bem Sex Role Inventory (BSRI) is a list of adjectives popularly seen as masculine, feminine or androgynous (separate dimensions rather than points in a continuum) which can be used to test how individuals rate on each scale. Masculine adjectives,

for example, include 'ambitious', 'dominant' and 'self-reliant'; feminine adjectives include 'affectionate', 'gentle', 'understanding' ('The Measurement of Psychological Androgyny', *Journal of Consulting and Clinical Psychology* no. 42 [1974]: 115–62). The author of the BSRI and other researchers have argued that androgynous characteristics are the most useful, for society and for the individual, on the grounds that the androgynous personality can utilize masculine or feminine behaviour as appropriate and androgyny breaks the tyranny of sex stereotyping. Different studies have shown androgynous personalities to be more self-confident, better adjusted, more socially skilled and better able to make and maintain intimate relationships than less flexible, sex-typed individuals. Other researchers, however, have been alarmed at what they see as sexism under another name.

25. For example Spence and Helmreich, 'Masculine Instrumentality and Feminine Expressiveness: Their Relationship with Sex Role Attitudes and Behaviours', *Psychology of Women Quarterly*, vol. 5 no. 2 (Winter 1980).

26. For instance Orbach and Eichenbaum, *Outside In, Inside Out* (Fontana, 1982): *What Do Women Want?* (Fontana, 1983).

27. Writing immediately after the 1960s, Maggie Angeloglou forecast that the next development in cosmetics would be cosmetics for men; and although glam rock, its revenants and punk in the 1970s established something of a tradition of face- and body-paint in male subcultures, this has not replicated the widespread use of cosmetics among upper-class men in Europe until the eighteenth century, or among tribal peoples (*A History of Make-up* [Studio Vista, 1970] p. 140).

28. While during the 1970s women espoused trade union-

ism at an unprecedented rate – female membership rose from 2,743,000 in 1970 to 3,902,000 in 1979 (*Employment Gazette*, January 1983) – trade unions were slower to embrace feminism and slower still to go further than lip service in pursuing the best interests of their women members. This schism between feminism and socialism was of long standing. Proudhon, the nineteenth-century socialist who furnished the world with the useful maxim 'Property is theft', petitioned for the enactment of a law to grant men the right to condemn to death wives who were disobedient or conducted themselves badly, and considered that women had no right to independence of any sort – certainly not economic.

29. See, for instance, Marshall, *Women Managers*.
30. For example the findings of the *Women and Men of Europe* survey (op. cit.) on traditional attitudes to women; there was no bastion of old values except among older people.

2: *History*

1. Piggott, *Ancient Europe* (Aldine, 1965) pp. 179, 181, 196–9, quoted in Fisher, *Women's Creation*.
2. Some, however, contend that the Amazons were a historical population; Ann Oakley, for instance, comments that they were a West African people, living in the ancient Kingdom of Dahomey, who recruited women into the army, of which they still formed an estimated 40 per cent in 1845. They were, she reports, armed with blunderbusses, muskets and knives with eighteen-inch blades and fought with the same energy and success as men. (Oakley [ed.] *Sex Gender and Society* [Gower/Maurice Temple Smith, 1985] p. 145).
3. Julie Wheelwright, *Amazons and Military Maids: an examination of female military heroines in British*

literature and the changing construction of gender (unpublished paper, University of Sussex).

4. Chadwick, *The Celts* (Pelican, 1970) p. 115.

5. Aristotle, *Politics*, Book VIII, ch. 1, line 1337, trans. Barker (Oxford University Press, 1948) p. 391.

6. 'A state composed of too many will indeed be self-sufficient in the matter of material necessities (as an uncivilized people may equally be); but it will not be a true state, for the simple reason that it can hardly have a true constitution. Who can be the general of a mass so excessively large? And who can give it orders, unless he has Stentor's voice?' (Book VII, ch. 4, line 1326.) 'Both in order to give decisions in matters of disputed rights and to distribute the offices of government according to the merit of candidates, the citizens of a state must know one another's characters.' (Book VII, ch. 4, line 1326; ibid., pp. 342, 343.)

7. Discussed in Ortner, 'Is Woman to Nature as Man is to Culture?', in Rosaldo and Lamphere (eds) *Women, Culture and Society* (Stanford, 1973).

8. Larissa Bonfante, 'Etruscan Couples and their Aristocratic Society', in Foley (ed.) *Reflections of Women in Antiquity* (Gordon & Breach, 1981).

9. Evelyn Sullerot, *Women and Love* (Jill Norman, 1980).

10. The poor, who were almost 40 per cent of the London working classes in the 1880s, 'hardly enjoyed the "barest decencies of existence", even by the austere standards then applied to the lower orders' (Hobsbawm, *The Age of Capital* [Abacus, 1977] p. 268).

11. *Social Trends* 15 (HMSO, 1985) p. 147. See also Leonard and Speakman, 'The Family', in Beechey (ed.) *The Changing Experience of Women*; *Working Women* (TUC, 1983) p. 3.

12. See Scott and Tilley, 'Women's Work and the Family',

in Rosenberg (ed.) *The Family in History* (University of Pennsylvania Press, 1975).

13. Jessie Bernard, *The Female World* (The Free Press, 1974) p. 161.

14. On average British women watch over 25 hours' television a week, but this includes periods of 'passive' viewing when the television is on but the woman is involved in other activities. So, for instance, the television programmes children watch after school while their mother attends to household affairs may count as her viewing. Figures for total leisure time show that men have more free time than women, whose unpaid time is occupied with looking after the household. British men in full-time work average 11.5 hours per day free at the weekends compared with 9 hours for women full-time employees. Per week, employed men have on average 42 hours free compared with full-time working women's 36 hours. Whereas working part-time means that men's leisure increases to 60 hours a week, for women it means a gain of only four more hours (*Social Trends* 15 [HMSO, 1985]).

15. The *Women and Employment* survey (HMSO, 1984) showed that 45 per cent of women returning to part-time work after a career break for family reasons move into occupations with less status and less remuneration than their previous job, while 30 per cent of those going back to full-time work after their first baby went to a worse job than they had left.

Alban-Metcalf and Nicholson (*The Career Development of British Managers*, British Institute of Management [1985] survey of managers' career changes) found that women change employers slightly more often than men and most frequently in their thirties, suggesting the influence of career breaks. Women also change jobs and occupations, or move from employed to self-employed both to accommodate the opposing demands of family and job and to escape their low ceiling of career development. Thus the researchers found that some women left management to work as consultants because they could see no further career progress in their organization.

16. Popay and Wicks *et al.*, *Values and the Changing Family* (Study Commission on the Family, 1982).

17. This is described as one of the reasons for growing cynicism about governments in particular and leaders in general by (for instance) Sennett in *Authority* (Sigmund Freud Lecture at London University [1980] published in the USA by Vintage) or Mant, *Leaders We Deserve* (Blackwell, 1985). Sennett argues that leaders have lost authority and increased in authoritarianism as the qualities of consensus and play diminish.

18. See Smith's Classification of Jobs in the 1970s for the Canadian Department of Immigration.

19. The function of this style, apart from identifying users as members of the class who use professional language and establishing a 'scientific', 'objective' rather than a personal tone, may also be to represent a consensus rather than to advance an opinion, by analogy with a passage in Trilling:

In the course of a call being paid by the [American] Ambassador, the Queen inquired whether he was by now settled and comfortable in his home, to which he replied: 'We are still, in the residence, subject to some discomfiture and inconvenience owing to certain elements of refurbishment' (footnote to p. 113, *Sincerity and Authenticity* [Oxford Paperbacks, 1974]).

Trilling makes this reference in the course of discussing de Tocqueville's comments on American speech styles referring to the circumlocutory, general and abstract style as the language of democracy, for it aims not to express a personal opinion but to voice public opinion.

3: *An Unstable State?*

1. Juliet Mitchell argues that much of Freud has been misconstrued by many feminists; she tries to rescue Freudian psychology for psychotherapists to use with women in *Psychoanalysis and Feminism* (Penguin, 1974).

2. J. A. Grimes, *The Probability of Admission to a Mental Illness Hospital or Unit* (In-Patient Statistics from the Mental Health Inquiry for England [1975, 1978]).

3. Average length of stay in hospital was 12 days for men and 17 for women, excluding women's visits to hospital to give birth, according to an extrapolation from *Hospital In-Patients Inquiry 1980*, Table 3.7: *Hospital In-Patients: Mean Duration of Stay* . . . in *Sex Differences in Britain*, ed. Reid and Wormald (Grant McIntyre, 1982) p.43.

4. Only 4.7 per cent of households conform to the stereotype of the four-person nuclear family: two parents and two children, one male breadwinner and an economically inactive wife. According to the 1982 General Household Survey, 10 per cent of households have one male breadwinner, an economically inactive wife and an unspecified number of children.

5. Anthea Duquemin, in *The importance of marital status for women's lives* (unpublished doctoral thesis), refers to *Why are Women Redundant?* by W. R. Greg (1862), which proposed sending 40,000 women per year to the colonies. At first feminists supported the notion, but after Greg's article had linked emigration with husband-hunting, feminist support of the education-employment option grew. The other option for genteel women was the life of

a governess or companion. But outside the working class, marriage was the only respectable career.

The situation which led to concern over 'redundant women' has been reversed since the middle of this century, with men outnumbering women in age groups up to fifty although women, being particularly well represented in the older groups, still outnumber men in the population as a whole. The change in the number of men in the population is due to the greater numbers surviving infancy – probably a result of better medical care during pregnancy and in child-hood – and of better diet and social conditions, which have reduced infant mortality.

6. Ehrenreich and English, in *Complaints and Disorders: The Sexual Politics of Sickness* (Writers & Readers, 1976), quote (p. 33) P. Moebius, *Concerning the Physiological and Intellectual Weakness of Women*:

> If we wish woman to fulfil the task of motherhood fully she cannot possess a masculine brain. If the feminine abilities were developed to the same degree as those of the male, her material organs would suffer and we should have a repulsive and useless hybrid.

In 1873 Dr Edward Clarke wrote in his influential *Sex and Education* that 'higher education [was] already destroying the reproductive abilities of Ameri-can women' (Ehrenreich and English, p. 33).

Stanley Hall, in *Principles of Biology*, commented that too much intellectual activity made women sterile and that educated women frequently had difficulty breastfeeding (quoted in Duquemin, *The importance of marital status . . .*).

7. McClelland, *The Achievement Motive* (Appleton-Century-Crofts, 1953) and *The Achieving Society* (Van Nostrand, 1961).

8. See, for instance, the seminal works *The Development*

of Sex Differences (ed. Eleanor Maccoby [Stanford, 1966]) and *The Psychology of Sex Differences* (ed. Maccoby and Jacklin [Stanford, 1974]) which review studies on sex differences and generally conclude that the evidence is contradictory or unclear in most cases for consistent differences in ability.

9. Reported in Table 3.3 of *Sex Differences in Britain*, ed. Reid and Wormald (Grant McIntyre, 1982) p. 35.

10. According to information from the 1982 General Household Survey, 37 per cent compared to 33 per cent of men. Women see the doctor more often (*Social Trends* [HMSO, 1985]). On average women visit the doctor 4.4 times a year, compared to 3.3 visits per year per man, and have twice as many operations (Reid and Wormald, *Sex Differences*, p. 42).

11. The memorandum sent from the World Medical Association for Perfect Health to the Secretary of State for Social Services called for the National Health Service to adopt a system of herbal remedies and meditation, traditional in India, in order to reduce stress, which the doctors believed lay behind 80 per cent of diseases (reported in *The Guardian*, 29 December 1986).

12. Quoted in 'Anxieties: Agoraphobia and Hysteria', by Dianne L. Chambless and Alan J. Goldstein, in *Women and Psychotherapy*, ed. Brodsky and Hare-Mustin (Guilford Press, 1980).

13. A. J. Blair, *Social Class and Representations of Cancer*: paper to the British Psychological Society Annual Conference (1987).

14. Shirley Pearce and R.W. Beard, 'Chronic Pelvic Pain', in *Psychology and Gynaecological Problems*, ed. Broome and Wallace (Tavistock, 1984).

15. Perhaps the biggest indicator of how widespread chronic pelvic pain without obvious pathology might be comes from two studies of people who had appen-

dectomies for acute abdominal pain, both of which found that biopsies showed a 'large proportion' to have had normal appendixes. Creed, 'Life Events and Appendectomy', *The Lancet* 1381–5 (1981); Crossley, 'Hospital Admissions for Abnormal Pain in Childhood', *Journal of the Royal Society of Medicine* [1982], quoted in Pearce and Beard, 'Chronic Pelvic Pain'.

16. The same differences in private self-attention might also account for some of the differences in response to pain, including pain in childbirth. It is usually assumed that the experience of a symptom begins with the deviation of some physiological internal state from a normal baseline, and it has been implicit for a long time that the intensity with which such events are experienced, or the probability of experiencing them, is influenced by attentional factors. Someone who carefully scrutinizes his or her internal state is especially likely to notice changes from resting levels and may be more likely to perceive these as symptoms. Indeed, a person who is overly attentive may be classified as a hypochondriac. Someone who carefully diverts attention from such changes may remain unaware of them. But there is growing emphasis on other factors that influence just how a given internal sensation is experienced. In particular, it is being argued with increasing conviction that the schemas with which people approach these sensations have a profound impact on the subjective nature of the perception of the physiological event and thus the secondary affective reaction that the experience induces (Carver and Scheier, *Attention and Self-Regulation* [Springer-Verlag, 1981] p. 106).

17. Burnis and Thorpe, *National Survey of Agoraphobia* (1977).

18. Melville (*Phobias* [Unwin, 1977]) also reports that

phobics described their phobia as 'a nuisance', and Ruth Hurst Vose reports that only 2.2 people in a thousand suffer from severely disabling phobias, compared with 77 people per thousand suffering to some degree (*Agoraphobia* [Faber & Faber, 1987]).

19. *Personal Violence* (Home Office Research Study, 1986).

20. This symptom was noted by Ruth Hurst Vose (*Agoraphobia*), who gives a detailed account of her phobias and their treatment.

21. Freud, *The Psychopathology of Everyday Life* (Ernest Benn, 1914 [5th impression 1960]) pp. 62, 63.

22. The sense of fraudulence to which many women managers admit was noted by Judi Marshall in *Women Managers: Travellers in a Male World* (John Wiley, 1984) and has produced a crop of self-help books in the United States, such as: *If I'm so Successful, Why do I feel Like A Fake? The Imposter Phenomenon* (Pocket Books, 1986).

23. Chambless and Goldstein, *Women and Psychotherapy*.

24. Helen Petrie, Department of Applied Linguistics, Birkbeck College, University of London, private communication on unpublished research.

25. A comparison of an African people living in Sierra Leone with a Canadian Inuit (Eskimo) people showed that overall the Africans were more field-dependent than the Inuit and that among the Inuit there was no sex difference, while the Sierra Leone women were much more field-dependent than the men. The social structure of the two peoples was very different. While the African society was disciplinarian and conformist, with women and children subject to the rule of men, the Inuit society was liberal and encouraged autonomy among their children, regardless of sex. Berry,

'Temné and Eskimo perceptual skills', *International Journal of Psychology*, no. 1 (1966).

26. Comparisons of immigrants from developing countries adjusting to life in a technological society with people from the same culture living traditionally showed that people in transition were less field-dependent than those living traditionally. The study was interpreted as showing the effect of education on field dependency. See Doob, *Becoming More Civilized* (Yale, 1960); Lerner, *The Passing of Traditional Society* (Free Press, 1958) on the 'mobile personality' adapting from traditional to Western society.

27. Witkin and Goodenough, *Field Dependence Revisited* (Research Bulletin, Educational Testing Service [Princeton, 1976]) referred to in Lips and Colwill, *The Psychology of Sex Differences*.

28. See Lips, Myers and Colwill, 'Sex Differences in Ability', in Lips and Colwill (eds) *The Psychology of Sex Differences* (Prentice-Hall, 1978) pp. 168, 169.

29. Witkin and Goodenough, *Field Dependence Revisited*.

30. Carver and Scheier, *Attention and Self-Regulation*.

31. Rutter and O'Connell, 'The Relationship Among Sex-Role Orientation, Cognitive Complexity and Tolerance for Ambiguity', *Sex Roles*, vol. 8 no. 12 (1982).

32. Vonda Olson Long, 'Masculinity and Mental Health', *Journal of Consulting and Clinical Psychology*, vol. 54 no. 3 (1986).

33. Carver and Scheier, *Attention and Self-Regulation*.

34. Chambless and Goldstein, *Women and Psychotherapy*.

35. Joanna Bunker Rohrbaugh, *Women: Psychology's Puzzle* (Abacus, 1981) p. 422.

36. Bendefeldt, Miller and Ludwig, 'Cognitive Performance in Conversion Hysteria', *Archives of General Psychiatry*, vol. 33 (1976).

37. Hysterics have also been found to be more suggestible than most people, and suggestibility is a factor associated with high public but low private self-attention (Carver and Scheier, *Attention and Self-Regulation*). Although some of the experiments conducted by the authors involved all-female groups, they do not comment directly on any relationship between public and private self-attention and gender.

4: *Acting the Part*

1. Maggie Angeloglou, *A History of Make-up* (Studio Vista, 1970).

2. From Ben Barker-Benfield, *The Spermatic Economy*; quoted in Ehrenreich and English, *Complaints and Disorders: The Sexual Politics of Sickness* (Writers & Readers, 1973) p. 40.

3. 'The safety of walls with runic charms planted and erected round an encampment or village, would scare away the evil powers; but the unfortunate men had to travel outside the enclosures to find food, and so they needed disguises. Women, who sat at home and ground corn, could be left in their natural state, they had no enemies to frighten' (Maggie Angeloglou, *A History of Make-up*, p. 8).

4. Rayna Reiter, *Towards an Anthropology of Women*; Rosaldo and Lamphere (eds) *Women, Culture and Society*.

5. Zimbardo found that 42 per cent of his US sample were shy and 79 per cent emphasized their self-consciousness, compared to only 31 per cent of his Israeli sample who said they were shy and only 30 per cent who said they felt self-conscious (Zimbardo, *Shyness: What is it, what to do about it?* (Addison-Wesley, 1977).

6. Carver and Scheier, *Attention and Self-Regulation* (Springer-Verlag, 1981).

7. Sennett, *The Fall of Public Man*.
8. Goffman, *The Presentation Of Self In Everyday Life* (Penguin, 1974).
9. Clare, *In the Psychiatrist's Chair* (Chatto & Windus, 1984).
10. Simon Callow, *Being an Actor* (Methuen, 1984) p. 13.
11. Ibid., p. 23.

5: *The Mirror Crack'd*
1. Berger, *Ways of Seeing* (BBC, 1972) p. 46.
2. Irving Singer, *The Goals of Human Sexuality* (Wildwood House, 1973) p. 217; reproduced in 'The Sensuous and the Passionate', in Sobie (ed.) *The Philosophy of Sex* (Rowman & Littlefield, 1980).
3. Maccoby and Jacklin report in *Psychology of Sex Difference* (Stanford, 1974) that men do not prove less sensitive than women in terms of nurturant behaviour or of self-reported feelings. They conclude that the idea that women are more sensitive can be ascribed to sex stereotyping: 'It is our opinion that the social judgment skills of men and boys have been seriously underrated' (p. 214). Their review does show that boys socialize in groups where girls socialize with their best friend, but they do not consider that this shows a different level of sensitivity but different social skills. However, if sensitivity is understood to mean empathy rather than concern, then the sex roles inventory categorizes this as a feminine trait.
4. Four times as many women are marriage guidance counsellors. (Jeremy Laurance, 'Marital Breakdown' [*New Society*, 30 January 1987]: 18).
5. See, for instance, Williams, 'Gender, Masculinity and Femininity and Emotional Intimacy in Same Sex Friendships', *Sex Roles*, vol. 12 no. 5/6 (1985); Sollie and Fischer, 'Sex Role Orientation, Intimacy of Topic

and Target and Person Differences in Self Disclosure among Women', *Sex Roles*, vol. 12 no. 9/10 (1985), which reported that androgynous women were more willing to reveal themselves than sex-typed or undifferentiated women (women who were neither masculine nor feminine, as distinct from androgynous women who incorporate both feminine and masculine traits).

6. Sherry Ortner, 'Is Woman to Nature as Man is to Culture?', in Rosaldo and Lamphere (eds) *Woman, Culture and Society* (Stanford, 1976).

7. For instance, Rosalind Coward in *Female Desire* (Paladin, 1984), Richard Sennett in *The Fall Of Public Man* and Christopher Lasch in *The Culture of Narcissism* (Abacus, 1980).

8. Val Hey, *The Necessity of Romance* (University of Kent Occasional Papers, 1984).

9. Ibid., pp. 18, 20.

10. Unpublished research conducted by Helen Petrie of Birkbeck College, University of London, Department of Applied Linguistics; personal communication.

Women talk more freely and reveal more about themselves to one another, according to Aebischer, *Les Femmes et le Bavardage*, unpublished doctoral dissertation (1979) quoted in Gergen and Gergen, *Social Psychology* (Harcourt Brace Jovanovich, 1981); Sidney Jourard, *The Transparent Self* (Van Nostrand Reinhold, 1971) pp. 228–236.

Another difference between men and women relationships is that women's last longer (Wheeler and Nezlek, 'Sex Differences in Social Participation', *Journal of Personality and Social Psychology*, no. 35 (1977). Women are more likely than men to do things together spontaneously, to be warmly supportive of each other (Weiss and Lowenthal, 'Life-Course Perspectives on Friendship', in Lowenthal, Thurnher and

Chiriboga [eds] *Four Stages of Life* [Jossey-Bass, 1975]) and to have physical contact with one another (Rands and Levinger, 'Implicit Theories of Relationship: An Intergenerational Study', *Journal of Personality and Social Psychology*, no. 37 [1979]), according to a review in Gergen and Gergen, *Social Psychology*.

11. Argyle *et al.*, 'The Communication of inferior and superior attitudes by verbal and non-verbal signals', *Bulletin de Psychologie*, vol. 23; quoted in Cook, *Interpersonal Perception* (Penguin, 1971) p. 66.

12. Secord, 'The Role of Facial Features in Interpersonal Perception', in Tagiuri and Petrullo (eds) *Person Perception and Interpersonal Behaviour* (Stanford, 1958); referred to in Cook, *Interpersonal Perception*, 1971) p. 66.

13. Nicholson, *Men and Women: How Different are They?* (Oxford Paperbacks, 1984).

14. On how grown women passed for men: 'If a woman dressed, worked and behaved as a "man" she was accepted as such by other men and women . . .' But during the Victorian era, which shaped twentieth-century conceptions of femininity, Florence Nightingale and her nurses replaced women in the armed services, and: 'It was no longer accepted that women could simply change their attire and convincingly become men' (Julie Wheelwright, *Amazons and Military Maids: an examination of female military heroines in British literature and the changing construction of gender*: unpublished paper, University of Sussex).

15. *The Orcadian*, 1922.

16. Wilson, *Adorned in Dreams* (Virago, 1985) p. 117.

17. Sennett, 'The Body is a Mannequin', in *The Fall of Public Man* pp. 65–72.

18. Ibid., p. 67, referring to Braudel, *Capitalism and Material Life* (Harper & Row, 1973) p. 236.

19. Ibid., pp. 67–8.

20. Wilson (*Adorned in Dreams*) refers to David Kunzle, who suggests that a counterpart of make-up in dress, the practice of 'tight lacing' which was the main means of achieving the wasp waist fashionable in earlier periods, was also subversive. It attracted, as it still does, censure as an unhealthy custom, but was maintained in the face of this by women refusing to comply with the demands of moralizing reactionaries.

    Wilson also points out the practice's erotic and autoerotic dimensions as well as its masochistic element. She cites the women's dressing-rooms at the lawn tennis club at Wimbledon before the First World War, where a rail was provided near the fireplace to dry the steel-boned corsets most women tennis players wore – most of which, according to an observer, were bloodstained (p. 99). She places this discussion in the context of eroticism and fetishism, which she links etymologically with make-up, saying that the term 'fetish' '. . . originates from the Latin *facere*, which means to do or to make, and, through "make" (from Anglo-Saxon or German) it is related to "make-up" (in French, *maquillage*). A fetish is an alienated object that we ourselves make, but into which we then project magical properties. The magic of the fetish wards off or neutralizes fear' (p. 95). Hence using make-up is a fetish which enables women to face the public world.

21. A study comparing arranged marriages with love matches also found that as well as ending less often in divorce, arranged marriages held generally the same amount of affection. Although husbands in arranged marriages are less expressive towards their wives between the second and the ninth year, for the first two years and after the end of the eighth they are just as affectionate as husbands in love matches

(Blood, *Love Match and Arranged Marriage* [The Free Press, 1967]).

22. Ibid., p. 184.

6: *Barrier Zone*

1. Pinchot, from the original transcript of *The Entrepreneurs*, Programme 5 in *The Business of Excellence* (Thames Television, 1986).

2. 'Women are most often seen as achieving through luck or task ease rather than skill or effort. Skill is more favoured than effort for reward' (Heilman and Guzzo, 'The Perceived Case of Work Success as a Mediator of Sex Discrimination in Organizations', *Journal of Organizational Behaviour and Human Performance*, vol. 21 [1978]). O'Leary and Hansen, 'Trying Hurts Women, Helps Men: the Meaning of Effort', in Bernadin (ed.) *Women in the Workforce* (Praeger, 1982), contend, on the other hand, that women are perceived as achieving by working harder than men and are therefore seen as less able than men, who earn higher rewards for their greater natural ability, which corresponds to skill. Hence effort is more likely to be rewarded in men than in women.

3. Duval and Wicklund, 'Effect of Objective Self-awareness on Attribution of Causality', *Journal of Experimental Social Psychology*, vol. 9 (1973).

4. Fitch, 'Effects of Self-Esteem, Perceived Performance and Choice on Causal Attribution', *Journal of Personal Social Psychology*, no. 16 (1970). Both this and Duval and Wicklund's findings were linked and corroborated in Nadler, 'Objective Self-Awareness, Self-Esteem and Causal Attributions for Success and Failure,' *Journal of Personality and Individual Differences*, vol. 4 (1983).

5. For example Rivenbarle, 'Self-disclosure among adolescents', *Psychological Reports*, no. 28 (1971). Also

see Mark and Alper, 'Sex Differences in Intimacy Motivation', *Psychology of Women Quarterly*, vol. 5 no. 2 (1980) and Aries, 'Interaction Patterns and Themes of Male, Female and Mixed Groups', *Small Group Behaviour*, no. 7 (1976) on women's preference for talking to other women rather than men.

6. This has been shown in many studies, including Gauthier and Kjervik, 'Sex-Role Identity and Self-Esteem in Female Graduate Nursing Students', *Sex Roles*, vol. 8 (1982); DeGregorio and Carver, 'Type A Behaviour Pattern, Sex Role Orientation and Psychological Adjustment', *Journal of Personality and Social Psychology*, vol. 39 (1980); Colker and Widom, 'Correlates of Female Athletic Participation: Masculinity, Femininity, Self-Esteem and Attitudes towards Women', *Sex Roles*, vol. 6 (1980).

7. See, for example, a summary of the research in Nicholson, *Men and Women* (Oxford University Press, 1984) p. 107, and Archer and Lloyd, *Sex and Gender* (Pelican, 1982) p. 193.

8. Lasch, *The Minimal Self: Psychic Survival in Troubled Times* (Picador, 1985).

9. For example, a study by Jane Gregory of Western Ontario University showed that athletes were superstitious; the same author conducted a study comparing superstition in men and women in the 1970s and found a generally higher incidence of superstition among women except in sports, a finding corroborated by Graham Neil of McGill University, Montreal, who found men and women sports players were equally superstitious. All studies referred to by Judith Zimmer, 'Courting the Gods of Sport', *Psychology Today* (July 1984).

10. Erving Goffman, *The Presentation of Self In Everyday Life* (Penguin, 1982).

11. Horner, *Sex Differences in Achievement Motivation and Performance in Competitive and Non-competitive situations* (unpublished doctoral thesis, University of Michigan, 1968) and 'Feminity and Successful Achievement: a basic inconsistency', in Bardwick, Douvan, Horner and Gutmann, *Feminine Personality and Conflict* (Brooks/Cole, 1970).
12. Applegarth, 'Some Observations on Work Inhibition in Women', in Blum (ed.) *Female Psychology: Contemporary Psychoanalytic Views* (International Universities Press, 1977).
13. Ibid.
14. Marshall, *Women Managers: Travellers in a Male World.*
15. Horney, *The Overvaluation of Love in Feminine Psychology* (W.W. Norton, 1973).
16. David W. Krueger, *Success and the Fear of Success in Women* (The Free Press, 1984).
17. Ibid., pp. xiii–xiv.
18. Ibid., p. 13.

7: *Confidence Tricks*
1. Lasch, *The Culture of Narcissism* (Abacus, 1980).
2. See, for instance, Christine Griffin's paper circulated by the Centre for Cultural, Community and Social Studies in 1982 and her *Typical Girls* (Methuen, 1985).
3. The cost of having a child expressed in lost and reduced earnings through career break and part-time work and consequent reduced promotion prospects was put at £135,000 for a woman on average full-time earnings of £7,000 per year in 1986, in Roll, *Babies and Money* (Family Policy Studies Centre, 1986).
4. See Lasch, *The Culture of Narcissism.*
5. The General Household Survey shows that 90 per cent of all women in Britain now become mothers,

compared with an estimated 77 per cent two generations ago. See also Popay and Wicks, *Values and the Changing Family*, p. 9.

6. Analyses of fertility and social class by Jo Roll from Office of Population Censuses and Surveys General Household Survey 1983, in Roll, *Babies and Money*.

7. Daniels, *Maternity Rights: The Experience of Women* (PSI, 1986).

8. *In Public*

1. For instance, Roger Bennett, 'How Performance Appraisals Hurt Women Managers', *Women in Management Review*, no. 2/3 (1986).

2. Source: Burgoyne *et al.*, *Occupations 87* (COIC, 1986).

3. Women are 53 per cent of arts graduates, 70 per cent of literature and language graduates and 45 per cent of social science graduates – 1983 statistics from Table 2.8: *Women as a percentage of full-time undergraduates in universities by selected subjects Great Britain 1978–1984*, *Women and Men in Britain: A Statistical Profile* (EOC, 1986).

4. Source: André Clark and Jason Tarsh, *How Much is A Degree Worth in Education and Training UK: an economic, social and policy audit* (Policy Journals, 1987). The probable reason for social science graduates earning so much more than experts and professionals is that business studies, whose graduates enter management positions, is included in this category.

5. Bates and Kiersey, *Please Understand Me* (Prometheus Nemesis Book Company, 1984); quoted in Susan Vinnicombe, 'Drawing Out the Differences in Male and Female Managerial Styles', *Women in Management Review*, vol. 3 no. 1 (1987).

6. Details on labour market changes from 'Occupational Change', in Burgoyne *et al.*, *Occupations 87*.

7. Table 3.1: *Occupational Order for jobs of full and part-time working women, and working men,* in Martin and Roberts, *Women and Employment* (HMSO, 1984).

8. For instance, 50 per cent of women in predominantly men's jobs reported that they had been sexually harassed, while 40 per cent reported that they had been discriminated against on the basis of sex – being told that they were not going to be hired or promoted because they were women was a common experience – yet none had taken the matter further: because they did not know they could bring a case to an industrial tribunal; because they did not know how to do so; or because they feared the repercussions on their job prospects if they got a reputation as troublemakers, even if it was undeserved (Sarah Clements of Goldsmith's College, University of London, in a paper to the British Psychological Society London Conference, 1986).

9. For instance the annual survey by Remuneration Economics on behalf of the British Institute of Management generally finds few if any women in the top categories of job among the 25,000 British managers surveyed, and the highest-paid male managers earn a third again more than the highest-paid women directors. A Labour Research Department survey of the highly paid noted that researchers had been unable to locate one single highly paid woman ('More Pay Rises for Rich Directors', *Labour Research*, vol. 74 no. 10 (1985: 252).

10. Shareholder's question campaign by the Fawcett Society, reported in Alison Baines, 'What's In It for Women, Mr Chairman?' (*The Guardian*, May 1985) and elsewhere.

12. Sarah Clements, op cit.

13. Alice Leonard's analysis looked at figures available

then which covered the first eight years of the laws' operation, 1976 to 1984. *Pyrrhic Victories* (Equal Opportunities Commission, 1986)

14. Alice Leonard found, on analysing the result of claims brought under the Equal Pay and Sex Discrimination acts, that although 80 per cent of cases are brought by women, men's success rate was much higher. Only one in four women whose cases went before an industrial tribunal were successful, compared with one in three men. Further analysis showed that this related to different success rates for different sorts of cases: claims of discrimination in recruitment, more of which were made by men than women, were more successful than claims over dismissal, where five times as many women as men were involved. Victimization cases, none of which was brought by a man, were generally unsuccessful; so were equal pay claims involving grading schemes, where again no man brought a claim (Leonard, *Judging Inequality: The effectiveness of the industrial tribunal system in sex discrimination and equal pay cases* [The Cobden Trust, 1987]).

15. O'Leary and Hansen, 'Trying Hurts Women, Helps Men: the Meaning of Effort', in Bernardin (ed.) *Women in the Workforce*.

16. Chart 5.15: *Families with incomes at or below Supplementary Benefit Levels, Social Trends* 15 (HMSO, 1985) p. 85.

17. See, for example, Helen Franks, *Goodbye Tarzan: Men after Feminism*.

18. Personal communications supporting the findings of Bell, McKee and Priestley in a study of fathers' attitudes to the conflicts of work and family life (*Fathers, Childbirth and Work*) that more than 90 per cent of fathers felt strongly that there should be a statutory scheme of paid paternity leave, in addition

to annual holiday leave, in order to provide both practical and emotional support to their partners and other children, and because they wanted to establish an immediate emotional involvement with the new baby.

19. Quoted in Beverly Alban-Metcalf, *Current Career Concerns of Female and Male Managers and Professionals: An Analysis of Free-response Comments to a National Survey* (MRC/SSRC, Social and Applied Psychology Unit, University of Sheffield, 1984).

20. See, for instance, Alistair Mant, *Leaders We Deserve* (Blackwell, 1984) or C. Brooklyn-Derr, *Managing The New Careerists* (Jossey-Bass, 1986).

21. Conducted and published by Ashridge Management College with funding from the Manpower Services Commission.

22. For example, *Women and Men of Europe* (1984; published by Euromonitor, the EEC opinion poll).

23. For example, Isaacs, 'Sex Role Stereotyping and the Evaluation of the Performance of Women', *Psychology of Women Quarterly*, vol. 6 no. 2 (Winter 1981), which found that the power of stereotypes in the imagination had waned during the 1970s.

24. *Women and Men of Europe in 1983* (Commission of The European Communities, 1984).

25. He made the remark in a television programme on workplace equality training courses (*20:20 Vision*, 30 November 1984).

26. For instance, an annual survey of earnings among 25,000 managers across a representative spread of industries and areas in the UK (published by Remuneration Economics Ltd) has found no women at company chairman level for some years. Although there are women chairing the boards of a million companies in Britain, they tend to receive a volume of

publicity which masks the fact that they remain a statistically insignificant section of the population.

27. *Job Evaluation Schemes Free of Sex Bias* (Equal Opportunities Commission, 1984).

28. Susan Vinnicombe, 'Drawing Out the Differences in Male and Female Managerial Styles', *Women in Management Review*, vol. 3 no. 1 (1987).

29. *New Earnings Survey 1984*, quoted in Equal Opportunities Commission Ninth Annual Report (EOC, 1985).

30. Alban-Metcalf, *Current Career Concerns* . . . .

31. Official documents have been found so obscurantist that they could not be understood by the 'common man' – who has been the standard, in law and in concepts of the national character, by which understanding is measured – and in the late 1970s Chrissie Maher set up the Plain English Campaign, which now runs under the aegis of the National Consumer Council. It makes annual awards for the most and least clear official publications drawn to its attention.

32. Susan Brownmiller, *Femininity* (Paladin, 1985).

33. Clarke and Esposito, 'A Study of Occupational Advice for Women in Magazines', *Journalism Quarterly*, vol. 43 no. 3 (1966), reprinted in Theodore (ed.) *The Professional Woman* (Schenkman, 1971).

34. According to the Report of the Media and Women Topic Group, prepared for the UK delegate to the UN Decade for Women conference in Nairobi (1985).

35. In 1983 Professor Jean Millar undertook an analysis of the position of women in Fleet Street for Women In Media, updating 1974 figures (from Roger Smith, *Women in the Press*). She found that over the ten years to 1983 women had doubled as a proportion of Fleet Street journalists to 22 per cent, but that they comprised half of all general news reporters and almost all the fashion journalists, 40 per cent of

features writers but only 12 per cent of features and news subs, which lies on the route up to senior editorial responsibility. Only 7 per cent of senior editors in 1983 were women.

Roger Smith's 1974 study also illustrated the ways and means by which women were excluded from the editorial process by which the media communicates information and opinion. He reported that one newspaper management claimed that no women applied for senior editorial jobs, but that a file had been found of women's applications for such jobs which had not been considered. He recorded that one woman subeditor believed, even after she had been in her job for some time, that when male colleagues said they were 'going on the stone' they meant they were going to the lavatory. Stone subbing meant seeing the pages made up and making any final alterations to the layout before printing – an important area of expertise for the career journalist.

36. Women are now absent from the labour force for less than four years on average when they have a child and increasingly return to work between births. Currently women can expect to spend 60 per cent of their lives at work (Roberts and Martin, *Women and Employment: A Lifetime Perspective* [HMSO, 1984]).

37. There are circumstances where public activities take place under conditions of privacy – cases heard in camera, Cabinet discussions, espionage and so forth – but these are not part of the personal realm.

9: *The Defence of Identity*
 1. Christie and Gies (eds) *Studies in Machiavellianism* (Academic Press, 1970); quoted in Westen, *Self and Society: Narcissism, Collectivism and the Development of Morals* (Cambridge University Press, 1985).

2. Whiting and Whiting (eds) *Children of Six Cultures: a Psychocultural Study* (Harvard University Press, 1975); quoted in Westen, *Self and Society*.

3. Kagan and Carlson, 'Development of Adaptive Assertiveness in Mexican and United States Children', *Developmental Psychology*, no. 11 (1975); quoted in Westen, *Self and Society*.

4. Marin, Mejia and deOberle, 'Cooperation as a Function of Place of Residence in Colombian Children', *Journal of Social Psychology*, no. 51 (1975); quoted in Westen, *Self and Society*.

5. Madsen, 'Developmental and Cross-cultural Differences in the Cooperative and Competitive Behaviour of Young Children', *Journal of Cross Cultural Psychology*, no. 2 (1971); quoted in Westen, *Self and Society*.

6. See Carver and Scheier, *A Control Theory Approach to Human Behaviour* (Springer-Verlag, 1981).

7. Adorno, *The Authoritarian Personality* (Suhrkamp-Verlag, 1951).

8. Strauss, *Mirrors and Masks* (Martin Robertson, 1977) p. 26.

9. For instance: 'The disposition towards originality may thus be seen as a highly organized mode of responding to experience including other persons, society, and oneself. The socially disrated traits which may go along with it include rebelliousness, disorderliness and exhibitionism, while the socially valued traits which accompany it include independence of judgment, freedom of expression and novelty of construction and insight' (Barron, 'The Disposition Towards Originality', in the 1955 Yearbook of the *Journal of Abnormal and Social Psychology*; see also Barron, 'The Creative Personality', *Scientific American* (June 1959).

10. Lynn Spender, *Intruders on the Rights of Men: Women's Unpublished Heritage* (Pandora, 1983).

11. Dale Spender, *A Difference of View: Reviewing Male Reviewers*: paper presented at Cambridge University, 26 April 1984.

12. Guilford, *The Nature of Human Intelligence* (McGraw Hill, 1967).

13. Terman, *Genetic Studies of Genius* (Stanford, 1975).

14. Ravenna Helson, *Women Mathematicians and the Creative Personality* (American Association of Women in Mathematics, 1976).

15. Such a brief discussion must omit the fact that many artists have worked co-operatively to produce artworks, some of which satisfy the criteria of greatness (artists working in a master's studio; artists' collectives and anonymous Masters). Some perceive the cult of the individual and the quest for personal fame as an impediment to authentic creativity; accordingly they choose either a reclusive life or collaborative work so that the product cannot be ascribed to any individual.

16. D. W. Winnicott, *Playing and Reality* (Penguin, 1969) p. 125.

17. Erving Goffman, *The Presentation of Self In Everyday Life*.

18. Bernard, *The Female World* (The Free Press, 1974) p. 161.

19. See Bell, McKee and Priestley, *Fathers, Childbirth and Work*; Franks, *Goodbye Tarzan*.

20. According to a survey by Harris Polls for the *London Daily News*, reported 2 March 1987.

21. See Agassi, *Comparing Work Attitudes of Women and Men* D.C. Heath, 1982); *Women on the Job* (Lexington, 1982) and Bernadin (ed.) *Women in the Workforce*.

22. Two-thirds of the self-employed work in construction,

distribution and services like hotels, catering and repair work. The rate of self-employment is highest in the south of England and lowest in the north and Scotland. Over 60 per cent of the self-employed work more than a forty-hour week compared with less than 35 per cent of the PAYE employees. Elizabeth Ingleton, 'Enterprise', *Occupations 87* (COIC, 1986) p. xxxiii.

23. See Glover, *Working from Home* (Post Office Social Forecast, 1974).

24. See chapter 1, note 11. For the estimates of the size of the black economy and its consequences on personal life, see Hermione Parker, *The Moral Hazards Of Social Benefit* (IEE, 1982); for a projection of the adjustments to conventional conceptions of work and home, see Postgate, *Home-based Employment* (Gulbenkian, 1985).

25. See, for instance, Dale Spender, *Man Made Language* (Routledge & Kegan Paul, 1980); also unpublished research by Sara Mills ('Women and Politeness'); the author found in general substantial (mainly quantitative) differences between male and female politeness strategies, but these seemed to be of much the same order as males in an authority position speaking to subordinate males: 'In my research, it seemed to be far more a question of power than of gender, although gender does seem to be a form of power relation' (personal communication).

26. Rosalind Coward, *Female Desire* (Paladin, 1984) p. 137.

27. Ibid., p. 138.

28. Susan Condor researched women's social relationships with each other while at Kent University and dismissed the myth of women's competitiveness, and competition to attract men, in a paper to the British Psychological Society London Conference, 1984 and

also in 'Sex Role Belief' in Wilkinson (ed.) *Feminist Social Psychology* (Open University, 1986).

29. Sennett, *The Fall Of Public Man* p. 6.
30. Ibid., p. 8.
31. Women working full-time average 36 hours a week; men 38 hours (*Social Trends 15* [HMSO] p. 66).
32. Sennett, *The Fall Of Public Man*. His views are clearly formed on American political responses, though the same things are widely believed to be true – and particularly so of women – in the UK.

Bibliography

Adorno, T. *The Authoritarian Personality* (Suhrkamp-Verlag, 1951).

Agassi, J. *Comparing Work Attitudes of Women and Men* (D.C. Heath, 1982).

—*Women on the Job* (Lexington Books, 1982).

Alban-Metcalf, B. *Current Career Concerns of Female and Male Managers and Professionals: An Analysis of Free-Response Comments to a National Survey* (MRC/SSRC Social and Applied Psychology Unit, University of Sheffield, 1980).

Alban-Metcalf, B. and Nicholson, N. *The Career Development of British Managers* (British Institute of Management, 1985).

Allin, P. and Hunt, A. 'Women In Official Statistics', in *The Changing Experience of Women* (Martin Robertson, 1982).

Angeloglou, M. *A History of Make-up* (Studio Vista, 1970).

Anon., 'More Pay Rises for Rich Directors', *Labour Research* 74 (10) (1985).

Applegarth, A. 'Some Observations on Work Inhibition in Women', in Blum (ed.).

Archer, J. and Lloyd, B. *Sex and Gender* (Pelican, 1982).

Ardener, S. (ed.) *Defining Females: The Nature of Women in Society* (Croom Helm, 1978).

—*Women and Space: Ground Rules and Social Maps* (Croom Helm, 1981).

Arendt, H. *The Human Condition* (Chicago, 1958).

Argyle, M. *et al.* 'The Communication of Inferior and Superior Attitudes by Verbal and Non-Verbal Signals', *Bulletin de Psychologie* 23.

Arieti, S. *Creativity: The Magic Synthesis* (Basic Books, 1976).

Aristotle, *Politics*, trans. Barker (Oxford University Press, 1948).

Baines, A. 'What's In It for Women, Mr Chairman?' (*Guardian*, May 1985).

Bardwick, J., Douvan, E., Horner, M. and Gutmann, D. *Feminine Personality and Conflict* (Brooks/Cole, 1970).

Barron, F. 'The Disposition Towards Originality', *Journal of Abnormal and Social Psychology Yearbook* (1955).

—'The Creative Personality', *Scientific American* (June 1959).

Beechey, V. (ed.) *The Changing Experience of Women* (Martin Robertson, 1982).

Bell, C., McKee, L. and Priestley, K. *Fathers, Childbirth and Work* (Equal Opportunities Commission, 1983).

Bem, S. 'The Measurement of Psychological Androgyny', *Journal of Consulting and Clinical Psychology* 42 (1974).

Bendefeldt, Miller and Ludwig 'Cognitive Performance in Conversion Hysteria', *Archives of General Psychiatry* 33 (1976).

Bennett, R. 'How Performance Appraisals Hurt Women Managers', *Women in Management Review* 2 (3) (1986).

Bennett, Y. and Carter, D. *Sidetracked? A Look at the Careers Advice Given to Fifth-Form Girls* (Equal Opportunities Commission, 1982).

Berger, J. *Ways of Seeing* (BBC, 1972).

Bernadin, J. (ed.) *Women in the Workforce* (Praeger, 1982).

Bernard, J. *The Female World* (The Free Press, 1974).

Berry, J. 'Temné and Eskimo Perceptual Skills', *International Journal of Psychology* 1 (1966).

Blair, A. *Social Class and Representations of Cancer*, paper to the British Psychological Society Annual Conference (1987).

Blood, R. *Love Match And Arranged Marriage* (The Free Press, 1967).

Blum, H. (ed.) *Female Psychology: Contemporary Psychoanalytic Views* (International Universities Press, 1977).

Bonfante, L. 'Etruscan Couples and their Aristocratic Society', in Foley (ed.).

Braudel, F. *Capitalism and Material Life* (Harper & Row, 1973).

Brodsky, A. and Hare-Mustin, R. *Women and Psychotherapy* (Guilford, 1980).

Brooklyn-Derr, C. *Managing The New Careerists* (Jossey-Bass, 1986).

Broome A. and Wallace, L. (eds) *Psychology and Gynaecological Problems* (Tavistock, 1984).

Brownmiller, S. *Femininity* (Paladin, 1985).

Burgoyne, M. *et al.* (eds) 'Occupational Change', *Occupations 87* (COIC, 1987).

Burnis, L. and Thorpe, G. *National Survey of Agoraphobia* (Sparthfield Clinic, Rochdale, 1977).

Burns, R. (ed.) *Work and the Family*, Research Bulletin No. 8 (Equal Opportunities Commission, 1984).

Callow, S. *Being an Actor* (Methuen, 1984).

Carver, L. and Scheier, M. *Attention and Self-Regulation: A Control-theory Approach to Human Behaviour* (Springer-Verlag, 1981).

Chadwick, N. *The Celts* (Pelican, 1970).

Chambless, D. and Goldstein, A. 'Anxieties: Agoraphobia and Hysteria', in Brodsky, A. and Hare-Mustin, R. (eds).

Christie, R. and Gies, F. (eds) *Studies in Machiavellianism* (Academic Press, 1970).

Clare, A. *In the Psychiatrist's Chair* (Chatto & Windus, 1984).

Clark, A. and Tarsh, J. 'How Much is A Degree Worth?', in *Education and Training UK: an economic, social and policy audit* (Policy Journals, 1987).

Clarke, P. and Esposito, V. 'A Study of Occupational Advice for Women in Magazines', *Journalism Quarterly* 43 (3) (1966); in Theodore (ed.).

Colker, R. and Widom, C. 'Correlates of Female Athletic Participation: Masculinity, Femininity, Self-Esteem and Attitudes towards Women', *Sex Roles* 6 (1980).

Condor, S. 'Sex Role Belief and "Traditional" Women: Feminist and Intergroup Perspectives', in Wilkinson (ed.).

Cook, E. *Psychological Androgyny* (Pergamon, 1985).

Cook, M. *Interpersonal Perception* (Penguin, 1971).

Cooper, C. and Davidson, M. *High Pressure: Working Lives of Women Managers* (Fontana, 1982).

Cooper, C. and Thompson, L. *Public Faces, Private Lives* (Fontana, 1984).

Coward, R. *Female Desire* (Paladin, 1984).

Cragg, A. and Dawson, T. *Qualitative Research Among Homeworkers*, Research Paper No. 21 (Department of Employment, 1981).

Crozier, R. Paper on shyness to British Psychological Society London Conference (December 1984).

Daniels, W. *Maternity Rights: The Experience of Women* (PSI, 1986).

DeGregorio, E. and Carver, C. 'Type A Behaviour Pattern, Sex Role Orientation and Psychological Adjustment', *Journal of Personality and Social Psychology* 39 (1980).

Douglas, M. *Purity and Danger: An Analysis of the Concepts of Pollution and Taboo* (Routledge & Kegan Paul, 1966).

Dowling, C. *The Cinderella Complex* (Fontana, 1982).

Duquemin, A. *The Importance of Marital Status for Women's Lives* (unpublished thesis for Plymouth Polytechnic, 1982).

Duval, S. and Wicklund, R. 'Effect of Objective Self-awareness on Attribution of Causality', *Journal of Experimental Social Psychology* 9 (1973).

Ehrenreich, B. and English, D. *Complaints and Disorders: The Sexual Politics of Sickness* (Writers & Readers, 1976).

Elshtain, J. *Public Man, Private Woman: Women in Social and Political Thought* (Princeton, 1981).

Fisher, E. *Women's Creation: Sexual Evolution and the Shaping of Society* (Wildwood, 1980).

Fitch, F. 'Effects of Self-Esteem, Perceived Performance and Choice on Causal Attribution', *Journal of Personal Social Psychology* 16 (1970).

Foley, H. (ed.) *Images of Women in Antiquity* (Gordon & Breach, 1981).

Franks, H. *Goodbye Tarzan: Men After Feminism* (Allen & Unwin, 1984).

Freud, S. *The Psychopathology of Everyday Life* (Ernest Benn, 1960 edn).

Gauthier, J. and Kjervik, D. 'Sex-role Identity and Self-esteem in Female Graduate Nursing Students', *Sex Roles* 8 (1982).

Gavron, H. *The Captive Wife* (Penguin, 1966).

Gergen, K. and Gergen, M. (eds) *Social Psychology* (Harcourt Brace Jovanovich, 1981).

Gershuny, J. *Household Work Strategies: Sexual Segregation and Inequality* (paper to International Sociological Association Conference, Mexico, 1982).

Glover, J. *Working from Home* (General Post Office Long Range Survey Intelligence Unit, 1974).

Goffman, E. *Interaction Ritual: Essays on Face-to-Face Behaviour* (Anchor Books, 1967).

—*The Presentation of Self In Everyday Life* (Penguin, 1974).

—*Gender Advertisements* (Macmillan, 1985).

Greer, G. *The Obstacle Race* (Secker & Warburg, 1979).

Grey, S. *Domestic Technology: an Investigation into the Relationship Women have with Technology in the Home* (unpublished research for the Open University, 1983).

Griffin, C. *Typical Girls: Young Women from School To the Full-time Job Market* (Methuen, 1985).

Hakim, C. *Occupational Segregation: A Comparative Study of the Degree and Pattern of the Differentiation between Men and Women's Work in Britain, the United States and Other Countries*, Department of Employment Research Paper No. 9 (Department of Employment, 1979).

—'Job Segregation: Trends in the 1970s', *Employment Gazette* (Department of Employment) (December 1981).

Harvey, J. with Katz, C. *The Imposter Phenomenon* (Pocket Books, 1985).

Hay-Davidson, I. (ed.) *The Business of Excellence* (Thames Television, 1987).

Heilman, M. and Guzzo, M. 'The Perceived Case of Work Success as a Mediator of Sex Discrimination in Organizations', *Journal of Organizational Behaviour and Human Performance* 21 (1978).

Helson, R. *Women Mathematicians and the Creative Personality* (American Association of Women in Mathematics, 1976).

Hennig, M. and Jardim, A. *The Managerial Woman* (Marion Boyars, 1978).

Hey, V. *The Necessity of Romance* (University of Kent Occasional Papers, 1984).

Hobsbawm, E. *The Age of Capital* (Abacus, 1977).

Holmstedt, M. (ed.) *Women in Statistics*, Research Bulletin No. 10 (Equal Opportunities Commission, 1987).

Horne, D. *The Public Culture: The Triumph of Industrialism* (Pluto, 1986).

Horner, M. 'Femininity and Successful Achievement: a basic inconsistency', in Bardwick, J. Douvan, E. Horner, M., and Gutmann, D. (eds).

Ingleton, E. 'Enterprise', *Occupations 87* (COIC, 1986).

Isaacs, M. 'Sex Role Stereotyping and the Evaluation of the Performance of Women', *Psychology of Women Quarterly* 6 (2) (1981).

Job Evaluation Schemes Free of Sex Bias (Equal Opportunities Commission, 1984).

Jourard, S. *The Transparent Self* (Van Nostrand Reinhold, 1971).

Kagan, S. and Carlson, H. 'Development of Adaptive Assertiveness in Mexican and United States Children', *Developmental Psychology* 11 (1975).

Krueger, D. *Success and the Fear of Success in Women* (The Free Press, 1984).

Laing, R. *The Divided Self* (Pelican, 1965).

—*Self and Others* (Pelican, 1971).

Land, H. *Parity Begins At Home: Women's and Men's Work in the Home and its Effects on their Paid Employment* (EOC/SSRC, 1981).

Lasch, C. *The Culture of Narcissism* (Abacus, 1980).

—*The Minimal Self: Psychic Survival in Troubled Times* (Picador, 1985).

Laurance, J. 'Marital Breakdown', *New Society* (30 January 1987).

Leonard, A. *Pyrrhic Victories* (Equal Opportunities Commission, 1987).

—*Judging Inequality: The Effectiveness of the Industrial Tribunal System in Sex Discrimination and Equal Pay Cases* (The Cobden Trust, 1987).

Leonard, D. and Speakman, S. 'The Family', in Beechey (ed.).

Lerner, D. *The Passing of Traditional Society: Modernizing the Middle-East* (The Free Press, 1958).

Lewenhak, S. *Women and Work* (Fontana, 1980).

Lips, H., Myers, A. and Colwill, N. 'Sex Differences in Ability', in Lips, H. and Colwill, N. (eds).

Lips, H. and Colwill, N. (eds) *The Psychology of Sex Differences* (Prentice-Hall, 1978).

Long, V. 'Masculinity and Mental Health', *Journal of Consulting and Clinical Psychology* 54 (3) (1986).

Lowenthal, M., Thurnher, M. and Chiriboga, D. (eds) *Four Stages of Life* (Jossey-Bass, 1975).

Maccoby, E. (ed.) *The Development of Sex Differences* (Stanford, 1966).

Maccoby, E. and Jacklin, C. (eds) *The Psychology of Sex Differences* (Stanford, 1974).

McClelland, D. *The Achievement Motive* (Appleton-Century-Crofts, 1953).

—*The Achieving Society* (Van Nostrand, 1961).

Madsen, M. 'Developmental and Cross-Cultural Differences in the Cooperative and Competitive Behaviour of Young Children', *Journal of Cross Cultural Psychology* 2 (1971).

Mant, A. *Leaders We Deserve* (Blackwell, 1985).

Marcuse, H. *One-Dimensional Man* (Ark, 1986).

Marin, G., Mejia, B. and deOberle, C. 'Cooperation as a Function of Place of Residence in Colombian Children', *Journal of Social Psychology* 51 (1975).

Marshall, J. *Women Managers: Travellers in a Male World* (Wiley, 1984).

Meehan, E. *Women's Rights at Work: Campaigns and Policy in Britain and the United States* (Macmillan, 1985).

Miller, J. *Towards a New Psychology of Women* (Penguin, 1976).

Mitchell, J. *Psychoanalysis and Feminism* (Penguin, 1974).

Modleski, T. *Loving with a Vengeance: Mass-Produced Fantasies for Women* (Methuen, 1982).

Moore, B. *Privacy: Studies in Social and Cultural History* (Sharpe, 1984).

Nadler, A. 'Objective Self-Awareness, Self-Esteem and Causal Attributions for Success and Failure', *Journal of Personality and Individual Differences* 4 (1983).

New Earnings Survey, Department of Employment.

Nicholson, J. *Men and Women: How Different are They?* (Oxford Paperbacks, 1984).

Oakley, A. *Housewife* (Penguin, 1974).

—*Sex, Gender and Society* (Gower/Maurice Temple Smith, 1985).

—*The Sociology Of Housework* (Basil Blackwell, 1986).

O'Leary, V. and Hansen, R. 'Trying Hurts Women, Helps Men: the Meaning of Effort', in Bernadin, J. (ed.).

Orbach, S. and Eichenbaum, L. *Outside In, Inside Out* (Fontana, 1982).

—*What Do Women Want?* (Fontana, 1983).

Ortner, S. 'Is Woman to Nature as Man is to Culture?', in Rosaldo and Lamphere (eds).

Parker, H. *The Moral Hazards Of Social Benefit* (Institute of Economic Affairs, 1982).

Pearce, S. and Beard, R. 'Chronic Pelvic Pain', in Broome, A. and Wallace, L. (eds).

Personal Violence, Home Office Research Study (Home Office, 1986).

Piggott, S. *Ancient Europe* (Aldine, 1965).

Popay, J. and Wicks, M. (eds) *Values and the Changing Family* (Study Commission on the Family, 1982).

Postgate, R. *Home-Based Employment* (Gulbenkian, 1985).

Rands, M. and Levinger, G. 'Implicit Theories of Relationship: an Intergenerational Study', *Journal of Personality and Social Psychology* 37 (1979).

Rapoport, R. and Rapoport, R. (with Strelitz, Z.) *Leisure and the Family Life Cycle* (Routledge & Kegan Paul, 1975).

—*Dual Career Families Revisited: New Integrations of Work × Family* (Martin Robertson, 1976).

Reid, I. and Wormald, E. (eds) *Sex Differences in Britain* (Grant McIntyre, 1982).

Reiter, R. 'Men and Women in The South of France: Public and Private Domains', in Reiter (ed.).

Reiter, R. (ed.) *Towards an Anthropology of Women* (Monthly Review Press, 1975).

Roberts, C. and Martin, J. *Women and Employment: A Lifetime Perspective* (HMSO, 1984).

Rohrbaugh, J. *Women: Psychology's Puzzle* (Abacus, 1981).

Roll, J. *Babies and Money* (Family Policy Studies Centre, 1986).

Rosaldo, M. and Lamphere, L. (eds) *Women, Culture and Society* (Stanford, 1976).

Rosenberg, C. (ed.) *The Family in History* (University of Pennsylvania Press, 1975).

Rutter, R. and O'Connell, C. 'The Relationship Among Sex-Role Orientation, Cognitive Complexity and Tolerance for Ambiguity'. *Sex Roles* 8 (12) (1982).

Sarsby, J. *Romantic Love and Society* (Penguin, 1983).

Scott, J. and Tilley, L. 'Women's Work and the Family', in Rosenberg (ed.).

Secord, M. 'The Role of Facial Features in Interpersonal Perception', in Tagiuri, R. and Petrullo, L. (eds).

Sennett, R. *The Fall of Public Man* (Vintage, 1980).

—*Authority* (Vintage, 1981).

Siltanen, J. and Stanworth, M. (eds) *Women and the Public Sphere* (Hutchinson, 1984).

Singer, I. *The Goals of Human Sexuality* (Wildwood, 1973).

Siward, R. *Women . . . A World Survey* (World Priorities, 1985).

Sobie, T. 'The Sensuous and the Passionate', in Sobie, T. (ed.) *The Philosophy of Sex* (Rowman & Littlefield, 1980).

Social Trends 15 (HMSO, 1985).

Sollie, D. and Fischer, J. 'Sex Role Orientation, Intimacy of Topic and Target and Person Differences in Self Disclosure among Women', in *Sex Roles* 12 (9/10) (1985).

Spence, J. and Helmreich, R. 'Masculine Instrumentality and Feminine Expressiveness: Their Relationship with Sex Role Attitudes and Behaviours', *Psychology of Women Quarterly* vol 5 (2) (Winter 1980).

Spender, D. *Learning to Fail* (Routledge & Kegan Paul, 1978).

—*Man Made Language* (Routledge & Kegan Paul, 1980).

—*A Difference of View: Reviewing Male Reviewers* (paper presented at Cambridge University, 26 April 1984).

Spender, L. *Intruders of the Rights of Men: Women's Unpublished Heritage (Pandora, 1983).*

Stacey, M. and Price, M. *Women, Power and Politics* (Tavistock, 1981).

Strauss, A. *Mirrors and Masks* (Martin Robertson, 1977).

Sullerot, E. *Women and Love* (Jill Norman, 1980).

Tagiuri, R. and Petrullo, L. (eds) *Person Perception and Interpersonal Behaviour* (Stanford, 1958).

Terman, L. *Genetic Studies of Genius* (Stanford, 1925).

Theodore, A. (ed.) *The Professional Woman* (Schenkman, 1971).

Trilling, L. *Sincerity and Authenticity* (Oxford Paperbacks, 1974).

Vallance, E. *Women in the House of Commons* (Blackwell, 1979).

—'Women in the House of Commons', *Political Studies* 29 (1982).

—'Women Candidates in the 1983 General Election', *Parliamentary Affairs* 37 (3) (1984).

Vinnicombe, S. 'Drawing Out the Differences in Male and Female Managerial Styles', *Women in Management Review* 3 (1) (1987).

Vose, R. *Phobias* (Faber & Faber, 1987).

Weiss, L. and Lowenthal, M. 'Life-Course Perspectives on Friendship', in Lowenthal, M., Thurnher, M. and Chiriboga, D. (eds).

Westen, D. *Self and Society: Narcissism, Collectivism and the Development of Morals* (Cambridge University Press, 1985).

Wheeler, L. and Nezlek, T. 'Sex Differences in Social Participation', *Journal of Personality and Social Psychology* 35 (1977).

Wheelwright, J. *Amazons and Military Maids: an Examination of Female Military Heroines in British Literature and the Changing Construction of Gender* (paper to Women and History Conference, Leeds, 1986, from research in progress for University of Sussex).

Whiting, B. and Whiting, J. (eds) *Children of Six Cultures: A Psychocultural Study* (Harvard, 1975).

Wilkinson, S. (ed.) *Feminist Social Psychology: Developing Theory and Practice* (Open University 1986).

Williams, J. *Psychology of Women: Behaviour in a Bio-Social Context* (Norton, 1977).

—'Gender, Masculinity and Femininity and Emotional Intimacy in Same Sex Friendships', *Sex Roles* 12 (5/6) (1985).

Wilson, E. *Adorned in Dreams* (Virago, 1985).

Winnicott, D. *Playing and Reality* (Penguin, 1969).

Witkin, H. and Goodenough, D. *Field Dependence Revisited*, Research Bulletin, Educational Testing Service (Princeton, 1976).

Women and Men in Britain: A Statistical Profile (Equal Opportunities Commission, 1986).

Women and Men of Europe (Commission of the European Communities, Euromonitor, 1979, 1986).

Women in the 80s (CIS, 1981).

'Women in Statistics', supplement No. 14 to *Women of Europe* (Commission of the European Community, Women's Information Service, 1984).

Working Women (TUC, 1983).

Zaretsky, E. *Capitalism, the Family, and Personal Life* (Pluto, 1976).

Zimbardo, P. *Shyness: What is it, What to do about it* (Addison-Wesley, 1977).

Index

Index

Sexual Politics in Paladin Books

The Female Eunuch   £3.95 ☐
Germaine Greer
The book that caused a revolution, the central focus of the Women's
Liberation movement.

Love, Sex, Marriage and Divorce   £2.95 ☐
Jonathan Gathorne-Hardy
Did sexual intercourse really begin in 1963? Can a feminist revolution ever succeed? Over the last decades our attitudes to sexual
behaviour have shifted dramatically. The whole complex of love,
sex, marriage and divorce has undergone a radical change. In this
entertaining and wide-ranging survey, Jonathan Gathorne-Hardy
questions where it all leads.

Female Desire   £2.95 ☐
Rosalind Coward
Vivid, genuinely thought-provoking essays on the symbols, emblems
and enigmatic codes – from romance to royalty, from food to fashion
– that still govern our perceptions of female sexuality.

What a Man's Gotta Do   £3.95 ☐
Antony Easthope
A stimulating analysis of a neglected aspect of contemporary sexuality – masculinity, and how it is portrayed and defined in contemporary culture. Illustrated.

Femininity   £2.95 ☐
Susan Brownmiller
An examination of femininity in all its complexities: its roots in
history, culture and religion; the points at which it mirrors biology,
and the points where the two diverge (and often conflict).

To order direct from the publisher just tick the titles you want
and fill in the order form.   PAL15082

Arts in Paladin Books

Moving into Aquarius   £2.50 ☐
Sir Michael Tippett
One of our greatest living composers asks: How does music, the most
expressive of all forms of communication, relate to a technology-
obsessed society in which aggression and acquisitiveness have
become an index of personal worth?

The Jazz Book   £4.95 ☐
Joachim Berendt
The revised edition of this authoritative and comprehensive guide
which documents over 100 years of jazz.

Miles Davis   £3.95 ☐
Ian Carr
Penetrating biography of one of the world's most original and
enigmatic jazz performers.

A History of Jazz in Britain 1919–1950   £4.95 ☐
Jim Godbolt
From the arrival of jazz in Britain with the Original Dixieland Jazz
Band in 1919 to the early postwar years, this is the first truly
comprehensive study of the phenomenon of jazz from a British
perspective. 'Friendly, refreshing sceptical, very well documented.'
Max Jones. Illustrated.

Cult Objects   £5.95 ☐
Deyan Sudjic
A witty and stylish guide to contemporary design successes – objects
that have a special kind of attraction and personality that has nothing
to do with cost, utility or even neccessarily fashion. Illustrated
throughout.

To order direct from the publisher just tick the titles you want
and fill in the order form.   PAL3082

Philosophy/Religion in Paladin Books

Mythologies   **£2.95** ☐
Roland Barthes
An entertaining and elating introduction to the science of semiology
– the study of the signs and signals through which society expresses
itself – from the leading intellectual star.

Frames of Mind   **£5.95** ☐
Howard Gardner
Gardner's controversial theory of multiple intelligences has major
implications for our view of intelligence and our view of education.

Infinity and the Mind   **£3.50** ☐
Rudy Rucker
In the wake of *Gödel, Escher, Bach* comes this exceptional book
which draws from a staggering variety of source material to explore
the concept of infinity and its effect on our understanding of the
universe.

Confucius and Confucianism   **£2.95** ☐
D. Howard Smith
A skillful and thoroughgoing study which illuminates the man and
his influence and the doctrines of Confucian thought.

Paladin Movements and Ideas Series Series editor Justin Wintle
The series aims to provide clear and stimulating surveys of the ideas
and cultural movements that have dominated history. The first six
volumes are:

Rationalism   **£2.50** ☐
John Cottingham

Darwinian Evolution   **£2.50** ☐
Antony Flew

Expressionism   **£2.50** ☐
Roger Cardinal

The Psychoanalytic Movement   **£3.50** ☐
Ernest Gellner

Western Marxism   **£3.95** ☐
J. G. Merquior

Structuralism   **£3.95** ☐
John Sturrock

To order direct from the publisher just tick the titles you want
and fill in the order form.   PAL13082

All these books are available at your local bookshop or newsagent, or can be ordered direct from the publisher.

To order direct from the publishers just tick the titles you want and fill in the form below.

Name _____

Address _____

_____

Send to:
Paladin Cash Sales
PO Box 11, Falmouth, Cornwall TR10 9EN.

Please enclose remittance to the value of the cover price plus:

UK 60p for the first book, 25p for the second book plus 15p per copy for each additional book ordered to a maximum charge of £1.90.

BFPO 60p for the first book, 25p for the second book plus 15p per copy for the next 7 books, thereafter 9p per book.

Overseas including Eire £1.25 for the first book, 75p for second book and 28p for each additional book.

Paladin Books reserve the right to show new retail prices on covers, which may differ from those previously advertised in the text or elsewhere.